CRITICAL INSIGHTS

Violence in Literature

CRITICAL INSIGHTS

Violence in Literature

Editor
Stacey Peebles
Centre College in Danville, Kentucky

SALEM PRESS
A Division of EBSCO Information Services, Inc.
Ipswich, Massachusetts

GREY HOUSE PUBLISHING

Library of Congress Cataloging-in-Publication Data

Violence in literature / editor, Stacey Peebles, Centre College in Danville, Kentucky. -- [First edition].

pages ; cm. -- (Critical insights)

Edition statement supplied by publisher.
Includes bibliographical references and index.
ISBN: 978-1-61925-409-1

1. Violence in literature. 2. War stories--History and criticism. I. Peebles, Stacey L. (Stacey Lyn), 1976- II. Series: Critical insights.

PN56.V53 V56 2014
809.933552

LCCN: 2014949050

Contents

About This Volume, Stacey Peebles   vii

On Violence, Stacey Peebles   xii

Critical Contexts

The Foundations of Violence in Ancient Greek Literature,
  Thomas Palaima   3

Blood, Force, Influence: Studying the Representation of Violence,
  Stacey Peebles   23

The Thing and the Image: Violence in Chinua Achebe's *Things Fall Apart*,
  Aaron Bady   38

Modern War and American Literature: Ironic Realism, Satire, and Escape,
  Ty Hawkins   54

Critical Readings

Violence in the Bible from Genesis to Job, David Mikics   71

Street Violence and Youth in Shakespeare's *Romeo and Juliet*,
  Philip White   87

Grappling with Violence in Latin American Literature,
  Núria Sabaté Llobera   103

Kill Lists: Sade, Cinema, and the Language of the Torturer,
  Lindsay Hallam   119

Intimate Subject(ivitie)s: Race, Gender, and Violence in Toni Morrison's
  Beloved, Aretha Phiri   136

Excess, (Ir)rationality, and Consumerism: Violence in *No Country for
  Old Men* and *Fight Club*, James R. Giles   153

"Bluffers and Blowhards": Speaking of Violence in Ben Fountain's
  Billy Lynn's Long Halftime Walk, Mark Bresnan   168

Contemporary War Narratives: Story-Truth, New Journalisms, and Why
  We Write, Lydia Neuman   182

The War in "Big Two-Hearted River," Allen Josephs   202

Resources

Works of Literature Exploring Violence   219

Bibliography   223

About the Editor   227

Contributors   229

Index   233

About This Volume

Stacey Peebles

Violence is a big topic. Not only because its incidence and experience in the world demands our attention and judgment, but also because it is such a constant in human history and in artistic representation. Violence shapes our oldest stories and our newest ones, and deciding precisely how an anthology like this one should address the topic— even when limited to the only-slightly-narrower focus of violence in literature—poses something of a challenge. (Salem Press' Critical Insights series includes other thematic volumes, and I wondered which editors might have had a similarly interesting problem. Maybe Margaret Sönser Breen did when she was tasked with rounding up "good and evil," or John V. Knapp when he covered "family." I should also mention Alex Vernon's excellent volume on war, which can be considered a kind of companion to this one.)

And so I probably don't need to mention that this collection is necessarily selective and that there are certainly interesting subjects left out—the way violence works in comedy, for instance, or in regional and national traditions not covered here, or how graphic novels depict it in a combination of text and image. But I will note what this volume succeeds in doing, which is to draw together smart, sometimes provocative essays about works that vary widely in their historical and cultural contexts, in their style and structure, and the ways that violence makes (or resists) meaning within them. While each essay is intelligent and thought-provoking on its own terms, what has fascinated me most in compiling them is the connections that can be made across radically different works.

Thomas Palaima, for instance, begins his essay about the violent stories of the ancient Greeks and the cultural contexts that made those stories appealing—for them, and for us, almost 2,500 years later—with Euripides' *Medea*, a play about a woman who kills her own children. As he notes, it is an act that the scholar Denys L. Page once called "outside our experience," beyond the possible.

But we know, sadly and excruciatingly, that it's not. The real-life stories of Andrea Yates and Susan Smith reveal as much, as does that of Margaret Garner, whose life provided inspiration for Toni Morrison's *Beloved*. That novel is the focus of Aretha Phiri's essay, which explores the protagonist's act of infanticide in the context of African-American history and the lived experience of slavery. *Medea* was first performed on the brink of the Peloponnesian War; *Beloved* takes place both before and after the Civil War. Different worlds in many ways, with different motivations and historical circumstances at stake, and yet each work of art gives us a similarly unspeakable act to contemplate. Unspeakable—except Euripides and Morrison both speak it, insisting that we consider what we as humans are capable of, what is indeed within our experience, and the reasons that this might be so.

In Genesis, Abraham also believes he must kill his own child, an episode that David Mikics discusses in his essay on violence in the Hebrew Bible. Abraham doesn't question God's demand and moves to fulfill it, only to be stopped at the last moment. (Isaac is thus saved from his father's act of pious violence, though what he might have thought and felt about the experience afterwards is left to our imagination.) The threat of a single act of violence here becomes violence repeatedly and seemingly arbitrarily enacted in the Book of Job, a theological conundrum if ever there was one. Again, children die: Job's are killed, taken from him along with his wealth and his good health. The losses keep coming, and unlike Abraham, Job questions God—though the answer he receives is not the one he expected. Job is not a lengthy tale, and its author doesn't describe the deaths or Job's boils in anything like gory detail. But the piling of violence on violence is what we remember and what provokes both Job and the reader to ask, as we inevitably do in such circumstances, why this is happening. It's not so different, surprisingly, from the writings of the Marquis de Sade, which are also characterized by violent act after violent act visited upon seemingly undeserving victims. But as Lindsay Hallam argues in her essay, Sade's writing thus avoids the cloaking or veiling common to institutionalized violence and reveals that violence is "an integral part of the 'civilized' human, no matter how much we try to silence these aspects." It's not a comforting thought, but then neither is God's response from the whirlwind.

Shakespeare seems to think that violence is similarly unavoidable for some, according to Philip White, who explains how the Bard's view of the physical self, and thus a person's disposition and resulting values, influences his portrait of violence in *Romeo and Juliet*—murderous acts that are not, upon careful reading, purely a product of the feud between families. James R. Giles addresses two contemporary American novels that also suggest something about what it means to have a "disposition" for violence, though the characters in Cormac McCarthy's *No Country for Old Men* and Chuck Palahniuk's *Fight Club* are inclined to take things a bit further than the Montagues and the Capulets—and are motivated to do so at least in part by the corrupt capitalist systems in which they function. Issues of scale, of degree, of motivation do lead to considerations of economic and political context, as Núria Sabaté Llobera and Aaron Bady show in their discussions of colonial and post-colonial portraits of violence in Latin America and Africa, respectively, and the legacy of violent cross-cultural contact in representations from both sides of the conflict. Sábate Llobera's essay engages the blurred boundaries between history and fiction that can happen as a result in narratives that attempt to make meaning out of violence perpetrated or violence suffered. Bady focuses on Chinua Achebe's novel *Things Fall Apart*, which is often read in dialogue with Joseph Conrad's *Heart of Darkness*. As Bady argues, however, the novel is more properly understood through the lens of Simone Weil and her reading of the *Iliad*. Colonization is indeed a destructive force, but force itself—the true hero and subject of the *Iliad*, according to Weil, and of *Things Fall Apart*, according to Bady—can erupt in human relationships for other, deeper reasons, even within a colonial context.

Like Sabaté Llobera, Ty Hawkins also focuses on literature as a sense-making exercise, particularly in response to modern war, and finds different paradigms of doing so in Stephen Crane's *The Red Badge of Courage*, Joseph Heller's *Catch-22*, and Ernest Hemingway's *A Farewell to Arms*. The essays in this volume cover violence in a variety of social contexts, and even though the subject of war is, as I mentioned, well covered in another volume in this series, America's modern and contemporary wars—namely, the twenty-first-century wars in Iraq and Afghanistan—have elicited so much creative production that attention to that work is warranted. Mark Bresnan writes about Ben Fountain's 2012 novel *Billy Lynn's Long Halftime Walk*, which follows a squad of soldiers enduring the bromides, glad-handing, and overstimulation that comes with being honored for their service during a Dallas Cowboys football game. It's not combat, but it's not easy either, as they are bombarded with all the noise of American sports, fandom, patriotism, and spectacle. Fountain builds a story out of fictional characters, but Lydia Neuman shows in her essay how contemporary journalists like David Finkel, Sebastian Junger, and Dexter Filkins write about real people undergoing violent experience, balancing the need to document reality with the need to shape the story most effectively. These writers embed themselves within the lives of soldiers in combat or on the home front, a heightened presence that fades in their finished work, which seeks, as much as possible, to reflect those soldiers' experiences—a challenging and potentially problematic practice, to say the least.

All of these essays reveal the often unexpected ways that violence can turn up in human lives, but in this volume's final essay, Allen Josephs reminds us that violence and its traumatic aftermath may not, in fact, appear in the places we assume them to be. Sometimes a story about fishing is just a story about fishing (well, and writing), as Josephs argues about Hemingway's "Big Two-Hearted River," with a careful and thoughtful intervention into the details of that story and its publication, the critical conversation surrounding it, and Hemingway's own comments about its creation and content. An appropriate final word on the subject of violence, I think, emphasizing that as much blood, force, and injury there is to be experienced and written about in the world, there are also moments of stillness and peace. If it's true that one shouldn't turn a blind eye to violence, past or present—as many of the essays in this volume insist—then neither should one ignore the sight of a trout breaking through the surface of the water and, just for an instant, catching the sun.

On Violence ───────────────────

Stacey Peebles

When Jane Eyre is ten, she is regularly bullied and beaten by her cousin, John Reed. "[E]very nerve I had feared him," she says, "and every morsel of flesh on my bones shrank when he came near" (Brontë 42). After she is set to Lowood School, she endures privation and strict discipline, as well as the death from consumption of a dear friend. Later in life, she takes a job and gets engaged, only to find that her would-be husband, Rochester, is already married to Bertha Mason, a figure of abjection and torment: "beast or human being," Bertha growls, cries out, shakes her wild hair, and attacks Rochester when he visits, "grappl[ing] his throat viciously, and [laying] her teeth to his cheek" (Brontë 321).

When Jane confronts Rochester about his marriage, he is furious at her for insisting that she must leave. He grabs and shakes her, noting how easily he could crush her small, slight frame. But the struggle is, for her, internal—between her love for Rochester and her "intolerable duty" to leave him. "I was experiencing an ordeal," she says, "a hand of fiery iron grasped my vitals. Terrible moment: full of struggle, blackness, burning!" (Brontë 342). She wrests herself away, and leaves Thornfield Hall alone, weak, and weeping "stormy, scalding, heart-wrung tears" (Brontë 348). Jane endures homelessness and a near-fatal illness as a result. In her absence, Bertha sets fire to the Hall and commits suicide by leaping from the roof; the Hall burns to the ground and Rochester is blinded and disabled by the blaze.

Is *Jane Eyre* a violent novel? There are no armies massing on the grounds of Thornfield Hall and no descriptions that we might call gory or gratuitous, but if you're paying attention, the story is devastating—both when taken as a straightforward tale or when considered through a critical lens. Bertha, after all, is figured as a monster, but can also be read as "Jane's truest and darkest double . . . the angry aspect of the orphan child, the ferocious secret self Jane has been trying to repress ever since her days at Gateshead," argue Sandra Gilbert and Susan Gubar (360), and Jean Rhys exposes the racism and sexism inherent in Rochester's treatment of Bertha in her re-imagining of the story *Wide Sargasso Sea* (1966).

What about the *Bhagavad Gita*? That story does take place on a battlefield, and portrays the prince Arjuna poised on the brink of war with an enemy that includes his family members and friends. Krishna, his charioteer, counsels him on how to best understand the situation, as well as the nature of the world and his place in it. The setting is the field of war; the potential for violence that is both political and intensely personal has incapacitated even this great warrior. Few, however, would call this a war story, as the narrative quickly ascends into philosophical and theological abstractions. "O Krishna, I will not fight," Arjuna says and falls silent, paralyzed by what he sees as his conflicting duties. "You speak sincerely, but your sorrow has no cause," Krishna responds. "The wise grieve neither for the living nor for the dead. There has never been a time when you and I and the kings gathered here have not existed, nor will there be a time when we will cease to exist" (89). He continues at length, telling Arjuna about the nature of the world and the self, and the "perfect evenness of mind" that is yoga (94). Not, perhaps, a typical war story, but a story that is nonetheless initiated by the moral confusion that war and its violence engenders.

What counts as violence, or as a violent story? Arguably every story is a violent one, if you take "violence" to simply mean "a conflict of any kind." (A story completely lacking conflict, after all, would be rather defiantly so, thus conferring a kind of violence on the expectations of the audience, if nothing else.) Even "the drama of a broken teacup," to use Frank Norris' famously scathing description of most literary realism, is drama nonetheless.

But most of the time, when we talk about violence and art, we're referring to art that takes something more extreme than broken china as its subject—and typically, this is violence that causes physical injury or threatens to, though, in many cases, emotional or psychological violence is inseparable from its more tangible counterpart. Art can follow instances of violence that are large-scale—wars that engulf the globe, genocide, institutionalized torture—but the representations themselves almost always give us individuals to consider. This person, that wound, this act of aggression, that resistance. We encounter other people in situations that must be considered on a case-by-case basis, and yet (because this is art) those situations are never just about the individual. They don't stand alone. They stand as re-presentations of something important—something that society values or condemns, perhaps, or something that we must decide ourselves if we condone or censure. How to understand or even identify that "something," however, isn't always clear, and can provoke extended, passionate, and sometimes centuries-long conversations. Because, again, this is art.

Acts of violence can be understood as atrocities, things to be lamented, sworn against, perhaps punished. They can be read as necessities, unfortunate but required, a means to an end. And they can be seen as pleasures, acts to be enjoyed, even savored. In America, the pleasures of violence are many—the well executed sack of a vulnerable quarterback, the child's righteous punch of a bully, the movie hero's final domination of the bad guy. Americans do love their vengeance, as demonstrated in the longstanding popularity of that most American of genres, the Western. The hero there will kill, but only reluctantly, judiciously, and justly. He may even be an outlaw, but we are still to understand him as a man with honor. The gun he wears "tells us that he lives in a world of violence, and even that he 'believes in violence,'" writes Robert Warshow. "But the drama is one of self-restraint: the moment of violence must come in its own time and according to its special laws, or else it is valueless" (Warshow 716). And so the Virginian shoots Trampas; Shane kills Wilson and his cronies; the Ringo Kid shoots Luke Plummer and his two brothers. The pleasures are obvious: wrongdoers are found, punished; victims find saviors; families and townsfolk can settle down and live peaceful lives as their hero rides off into the sunset, taking his guns with him.

But violence loses its pleasure for those who would see stories like these as, at best, escapist myth and, at worst, the mythology of oppression—of women, whose roles are minimized; of African and

Mexican Americans, who also assume lesser supporting positions; and, of course, Native Americans, who so often are the de facto enemy in classic Westerns, simply because they live on the land that white civilization wants to claim for its own. The power and satisfaction of the wielding of violence can be dampened if one is familiar with the pains of being its object. For those plagued in their real lives by domestic abuse, political terror, or gang violence, or for those who feel that, righteous or not, revenge is not a proper response to wrongdoing, even represented violence can lose its pleasure. For many, art that takes violence as its subject should be realistic about society's challenges, and forsake simple pleasures for hard truths.

But the pleasures of well-represented violence are never simple, even in a seemingly open-and-shut case like *Shane*. The Western hero, argues Warshow, is always a figure of moral ambiguity, since his justice is always violently delivered; it taints him, sets him apart from others, as Richard Slotkin has also noted. And defining morality by the actions of a single person is always a troubling, if seductive, inclination. In Jack Schaefer's original novel from 1949, which predated the Hollywood film by four years, the young narrator spies Shane on his way to that final showdown:

> He was the man I saw that first day, a stranger, dark and forbidding, forging his lone way out of an unknown past in the utter loneliness of his own immovable and instinctive defiance. He was the symbol of all the dim, formless imaginings of danger and terror in the untested realm of human potentialities beyond my understanding. The impact of the menace that marked him was like a physical blow. (Schaefer 134)

For a boy given completely to hero worship of this stranger, the description is striking—and more striking still when considered in the light of the novel's publication, just a few years after the United States had wielded its own kind of terror in World War II. Schaefer may not have been consciously thinking about Hiroshima, Nagasaki, and the firebombing of Tokyo when he wrote about "the untested realm of human potentialities," but the implications are there to explore.

This volume is, in many ways, dedicated to the pleasures of works of art that depict violence and the taxonomy of those pleasures—whether they are the pleasures of aesthetic satisfaction, of intellectual rigor, of escapism or of confrontation, of personal or political recognition, of giving voice to those in pain, or simply the realization that someone, somewhere, has captured something essential about the suffering that is an integral part of being human. These are pleasures that—even, or perhaps especially, in the most escapist of tales—should never be easy or unchallenging.

My own interests tend toward the exquisite articulation of extreme violence, the complex reactions engendered when poetic language rubs up against horror. My first encounter with this was in Cormac McCarthy's *Blood Meridian*, a historical novel that follows a group of men who are paid by the Mexican government to scalp Native Americans in 1849. The protagonist is an unnamed "kid" of sixteen who falls in first with a filibustering expedition led by Captain White, a man determined to militarily dispute the Treaty of Guadalupe Hidalgo, which ended the Mexican-American War and set the Rio Grande as the border between those two nations. "We fought for it. Lost friends and brothers down there. And then by God if we didnt give it back," White says to the kid, lamenting the territory he feels the United States gave up (McCarthy 33). "Back to a bunch of barbarians that even the most biased in their favor will admit have no least notion in God's earth of honor or justice or the meaning of republican government" (McCarthy 33). He goes on:

> What we are dealing with . . . is a race of degenerates. A mongrel race, little better than niggers. And maybe no better. There is no government in Mexico. Hell, there's no God in Mexico. Never will be. We are dealing with a people manifestly incapable of governing themselves. And do you know what happens with people who cannot govern themselves? That's right. Others come in to govern for them . . . We are to be the instruments of liberation in a dark and troubled land. (McCarthy 34)

It's perfect imperialist rhetoric, complete with dehumanizing language that is a denial of Mexican government, religion, and morality. The only thing to do, as the appropriately named White sees it, is to go there and take what rightfully belongs to the United States (as a number of filibustering expeditions really did attempt to do during this time period.)

As easy as White expects the mission to be for such clearly superior troops, they are undone in unexpected ways. An old Mennonite warns them before they depart: "The wrath of God lies sleeping," he says. "It was hid a million years before men were and only men have power to wake it. Hell aint half full. Hear me. Ye carry war of a madman's making onto a foreign land. Ye'll wake more than the dogs" (McCarthy 40). That warning is echoed in McCarthy's descriptions of the landscape, which grow cosmic as the men ride through an unforgiving desert:

> All night sheetlightning quaked sourceless to the west beyond the midnight thunderheads, making a bluish day out of the distant desert, the mountains on the sudden skyline stark and black and livid like a land of some other order out there whose true geology was not stone but fear. The thunder moved up from the southwest and lightning lit the desert all about them, blue and barren, great clanging reaches ordered out of the absolute night like some demon kingdom summoned up or changeling land that come the day would leave them neither trace nor smoke nor ruin more than any troubling dream. (McCarthy 47)

When they encounter other men to fight, the battle doesn't go as planned. It's not their stated opponent, and it's not even really a battle. When they see dust on the horizon, White at first takes it to be "a parcel of heathen stocktheives" with whom they may see "a little sport" (McCarthy 51). But it's an attacking party of Comanche warriors, painted and "clad in costumes attic or biblical or wardrobed out of a fevered dream with the skins of animals and silk finery and pieces of uniform still tracked with the blood of prior owners," howling and charging, "death hilarious" (McCarthy 52–53). The men can do no more than gasp out "oh my God" before they are shot by arrows, pierced by lances, and scalped. The scene is chaotic, excessive—the satisfaction at seeing White's racism turned on its ear is quickly tempered by the extreme violence of the attack,

---

and that violence is both heightened and made aesthetic by the way McCarthy describes it:

> Now driving in a wild frieze of headlong horses with clusters of arrows clenched in their jaws and their shields winking in the dust and up the far side of the ruined ranks in a piping of boneflutes and dropping down off the sides of their mounts with one heel hung in the withers strap and their short bows flexing beneath the outstretched necks of the ponies until they had circled the company and cut their ranks in two and then rising up again like funhouse figures, some with nightmare faces painted on their breasts, riding down the unhorsed Saxons and spearing and clubbing them and leaping from their mounts with knives and running about on the ground with a peculiar bandylegged trot like creatures driven to alien forms of locomotion and stripping the clothes from the dead and seizing them up by the hair and passing their blades about the skulls of the living and the dead alike and snatching aloft the bloody wigs and hacking and chopping at the naked bodies, ripping off limbs, heads, gutting the strange white torsos and holding up great handfuls of viscera, genitals, some of the savages so slathered up with gore they might have rolled in it like dogs and some who fell upon the dying and sodomized them with loud cries to their fellows. (53–54)

This reads like the climax of a story, but in fact it's just the opening salvo in a novel that portrays violence in almost every permutation, a Hobbesian war of all against all in a place "beyond men's judgments [where] all covenants were brittle" (McCarthy 106). The kid moves among these people, miraculously surviving the Comanche attack and later joining a gang of scalphunters, "a pack of viciouslooking humans" who are the worst yet, "dangerous, filthy, brutal, the whole like a visitation from some heathen land where they and others like them fed on human flesh" (McCarthy 78). This gang targets anyone with hair dark enough to pass for the Native Americans they have been contracted to eliminate, and their conflicts are numerous, deadly, and often arbitrary. When the leader of that group is finally killed himself, McCarthy writes that an old Yuman warrior raises an axe and "split the head of John Joel Glanton to the thrapple," using an archaic Scottish word for throat (McCarthy 275). McCarthy's descriptions and word choices reflect these moments' extremity and strangeness, as if his sentences' rhythms and vocabulary must necessarily push the boundaries of language in order to render such things.

But the point, ultimately, is a larger one, especially for readers who wonder early on who they're supposed to root for in such a ubiquitously violent world. If no one group is better than any other, if everyone is capable of such appalling action, then why tell the story, beyond pointing out that the Old West wasn't the land of mythic justice that it's so often cracked up to be? While I think there's a lot to think about simply in McCarthy's descriptive practices—can violence be beautiful? If so, what are the implications?—he's up to more here, and hints at as much in the opening pages. The kid, the novel's protagonist, leaves his drunken father at fourteen and heads to Texas by way of Memphis, St. Louis, and New Orleans. As he approaches his destination, McCarthy tells us that he is now "finally divested of all that he has been. His origins are become remote as is his destiny and not again in all the world's turning will there be terrains so wild and barbarous to try whether the stuff of creation may be shaped to man's will or whether his own heart is not another kind of clay" (McCarthy 4–5).

This statement can be interpreted a number of different ways, but at bottom it poses a question about how the kid—this blank slate of sorts, a person remote from both origin and destiny, the circumstances of his birth and death—will or won't be affected by his exposure to violence. Will he shape creation, or be shaped? If so, to what end? It's a question that is answered enigmatically if at all and has spawned a robust scholarly discussion over the years. As precise as the novel is about the workings of violent human interaction, and what happens when people come crashing into one another with lethal intent and ruthlessness, it offers less about what happens to the soul in such cases, even though that's the very question it begins by asking. Or if it does tell you about the soul, about the human spirit, it does so in ways that are not easy to parse— as is, perhaps, appropriate. (I've offered this discussion of the novel without touching on either the character of Judge Holden or the epilogue, both of which are essential but quite complex elements when considering what the novel has to say about violence and human nature. Too much, I think, for the space I have here.)

"Can you describe this?" a woman asks Anna Akhmatova during Stalin's Great Purge of the Soviet Union, as they stand together in a prison queue in Leningrad. "Yes, I can," she replies, as Akhmatova relates in the opening of her poem cycle *Requiem*. "And then something like the shadow of a smile crossed what had once been her face" (Akhmatova 2346). Horror that doesn't stay beyond language's reach, where all horror begins—it creates a small satisfaction, a realization that others will know, that the experiences won't fade into nightmare. Even when Akhmatova goes on to describe what happened in part as a denial, a veiling, the power is still there:

> No, it is not I, it is someone else who is suffering.
> I could not have borne it. And this thing which has happened,
> Let them cover it with black cloths,
> And take away the lanterns . . . Night. (2348)

Pleasure, then—even if it's just the shadow of a smile, someone else's story that seems like your own. Maybe it's your own because it creates the deepest kind of personal recognition, or maybe it becomes yours because it brings something utterly distant from your own life into sharp, exquisite focus, and that something stays with you. This is pleasure that provokes deep and often difficult reflection, even more so when you put those reflections in play with others'—in the kind of conversation that is perhaps more necessary than any other. "You saw nothing in Hiroshima. Nothing," the man tells the woman at the beginning of Marguerite Duras' *Hiroshima Mon Amour*. "I saw *everything*," she insists. "*Everything*" (15). And the story goes on from there.

Works Cited

Akhmatova, Anna. *Requiem*. Trans. D. M. Thomas. *The Norton Anthology of World*

Masterpieces. 5th ed. ed. Maynard Mack et al. New York: Norton, 1987. 2346–53. *The Bhagavad Gita*. Trans. Eknath Easwaran. Tomales, CA: Nilgiri Press, 2007.

Brontë, Charlotte. *Jane Eyre*. 1847. New York: Penguin, 1985.

Duras, Marguerite. *Hiroshima Mon Amour*. 1960. Trans. Richard Seaver. New York: Grove Press, 1994.

Gilbert, Sandra M., & Susan Gubar. *The Madwoman in the Attic: The Woman Writer and the Nineteenth-Century Literary Imagination*. New Haven: Yale UP, 1979.

McCarthy, Cormac. *Blood Meridian*. 1985. New York: Vintage, 1992.

Rhys, Jean. *Wide Sargasso Sea*. 1966. New York: Norton, 1992.

Schaefer, Jack. *Shane*. New York: Random House, 1949.

Warshow, Robert. "Movie Chronicle: The Westerner." 1954. *Film Theory and Criticism*. 6th ed. Eds. Leo Braudy & Marshall Cohen. New York: Oxford UP, 2004. 703–716.

CRITICAL
CONTEXTS

The Foundations of Violence in Ancient Greek Literature_____

In spring of 431 BCE, months before the beginning of what we may justly call the first long, continuous, and two-parted world war in Western history, the so-called Peloponnesian War (431–404 BCE) between the city-state of Athens and her subject allies and the Spartans and their allies, many thousands of adult male citizens of Athens sat together in the theater of Dionysus beneath the south wall of the acropolis and took in the play we now call Euripides' *Medea*. The preceding fifty years had seen almost constant localized warfare in the greater Greek world. Athenian citizens were major participants in that widespread recurring violence (Palaima, "Civilian Knowledge").

The *Medea* was the first of the set of four plays by Euripides produced on that given day and the only one to survive. The title it is known by rightly identifies the character who is the focus of the play: Medea, a non-Greek princess from the furthest eastern limits of the Black Sea, who, as she herself admits in the play, has betrayed her father and fatherland for love of the Greek adventurer-hero Jason. Medea kills her own younger brother and cuts his body into chunks of bloody flesh that she, then even more sacrilegiously (if we can put such matters on a sliding scale), flings from Jason's ship into the sea, in order to slow the pursuit of her country's royal fleet. When Jason and Medea reach Jason's home city of Iolcus in northern Greece, Medea tricks the daughters of Jason's uncle—who has usurped power from Jason—into killing their own father in an act of rejuvenation magic that Medea makes sure will fail. Jason and Medea then flee to Corinth where King Creon gives them refuge.

The play is set in Corinth. It lays out for us how and why this exotic, feared, socially isolated, non-Greek woman—a murderess who deals in the dark arts of magic—decides to kill her children and then does kill them. The trigger event is the news that Jason will

The Foundations of Violence   3 abandon Medea and their two children, in order to secure material well-being and a renewal of his faded fame and prestige by marrying a young princess, daughter of the king.

A definitive scholarly commentary on the *Medea*, written by Denys L. Page seventy-five years ago, just before the outbreak of another horrific world war, had this to say about the key action in the play:

> The murder of children, caused by jealousy and anger against their father, is mere brutality; if it moves us at all, it does so towards incredulity and horror. Such an act is outside our experience, we— and the fifth century Athenian—know nothing of it. (xiv)

The abominable violence of a mother killing her children is not outside our experience, and I doubt whether it was outside the experience of the ancient Athenians. The larger question, however, is what set of cultural conditions made the ancient Athenian audience and still makes modern readers and audiences want to know how and why a mother could be brought into a psychological state and mindset in which killing her own children with her own hands becomes, to her, what she has to do.

As with elements of the Old Testament, the earliest recorded literary texts in ancient Greek were songs from a long-standing oral tradition that were selected, edited, and written down in order to ensure their preservation. From the time when alphabetic writing was first introduced, around the eighth century BCE, down through the full development in fifth-century classical Athens of many of the literary genres, especially poetic forms that we still consider canonical, Greek literature is mainly a public performance literature embedded in a still primarily oral culture. And it is run through with violence.

This is true even if we leave aside the two famous early epics, the *Iliad* and the *Odyssey*, attributed to Homer. The two great Homeric song poems lay out, with an almost clinical accuracy, the hard realities—psychological, physical, emotional, and practical— of what human beings go through in practicing and experiencing violence: when state-sanctioned and state-organized armies are away at war; when the inhabitants of cities and countries are fighting in defense of their territories, homes, families, and ways of life (the ancient Greek *politeia*, from the word *polis*, was used by the ancient Greeks for their peculiar form of city and is related to our word "politics," that is, "matters having to do with living in a *polis*"); and when soldiers return home to their communities, where life has gone on without them and where even their closest friends and family members have not shared the sufferings and hardships they, as combat veterans, bring back hard-wired in their memories. These are aspects of violence we still want and need to know about as individuals and members of families and larger social groups when and after our country is at war.[1] So it is no wonder that the Homeric epics have survived and are translated anew generation after generation.

Violent acts and their immediate effects and after-effects, direct and indirect, on human beings consume the lengthy song poems—the *Iliad* is 15,693 lines long, the *Odyssey* 12,110. In the *Iliad*, over two hundred combat deaths are described in gruesomely graphic detail. They are so numerous and so grisly that one critic remarks, "in terms of sheer body count, most of those that perish in battle seem to have been created simply in order for others to kill them" (Marks 300).

In the *Iliad*, the goddess Hera offers up for annihilation the innocent citizens of the three friendliest cities (Argos, Sparta, and Mycenae) where she is worshiped dutifully and piously (Homer, *Iliad* 4.50–54). Agamemnon, commander-in-chief of the Greek forces attacking Troy, declares his aim to exterminate the Trojans as a people by killing all the males in the city, even male fetuses in their mothers' wombs (Homer, *Iliad* 6.51–65). Priam, king of Troy, conjures up a nightmare image of what will befall him once his son Hector is killed by Achilles in combat. The very dogs, to which Priam once fed scraps from his table, will feast upon and mutilate the genitals of his corpse (Homer, *Iliad* 22.66–76).

In the *Odyssey*, Odysseus, the returning king, slaughters the men who consumed his resources in his long absence and hangs the female servants who took pleasure with them. Earlier in the cave of the Cyclops, Polyphemus grabs several of Odysseus' men and smashes their heads open upon the rocks in the same violently matter-of-fact way that, Homer notes in a simile, human beings kill unwanted puppies in a new litter (Homer, *Odyssey* 9.289–290). In the same episode, we get what is to us a ghastly, detailed description of what happens to an eye—in this case, the giant eye of a Cyclops—when it is pierced by a sharpened and fire-hardened wooden staff (Homer, *Odyssey* 9.387–394). It is worthwhile thinking about what sensibilities, cultural values and histories, life experiences, and personal expectations the audiences, who received such violent scenes during their realization in recitation (for song poems) or enactment (for plays), must have had.

The hero of the *Iliad* is Achilles. His name means "he who causes hurtful woe to the male fighting force" (*akhi-* from Greek *akhos*; see our word "ache"; *-lleus* ultimately from *lāos*). As the story of the *Iliad* unfolds, we see that Achilles causes countless sufferings for soldiers in both the enemy Trojan *lāos* (army) and his own Greek *lāos* (army). The hero of the *Odyssey* is Odysseus. He is, as the Coen and Stanley brothers played with his name in the soundtrack to the film *O Brother, Where Art Thou?*, the "man of constant sorrow," literally "the man who *has to do with* painful sorrow."[2] These two heroes enact what their names signify through violence, what Simone Weil in her classic essay on the *Iliad* calls "the use of force" (Holoka).

Ancient Greek mythmakers (the word *muthos* means simply "something uttered," i.e., what we call a "story") did not shy away from describing brutally violent acts. They told stories that describe extreme violence, which causes severe psychological and physical trauma, including macabre forms of death. In Euripides' *Bacchae*, a mother with her aristocratic women friends, while in the ecstasy (literally *ekstasis*, emotionally and psychologically "standing outside yourself") of Dionysiac ritual in the mountainous countryside, tears apart her own son, the young King Pentheus, whose name comes from the root *path-* meaning "suffer" (see our English words "pathos," "pathetic" and "sympathy"), and fixes his severed head on a pike. They think they have killed and beheaded a lion. She and her fellow celebrants, carrying his mounted head, parade exultantly into the horrified city (*polis*, see *politeia* above) where the return to organized communal life brings them back to their senses.

The violence in Greek literature—excluding, hereafter, war literature *per se*—is wielded almost indiscriminately. Its targets include noble and reverent men and women, the old and the young, the strong and the weak, the helpless remnants of the fighting force of the hero Odysseus and newborn puppies, those who have sinned and those who are pure and righteous and helpless.

The violence often cascades and careens. In Euripides' play *Herakles*, performed in 430 BCE, a year after *Medea*, when the Peloponnesian War had begun and a devastating plague was breaking out in Athens, murders are planned and executed in mafia-like power struggles between the families of the hero Herakles and the usurping ruler Lycus. Put the word "don" in front of these two names, and it is easier to understand that we are seeing a clan blood feud play out between the family of Don Herakles and the families of two other ancient mafia godfathers. The violence here, however, is compounded by what our society would now diagnose as PTSD (post-traumatic stress disorder) affecting Herakles (Mercouri), and it is mixed in with intra-family violence and what human beings conceive of as divinely sanctioned killing.

Lycus sets in motion the slaughter of Megara, the wife of Herakles and daughter of the legitimate king, Creon, and their three children. When they take refuge at an altar of Zeus, Lycus orders a pyre to be built around them and Megara and her three children to be burned alive. Herakles returns from a harrowing and traumatizing labor in Hades—his task was to bring the hound of hell, Cerberus, out of the underworld. He kills Lycus, but is then driven mad at the instigation of the goddess Hera, wife of Zeus, for no better reason than that she has always disliked Herakles. Iris, the messenger of the gods, and the *daimōn* (see below) Madness come down from Olympus to effect her plan. In his deranged state of mind, Herakles thinks he is killing Eurystheus, another hated power rival, who had set him on his twelve labors, and Eurystheus' children. Instead, he kills his own wife Megara and their three children.

All this takes place in Thebes, a city of violence from the time it was founded:

> Thebes, where dragon teeth
> Were broadcast and sprouted full-grown fighters
> Berserk to kill each other.
> Ares kept a few back
> From the slaughter and they put down roots—their children's
> Children grew up here in this city Kadmos
> Built from the ground up.
> (Euripides, *Herakles* 8–13, translation Sleigh)

We sample the murderous fury that consumes Herakles when, having returned, he declares to Megara and the chorus of old men of Thebes what he intends to do.

> As for me, for the matter is now in my hands,
> first I'll go and tear down, foundations and all, the palace halls
> of this new self-installed ruling family. I'll slice off his fucking
>   head
> and throw it to the dogs to drag about like a chew toy. As for
>   the Thebans,
> whoever was one of us, whoever we treated well and went over
>   to them,
> I'll bring them down with this here unbeatable club of mine.
> As for the rest of them, I'll spray arrows all over the fucking
>   place
> and fill the entire sacred Ismenus river with corpses of all
>   kinds,
> an all out slaughter, and the clear spring waters of Dirce, I'll
>   make them run blood red.
> For who deserves my protection more than my wife, my kids
>   and my old man.
> (Euripides, *Herakles* 565–575, translation mine)

Herakles' acts in obtaining vengeance will include decapitation, sacrilegiously defiling a corpse, and rampant clubbing to death of all Thebans who in any way associated themselves with the usurper's family. He'll then create a bloodbath with his rapid-fire bow, a kind of ancient Bushmaster model XM-15. The slaughter it causes will pollute the sacred river Ismenus by choking it with dead bodies. And it will make what the Greeks literally call the "white" waters of the equally sacred Dirce spring and stream flow blood red.

Well before Alfred Hitchcock in his film *Psycho* (1960) orchestrated, with the body and eye of actress Janet Leigh in a scene set in a Bates Motel bathroom, the violent choreography of knife blade, shower head, tub drain, and shower curtain, Aeschylus in his tragedy *Agamemnon* has Agamemnon's unfaithful and long murderously hateful wife and queen Clytemnestra—hateful because Agamemnon had killed their daughter Iphigeneia in blood sacrifice to the goddess Artemis at the start of the Trojan expedition, in order to gain fair winds for the sailing of his armada—fawningly seduce him, on his triumphal return from Troy, into entering into the palace at the top of the site of Mycenae. There, she kills him with knife blow after knife blow in the royal bathtub (a rare luxury even in fifth-century Athens).

Clytemnestra comes out on stage afterwards, spattered with his blood, and describes her act in an orgasmic ecstasy:

> I stand here where I struck, and the deed is done.
> This was my work, I do not deny it.
> I cast my vast net, tangling around him,
> wrapping him in a robe rich in evil.
> I struck him twice and he screamed twice,
> his limbs buckled and his body came crashing down,
> and as he lay there, I struck him again, a third blow
> for underworld Zeus, the savior of the dead.
> He collapsed, gasping out his last breath,
> his life ebbing away, spitting spurts of blood,
> which splattered down on me like dark sanguine dew.
> And I rejoiced just as the newly sown earth rejoices,
> When Zeus send the nourishing rain on the young crops.
>   (Aeschylus, *Agamemnon* 1380–1392, translation Meineck)

Clytemnestra shows pride in her plan and its execution. She has finally outwitted and put to death arguably the most powerful man in all of Greece, the commander-in-chief of the allied forces that took the citadel of Troy. She revels in giving the details of the three knife blows, as if she is a holy priestess blood-sacrificing a male victim in full prime in long-delayed compensation for the young daughter whom ten years before, Agamemnon, husband and father, had ritually slain (slitting her throat with a knife) before she had even reached marrying age. The blood that pulses from Agamemnon's wounds, wounds Clytemnestra has made, spurts upon her like refreshingly welcome bloody dew, a morning mist that falls upon and nourishes young plants growing in the field. No one who did not understand the psychological states of people committing violent acts could have written so macabrely vivid and riveting a passage. Aeschylus was a combat veteran. He had fought at the plain and beach of Marathon during the first Persian War (490 BCE), the Normandy of ancient Athenian history (Palaima, "When War").

How and why was extreme violence so prevalent in Greek literature? Why was it depicted so graphically in plays that were publicly performed at large-scale annual ritual dramatic festivals in the *polis* of Athens and songs that were publicly sung at other public festival competitions? What atmosphere, social norms, and worldviews made violence in literature commonplace? Why does it fascinate us now?

Violence had to be of interest and pleasing to the audience, or else the playwrights and singers would not have chosen violent themes for their tragedies and song poems. They were, after all, in serious public competitions and, to focus on tragedy, the subject matter of a play and its treatment were crucial for its success in performance. A chief social motivation for good behaviors or excellent achievements among men in Greek culture was the *kleos*, "communal fame," that they would win by performing well in what they were obliged to do as soldiers, citizens, athletes, and what we would call politicians—and in the simultaneously civic and religious song, dance and theatrical competitions put on within their *poleis* (plural of *polis*). Archetypically, Achilles was willing to trade a long life in enjoyable and undisturbed obscurity for a short life with *kleos* as a soldier and field commander. For the tragic playwrights, victory at the festivals was serious business to a degree that we cannot fully comprehend.

One set of clues about the cultural environment for Greek literature of violence comes from what we know about Greek religious thought from the central text called Hesiod's *Theogony* (*Birth of the Gods*). Other insights come from Hesiod's *Works and Days*. In the W*orks and Days*, Hesiod examines through a moral filter the history of Greek culture and the moral and ethical codes and behavior patterns that prevail in contemporary Greek society. The *Theogony* is generally compared, as a creation myth, to the book of *Genesis.* The *Works and Days* has elements that are parallel to biblical parainetic or morality literature.

As with the cultures of Egypt, Israel, and the Near and Middle East, the supernatural world that the Greeks, from 800 to 400 BCE, posited as affecting, if not fully controlling, human affairs was permeated with violence. The chief gods in these cultures were essentially "warrior kings" (Hiebert 876–880), who used violence or the threat of violence to maintain their dominance, to subject other forces (both spiritual entities and what we would consider natural forces within the physical universe) to their wills, and to keep the *kosmos* (the organized and orderly world) stable. The violence on high, as it were, reflected the conditions of power relationships in Greek culture of the period—recall here how violently Herakles exerts his power in the bloodbath he envisions and how Clytemnestra achieves her vengeance by using a bath as a sacrificial altar. Violence was wielded among the gods to establish and maintain a stable *status quo* under Zeus. This served as a paradigm for human beings who hoped that otherwise unattainable justice would prevail on earth through at least the threat of violent intervention from the divine sphere.

The *Works and Days* and *Theogony* of Hesiod, both song poems of about 1,000 lines in length using the same artificial dialect and dactylic hexameter verse form as the Homeric poems, reflected the view of natural and supernatural worlds imbued with violence that prevailed throughout Greek culture from the time when these poems coalesced into their present forms ca. 700 BCE through the following three centuries.

The ancient Greeks in historical times, and even earlier, so far as we can tell from the economic documents (Palaima, "Linear B Sources") and depictions on wall paintings and man-made artifacts from the major palatial centers of the late Greek Bronze Age (e.g., Pylos, Mycenae, Thebes, Tiryns, Knossos) ca. 1600–1200 BCE, were polytheistic and held a shared belief in an eventually fixed pantheon of deities, who dwelled on Mount Olympus. In both works of Hesiod, however, the focus on an all-powerful storm god named Zeus, who can violently force natural and supernatural powers to his will, verges on monotheism.

The *Works and Days* opens with a short hymn to the Muses. They themselves, Hesiod tells us, sing in celebration about:

> the will of great Zeus.
> Easy for Him to build up the strong
> And tear the strong down.
> Easy for Him to diminish the mighty
> And magnify the obscure.
> Easy for Him to straighten the crooked
> And wither the proud.
>
> (Hesiod, *Works and Days* 6–12, translation Lombardo)

The Muses' own song makes clear that justice (*dikē*) ultimately resides in Zeus, a great hope for mortal human beings whose lives, as Hesiod describes prevailing conditions, are generally worse than Thomas Hobbes' famous description. Most human beings in rural areas in the early seventh century BCE lived in "continual fear and danger of violent death, and the life of man [was] solitary, poor, nasty, brutish, and short" (Hobbes 76).

No small wonder, then, that the first principle of society that Hesiod takes up in the *Works and Days* is *eris*, which has a range of related meanings: "political or domestic strife," "conflict in battle," and most neutrally "a spirit of competition." In Homer, *Eris* is personified as a *daimōn*, a supernatural force that "distributes" whatever powers it controls to mortals for good or for ill. *Daimones* (the plural form) are not what we would call full-fledged "gods," but they affect human behaviors, lives, and societies. *Eris*, as a *daimōn*, is a sister of the dreaded god of war Ares. *Eris* drives men on to war with one another.

Hesiod soon takes up why life is so difficult for human beings, why we have to strive and struggle, often with no real gain. At one time:

> the human race
> had lived off the land without any trouble, no hard work,
> No sickness or pain that the Fates give to men
> (and when men are in misery they show their age quickly).
> (Hesiod, *Works and Days* 111–114, translation Lombardo)

But because Prometheus stole fire and brought it to mortals, Zeus ordered other divine beings (Hephaestus, Athena, Aphrodite, Hermes, the Graces, Persuasion and the Seasons) to construct for mortal men an irresistible "evil thing" (*kakon*), in fact their *very own* "evil thing," in which they would delight, embracing it in love. This evil thing was the first woman, infused by Aphrodite with "painful desire and knee-weakening anguish," supplied by Hermes with a "bitchy mind and a cheating heart" and "lies and wheedling words," and built by Hephaestus with a "face like an immortal goddess'" and "the figure like a beautiful desirable virgin's" (Hesiod, *Works and Days* 77–102). Thus was Pandora brought into being. Her name is understood either as meaning "all-giver" of gifts, good and bad, or herself "all-gifted" with attributes by this consortium of divine designers and manufacturers.

Daily life was so bleak, hard, and randomly violent that what Pandora lets loose upon the world is not a small perfume jar, cosmetic case, or jewelry box of evils, as in many later and modern European depictions, but an entire large clay storage jar (*pithos*) full of *kēdea lugra* (literally "miserable or mournful troubles," with the words here having the full force of the roots on which they are built: "misery" and "mourning") (Hesiod, *Works and Days* 115–116). A few lines later, Hesiod emphasizes that there are *muria lugra*, or "tens of thousands of miseries"—a "myriad" is the highest number for which the Greeks had a word—now wandering throughout the world (Hesiod, *Works and Days* 121–122, li. 100). The verb "wander" is important because it emphasizes the randomness with which violent evil can strike human beings, a notion that Herodotus, the first major Greek historian, almost three centuries later picks up on in his encapsulation of what it means to be a human being: *pan ho anthrōpos sumphorē*, "a human being is entirely a matter of chance coincidence." The very period in which Hesiod is living and singing shares in the conditions he puts *in illo tempore*, in mythic time. The earth is full of evils (*kaka* "bad things"). The sea is full of evils, too. And diseases voicelessly prey in silence upon human beings, day and night.

This prompts Hesiod then to tell us how the hard times in the world came about. It is here we may note the centrality of violence as a key to the wretched and disordered state of humankind. The story Hesiod tells, an adaptation of Near Eastern models, is the Myth of the Five Ages (Hesiod, *Works and Days* 129–234).

Human beings once dwelled in a Golden Age created for them by the "immortals dwelling in heavenly halls" in the time when Kronos—the major male Greek deity, whom Zeus, son of Kronos, overthrew—was dominant. This period was without diseases, without hard labors and without the pains of work. There was no getting old. Grain-giving cropland produced food abundantly of its own accord. Human beings did not go to war or murder one another, but they lived congenially at ease in fine cities and peacefully shared their products among each other. They were rich in healthy livestock, and they were *philoi*, "friends," in the narrow Greek sense, with the blessed gods.

A *philos*, "friend," is someone with whom one shares a reciprocal and mutually beneficial relationship. A common Greek tagline in tragedies and other works of literature bearing on the nature of friendship and the realities of living in Greece is that the best thing that one can do in life is "help your friends and harm your enemies." In the hyper-pragmatic Greek moral world, however, this is dependent upon both parties in a friendship maintaining the capability to be of benefit to each other. A downturn in health or personal fortunes or a wrong turn in choosing social alliances could turn former friends into non-friends or enemies. That everyone was a friend in the Golden Age shows that it is a true Never-never Land, an impossible condition to maintain in the real world that human beings continue to inhabit. In the real world, violence and sheer bad luck disrupt peaceful, and what we would call healthy, relationships.

This paradise of sorts came to an end. Hesiod remarks that the human beings of this Golden Age have become now themselves holy and good *daimones*. These Golden-Age *daimones* act as guardians of human beings and do their best to ward off evils, safeguard just acts, and "repay criminal acts." Note what these three functions reveal about the non-paradisiacal outlook on human society of the audience for Hesiod's song poems. For them the everyday expectation is that evils are prevalent, justice is endangered, and retribution needs to be sought for criminal acts. The guardian spirits from the golden age are givers of "abundance," a true benefaction in an environment that yields the basic necessities of life begrudgingly and only when compelled to do so by continual hard work, human ingenuity and good luck with the weather, the environment and the dispositions and actions of other human beings in your family, clan and broader community.

The human beings of the succeeding Silver Age took a long time to mature and then lived short adult lives. Far from being *philoi* of the blessed gods, they had no desire even to attend upon the gods (*therapeuein*, cf. English "therapy") or to make sacrifices on the holy altars dedicated to the gods, pious behavior that Hesiod says is *themis* (a "set down law") for human beings who act according to established customs. But the fatal flaw of the humans of the Silver Age was that they could not keep themselves from *atasthalos hubris,* "reckless or wicked violent action" (Hesiod, *Works and Days* 155–156, li. 134).

Hubris, or in its Latinized form *hybris,* is the Greek value word that stands for various forms of violence that has social consequences. There is no generally accepted etymology for the word, though one attractive proposal derives it from two roots that mean "high" and "heavy." It, then, literally means something that defies or violates the law of nature, whereby objects that have weight fall down under the force of gravity—i.e., something that is heavy should not, and actually cannot, be high. *Hubris* generally has the sense of violating a set boundary or the established rules of the physical world, human society, or prescribed behavior towards the gods. For this reason, it is used in modern English to describe hybrid plants and animals. In producing hybrids, human thought and skill have defied the laws of nature.

Angry with their impious acts, Kronos does away with men of the Silver Age. His successor as "warrior king" of the gods, Zeus, creates men of the Bronze Age (Hesiod, *Works and Days* 164–177). These human beings epitomize violence. They are characterized as a race (*genos*, see our English word "*geno*cide") that is *deinon*, "terrifying," and *obrimon,* "mighty, strong." We are told these men were preoccupied with *hubries* (plural), "wantonly violent acts," and *stonoenta,* "acts that are literally made of groans, wailings, lamentations." They kill each other off and death takes them, although they are *ekpagloi,* "frighteningly terrifying."

Next came a "divine race of heroes" made by Zeus (Hesiod, *Works and Days* 180–194). This race behaves more justly and nobly. They are even called demigods (*hēmitheoi*). They precede the race of human beings of Hesiod's own time, the Iron Age. This stage is a clear interpolation into the scheme of generations of human beings in steady decline and designated by metals of decreasing value. The cycles of Greek myths about heroes made the addition of this phase necessary in order to make sense of traditional history.

The heroes are killed off, however, through the violence of evil war (*polemos kakos*) and the dread battle cry or din of war (*phulopis ainē*) in such monumental war adventures as the *Seven Against Thebes* (the prototype for Kurosawa's *The Seven Samurai* and the Hollywood western *The Magnificent Seven*) and the Trojan War.

With this background of the negative evolution of human beings, Hesiod arrives at the Iron Age in which he lives. His view of the Iron Age (Hesiod, *Works and Days* 200–234) is violently apocalyptic. Here, even toil and labor have an inherent violence that ceaselessly, day and night, wears down and destroys men. Like an Old Testament prophet, Hesiod proclaims that Zeus will destroy men of this age on moral grounds. There will be a dissolution of all the social connections and interactions that make society function and life worthwhile.

Fathers will be at odds with their sons. Guests will be disconnected from hosts. The so-called *xenia* relationship between arriving outsiders and unrelated heads of households reduced and curtailed violence by obliging strangers to behave respectfully towards one another in codified roles as guests and hosts.

In Hesiod's Iron Age, brothers will be at odds with each other and children will disrespect parents once the parents have become old. Cities will be stormed and sacked. Men who respect oaths, adhere to justice and are just plain good will be out of favor. Evil-doers and men who are "violence incarnate" will be held in high esteem. The end game will see the two socially significant *daimones* named *Aidōs* (social shame that assures right, proper, and good behavior) and *Nemesis* (retribution for wrongdoing) abandon the earth, leaving behind *algea lugra* ("mournful pains") for death-beset human beings. In the end, there will be no defense at all against evil:

> There go Shame and Nemesis. And horrible suffering
> Will be left for mortal men, and no defense against evil.
> (Hesiod, *Works and Days*, 233–234, translation Lombardo)

At this point, Hesiod offers his most famous story, besides the tale of Pandora, in the *Works and Days*. The tale of the hawk and the nightingale (Hesiod, *Works and Days* 235–245) is a stunningly raw description of the law of tooth-and-claw violence. Its only saving grace is that its message that "might makes right irrelevant" just might persuade the corrupt petty kinglets who wield power and authority in backwater territories in Hesiod's time to be fearful that Zeus might assert his power over them. In fact, Hesiod says explicitly that it is a "fable for kings" (Hesiod, *Works and Days* 235), i.e., a story that they need to think about.

The hawk says to the nightingale, as he flies on high with her in his talons:

> No sense in your crying. You're in the grip of real strength now.
> And you'll go where I take you, songbird or not.
> I'll make a meal of you if I want, or I might let you go.
> Only a fool struggles against those who are stronger.
> He will not win and he suffers pains in addition to disgrace.
> (Hesiod, *Works and Days* 240–244, translation Lombardo)

Indeed, Hesiod summons up an apocalyptic vision of what the warrior sky god Zeus, dispenser and protector of Justice, will bring to pass for human beings who behave violently and lawlessly.

> But for those who live for violence and vice,
> Zeus, son of Kronos, broad-browed god, decrees
> A just penalty, and often a whole city suffers
> For one bad man and his damn fool schemes.
> The son of Kronos sends them disaster from heaven,
> Famine and plague, and the folk wither away,
> Women stop bearing children, whole families
> Die off, by Zeus' Olympian will. Or another time
> He might lay low their army, or tumble down
> Their Walls, or sink all their ships at sea.
> (Hesiod, *Works and Days* 276–285, translation Lombardo)

The *Theogony* of Hesiod reinforces in the divine sphere the violence and instability that in the *Works and Days*, after the golden age, have pervaded the human sphere. In the *Theogony*'s scheme, one epoch ruled by a chief male deity succeeds the next. Kronos, the youngest son of the earth mother Gaea and the first supreme male god Ouranos (the vault of the sky), in complicity with his mother, castrates his father. As we might now expect, Hesiod describes the scene in all its gloriously gory splendor:

> From his dark hiding-place, the son reached out
> With his left hand, while with his right he swung
> The fiendishly long and jagged sickle, pruning the genitals

Of his own father with one swoop and tossing them
Behind him, where they fell to no small effect.
Earth soaked up all the bloody drops that spurted out,
And as the seasons went by she gave birth to the Furies
And to great Giants gleaming in full armor, spears in hand.

        (Hesiod, *Theogony* 179–186, translation Lombardo)

Later, Zeus, with the assistance of three fantastically powerful, early-born monsters known as the *Hekatonkheires*, the "Hundred-Handers," comes to power in an all-out war against the monstrous Titans, who were born from Ouranos before his castration. Zeus unleashes his own violence to subdue opposing supernatural forces and demonstrate his power to one and all:

And now Zeus no longer held back his strength.
His lungs seethed with anger and he revealed
All his power. He charged from the sky, hurtling
Down from Olymp[u]s in a flurry of lightning,
Hurling thunderbolts one after another, right on target,
From his massive hand, a whirlwind of holy flame.

        (Hesiod, *Theogony* 690–695, translation Lombardo)

Yet mortal human beings still lived in the world that Hesiod, Homer, Herodotus, and the tragic playwrights preserve for us. It is a violent world in which:

. . . Night bore hateful Doom and black Fate
And Death and Sleep and the brood of Dreams.

And deadly Night bore Nemesis too, more misery
For mortals; and after her, Deception and Friendship
And ruinous Old Age, and hard-hearted Eris.
And hateful Eris bore agonizing Toil,
Fortgetfulness, Famine and tearful Pains,
Battles and Fights, Murders and Manslaughters,
Quarrels, Lying Words and Words Disputatious,
Lawlessness and Recklenssness.

        (Hesiod, *Theogony* 211–212, 223–230, translation Lombardo)

This is the world the ancient Greeks learned of and knew from their central enculturating texts. They knew and feared that sons could kill their fathers and vice versa. They knew about incest, fratricide, frenzied mass killing, and infanticide. They knew a mother could kill her children. They explored the circumstances, conditions, inner psychological state, and triggering events that could cause a mother to kill her children. And in Aristotle's view, what they witnessed aroused in them pity and fear, and it then somehow purified or distilled those natural emotions surrounding their reality-based anxieties.

Euripides' *Medea* appeals to us now, not as an unrealistic horror film, but because we, along with the ancient Greeks, understand that the world is a violent place and it pays for us to know what leads to violent acts that only seem to have been ruled out by strong social, religious, educational, and legal principles and taboos.

The play offers a stunning psychological portrait of a powerful woman brought by powerful erotic emotions into a position of isolation and powerlessness in a culture not her own, but one she chose, while betraying every important social link to her own culture: fatherland, father, and brother. Medea is a woman with strong powers in the black arts and with strong passions. She has a strong love for her children. She has religiously deep feelings of oath-bound love for the now middle-aged Greek adventurer hero Jason, whom she considers her husband. She is a woman betrayed by a shell of a hero, an anxious middle-aged man looking now for comfort and position, trading his reputation, his *kleos*, for security and status. Jason is a man capable of believing his own lies.

Like so many ancient Greek texts, Euripides' *Medea* uses violence to make us see who we are as human beings and how artificial the limits on our violent instincts and actions are. *Medea* helps us not to tell so many lies about human violence and not to trust fully in the lies we do tell.

Notes

1. For more on this issue, see Jonathan Shay's *Achilles in Vietnam* and *Odysseus in America.*

2.   See our English word "anodyne."

Works Cited

Aeschylus. *Oresteia*. Trans. Peter Meineck. Introduction by Helene P. Foley. Indianapolis & Cambridge, MA: Hackett Publishing Company, Inc., 1998.

Euripides. *Herakles*. Trans. Tom Sleigh. Oxford & New York: Oxford UP, 2001.

_____. *Medea*. Trans. Diane Arnson Svarlien. Indianapolis & Cambridge, MA: Hackett Publishing Company, Inc., 2008.

_____. *Medea*. Ed. Denys L. Page. Oxford, UK: Clarendon Press, 1938.

Hesiod. *Works and Days. Theogony.* Trans. Stanley Lombardo. Indianapolis & Cambridge, MA: Hackett Publishing Company, Inc., 1993.

Hiebert, Theodore. "Warrior, Divine." *The Anchor Bible Dictionary*. Ed. David Noel Friedman. New York: Doubleday, 1992. 876–880.

Holoka, James P., ed. *The* Iliad *or The Poem of Force: A Critical Edition.* By Simone Weil. New York: Peter Lang, 2003.

Hobbes, Thomas. *Leviathan*. Ed. Edwin Curley. Indianapolis: Hackett Publishing Company, Inc., 1994.

Homer. *Iliad*. Trans. Stanley Lombardo. Indianapolis & Cambridge, MA: Hackett Publishing Company, Inc., 1997.

_____. *Odyssey*. Trans. Stanley Lombardo. Indianapolis & Cambridge, MA: Hackett Publishing Company, Inc., 2000.

Marks, Jim. "Context as Hypertext: Divine Rescue Scenes in the *Iliad*." *Trends in Classics* 2.2 (2010): 300–322.

Mercouri, Natasha. "Combat Veterans, Neuroscience, and the Tragic Mask: Euripides' *Herakles*." *Didaskalia* 10.5 (2013). Web. 10 Aug. 2014. <http://www.didaskalia.net/issues/10/5/>.

Palaima, Thomas. "Linear B Sources." *Anthology of Classical Myth: Primary Sources in Translation*. Eds. Stephen Brunet, R. Scott Smith, & Stephen Trzaskoma. Indianapolis & Cambridge, MA: Hackett Publishing Company, Inc., 2004. 439–454.

_____. "Civilian Knowledge of War and Violence in Ancient Athens and Modern America." *Experiencing War: Trauma and Society from Ancient Greece to the Iraq War*. Ed. Michael Cosmopoulos. Chicago: Ares, 2007. 9–34.

_____. "When War Is Performed, What Do Soldiers and Veterans Want to Hear and See and Why?" *Combat Trauma and the Ancient Greeks*. Eds. Peter Meineck & David Konstan. New York: Palgrave MacMillan, 2014. 261-285.

Shay, Jonathan. *Achilles in Vietnam. Combat Trauma and the Undoing of Character*. New York: Scribner, 1994.

_____. *Odysseus in America. Combat Trauma and the Trials of Homecoming*. New York: Scribner, 2003.

Tritle, Lawrence A. *A New History of the Peloponnesian War*. Malden, MA: Wiley-Blackwell, 2010.

Blood, Force, Influence: Studying the Representation of Violence_____

Stacey Peebles

In Homer's *Iliad*, which was first written down in the eighth century BCE but contains stories that likely date back much further, the great Greek warrior Achilles sends his close friend and companion Patroclus to fight the Trojans while wearing Achilles' armor. Though he warns Patroclus not to advance too far against the enemy, the young man is ignited by success; eventually, he is undone and dies as a result of a well-timed shove from Apollo, a spear thrust from Euphorbus, and a fatal wound from Hector, the Trojan prince. Achilles vows to avenge his friend's death—but to do so, he needs new armor.

Luckily, his mother is a goddess, and she has connections. She asks Hephaestus, god of the forge, to craft a breastplate, helmet, and leg-armor for her son. Hephaestus' masterpiece, however, is Achilles' shield. That piece is large and strong, of course, but also boasts a design of such breadth and intricacy that it could only be of divine origin. Not only does it contain the earth, sky, sea, sun, moon, and stars, but it also reveals farmers tending the countryside, a great vineyard, and youths reveling in dance. Two cities appear—in one, people gather for weddings and to see a disagreement arbitrated by the city elders. But in the other city, violence is not restrained by mediation. That second city is at war, guarding its wealth and citizenry against an attacking army. The forces clash outside the wall, "Hate and Din and the Angel of Death" fighting among them, and in the battle, one man is dragged dead by his heels (371).

It's not hard to see Achilles' shield as a microcosm of the *Iliad* itself, or indeed the wider world of human experience. People tend livestock, grow crops, and celebrate with each other, but they also fight. Sometimes, eruptions of violence can be contained by the structures of society, as in the first city. Other times, however, violence takes over society and becomes its purpose, as in the second. The image of the dead, dragged man that Achilles will wear on his person presages what he will do to Hector after he kills him, dragging his corpse around the city of Troy. It's an outrage, and everyone, mortal and divine, will agree that Achilles has gone too far. But what is war, after all, if not violence that has gone too far? Considering this, Simone Weil's understanding of the poem becomes clear—that "the true hero, the true subject, the center of the *Iliad* is force . . . that *x* that turns anybody who is subjected to it into a *thing*. Exercised to the limit, it turns man into a thing in the most literal sense: it makes a corpse out of him" (3). But Achilles is as doomed as Hector here. As Weil argues, force, that double-edged sword, turns the killer to stone even as it turns his target into a corpse. "This petrifactive quality of force, two-fold always, is essential to its nature; and a soul which has entered the province of force will not escape this except by a miracle" (Weil 27). Thus is the *Iliad* honest, disturbing, and required reading.

The *Iliad*, that ancient, long-form story of force and its effects, embeds significant representations of violence—notably Achilles' shield—within the larger war story itself. (The *Odyssey* does something similar when Odysseus, on his long, difficult journey home after the war, dines at the court of the Phaeacians and hears a bard sing stories about the Trojan War, about Achilles, and even about himself. The experience moves him to tears.) These epics draw our attention to the ways that violence becomes narrative—how it becomes art—both within the tale and, of course, by the example of the broader tale itself.

The *Iliad* and the *Odyssey* are many things—they can be read with an eye to history, poetry, politics, theology, philosophy, and, as Jonathan Shay has argued, the psychological effects of war. As subjects for study, both art and violence necessarily relate to these other areas of inquiry, and so Homer is a good place to start in a critical history of violence and literature. What follows are some (inevitably selective) thoughts on the roots and branches of that history—intertwined, as they must be, with those of other disciplines, such as military history, psychology, trauma studies, sociology, and media studies. And it's a history that is both ancient and contemporary, evidence of the continual need to consider and reconsider the ways that violence and its representation figure into our understanding of the human community.

With the possible exceptions of myth and theology, as Tom Palaima and David Mikics explore in their essays, the oldest method of systematically studying violence and the ways that violence becomes meaningful within that community is military history. The most famous treatises engage philosophically with their subject, such as Sun Tzu's *The Art of War* (c. 510 BCE), Thucydides' account of the Peloponnesian War (431–404 BCE), and Carl von Clausewitz's *On War* (1832), in which he asserts that war is the continuation of politics by other means—or, as he put it, that "War is not merely a political act, but also a real political instrument, a continuation of political commerce, a carrying out of the same by other means" (119). Ancient and modern military histories of particular wars and battles are very, very numerous, and if you want to know how Scipio Africanus avoided the destructive power of Hannibal's elephants at the Battle of Zama, or how Genghis Khan united the Mongols to conquer much of Asia, or why so many died at the Battle of the Somme, you can easily find a book—or a shelf of them—to answer your questions. But until relatively recently, those books focused on large-scale issues: the movements of troops, the decisions of leaders, the advantages or disadvantages of different kinds of weapons. It was less common to draw attention to the experience of the common soldier, the cog in the midst of such vast machinery. Then in 1985, Richard Holmes published *Acts of War: The Behavior of Men in Battle*, which draws on written and oral memoirs of war to explore the psychological effects of things like homesickness, encounters with the dead, drinking and drugs, coming home, and, of course, killing other people and having them try to kill you. The individual's experience of war has always mattered—and mattered intensely—in stories, music, and visual art; in using memoir to draw conclusions about the psychological effects of combat, however, Holmes legitimized an academic approach to that individual's narrative.

But it was Jonathan Shay, whom I mentioned above, whose work brought the most popular attention to the psychological effects of war trauma, and he did so by making connections between the oral accounts of Vietnam War veterans and the *Iliad*, that many-layered war story. In his *Achilles in Vietnam: Combat Trauma and the Undoing of Character* (1994), Shay shows the similarities of soldiers' experiences even in such vastly different historical contexts. He describes reactions to the betrayal of *thémis,* or "what's right," as when Achilles' war prize is seized by his leader Agamemnon, or when a soldier in Vietnam is ordered to open fire on civilians. He talks about the "berserk state," using a Norse word for a frenzied warrior to show how a soldier can lose all restraint and engage in a killing spree, often triggered by factors like the death of a close comrade—just as Achilles did after Patroclus was killed. And he talks in detail about the symptoms of Post-Traumatic Stress Disorder, or PTSD.

Shay continued this work in another book, *Odysseus in America: Combat Trauma and the Trials of Homecoming* (2002), in which he discusses veterans' difficulties in reintegrating into civilian life, and his general approach has been mirrored by Lawrence Tritle in his *From Melos to My Lai: War and Survival* (2000). Both writers emphasize the importance of community and communication in overcoming the traumatic effects of war, though certainly discovering how to tell your own war story, and finding people to share it with, can be a difficult task. Tritle addresses just how hard it can be for veterans to communicate with non-combatants because the way we commonly use language tends to fail when a solider attempts to describe some important aspect of war. Violence, Tritle argues, creates its own language, whether to veil a harsh truth, make sense of a mind-altering situation, or, on the part of the authorities, to manipulate or spin a situation in order to give an illusion of control. He cites phrases common in Vietnam, such as the all-encompassing "It don't mean nothin," calling napalm-blasted bodies "crispy critters," and the government's method of charting progress with numbers to represent dead bodies. Language is simultaneously too much and too little, and "both definitions explain what processes are at work in creating such language: experiences so brutal and extreme that they lie outside normative language and represent events that run counter to every principle, value, and right one has been taught" (Tritle 132).

In speaking specifically about the soldier's experience, Tritle's observations here are reflected in many studies of trauma generally. As a field, trauma studies gained steam in the 1970s, growing out of both the historically male sphere of war and combat as well as feminist theory and the women's liberation movement; the latter branch brought critical attention to women's narratives of violation and oppression. Studies by Deborah Horvitz and Suzette Henke, for instance, explore issues of voicing trauma in the work of authors like Leslie Marmon Silko, Charlotte Perkins Gilman, Colette, and Anaïs Nin. Cathy Caruth takes Tritle's point about how trauma defies the boundaries of normative language by using works by Freud, Lacan, Resnais, de Man, and Kant to explore the referentiality of trauma—the belated experience of a violent event that one can never precisely assimilate. Therefore, she argues in *Unclaimed Experience* (1996), one must interrogate the narratives of trauma as crises that both defy and demand witness and are spoken in language that both refutes and claims understanding (Caruth 5).

Trauma studies' most influential text, however, is Judith Herman's *Trauma and Recovery* (1992), in which she addresses both rape and combat as well as political terror. Herman explains the response to trauma as a dialectical one, a "conflict between the will to deny horrible events and the will to proclaim them aloud," as well as an alternation between "feeling numb and reliving the event" (1). Like Shay, Tritle, and others, she emphasizes the construction of a personal narrative as the crucial element in the healing process; thus the "work of reconstruction actually transforms the traumatic memory, so that it can be integrated into the survivor's life story" (Herman 175). She contrasts this "trauma story" with the traumatic memory itself, which she says is "wordless and static":

> The survivor's initial account of the event may be repetitious, stereotyped, and emotionless. One observer describes the trauma story in its untransformed state as a "prenarrative." It does not develop or progress in time, and it does not reveal the storyteller's feelings or interpretation of events. Another therapist describes traumatic memory as a series of still snapshots or a silent movie; the role of therapy is to provide the music and the words. (Herman 175)

Rendering trauma into language, as all of these scholars suggest, is a challenge for the individual as well as the artist, and that friction is often what gives masterful stories about violence their power. As Kalí Tal argues, however, putting trauma into words also has great political significance. "Bearing witness is an aggressive act," she writes in her book *Worlds of Hurt: Reading the Literature of Trauma* (1996):

> It is born out of a refusal to bow to outside pressure to revise or to repress experience, a decision to embrace conflict rather than conformity, to endure a lifetime of anger and pain rather than to submit to the seductive pull of revision and repression. Its goal is change. The battle over the meaning of a traumatic experience is fought in the arena of political discourse, popular culture, and scholarly debate. The outcome of this battle shapes the rhetoric of the dominant culture and influences future political action. (Tal 7)

The relationships that Tal delineates between violence, trauma, expression, and politics might seem familiar to readers of post-colonial criticism, an area of study focusing on the narratives of colonial powers and those who have been colonized. The connections between representation and ideology are central to scholars like Edward Said, Gayatri Spivak, and Homi Bhabha, as well as writers like Chinua Achebe, Ngugi wa Thiong'o, Sembene Ousman, Bharati Mukherjee, Keri Hulme, and many others. The world has seen imperialism in practice in a variety of regions and eras. "As a result of this complex development something occurred for which the *plan* of imperial expansion had not bargained," write Bill Ashcroft, Gareth Griffiths, and Helen Tiffin in their introduction to *The Post-Colonial Studies Reader*. They continue:

> The immensely prestigious and powerful imperial culture found itself appropriated in projects of counter-colonial resistance which drew upon the many different indigenous local and hybrid *processes* of self-determination to defy, erode and sometimes supplant the prodigious power of imperial cultural knowledge. Post-colonial

literatures are the result of this interaction between imperial culture and the complex of indigenous cultural practices. (Ashcroft, et al. 1)

Weil wrote that force can turn a person into a thing. But sometimes art can respond to that force with its own kind of power.

Other studies have taken an even broader view, examining artistic and cultural expression to help unravel humanity's longstanding affinity for violence. René Girard pays particular attention to Greek and Shakespearean tragedy in his *Violence and the Sacred* (1972), in which he argues that sacrifice is a generative act of violence that temporarily purges more destructive forms of violence from a community and is the foundation of religion and social structure. James Twitchell carries Girard's argument further and claims in *Preposterous Violence: Fables of Aggression in Modern Culture* (1989) that, in contemporary culture, the experience of represented violence in mass media has taken the place of religious rites as the purgative catalyst. The breadth of Girard's study has made it useful for scholars of different literary periods, and the same is true of philosophical works like Michel Foucault's *Discipline and Punish* (1975). His examination of the historical shift in Europe and America from public torture to private, institutionalized punishment allows Foucault to theorize about the many vectors of disciplinary power in modern life, power that works on the body and the self in more subtle, hidden, and insidious ways; his arguments provide foundations for fields like post-colonial studies, queer theory, and film studies. Though less influential, Hannah Arendt's *On Violence* (1969) is significant in that it rearranges the equation of power and violence, arguing (contra Hegel, Marx, and, indirectly, Foucault) that the two are "not the same," that in fact they "are opposites; where the one rules absolutely, the other is absent" (56). More recently, in his book *Violence* (2008), Slavoj Žižek casts what he calls "six sideways glances" at the problem of violence, using an eclectic mix of film, journalism, history, philosophy, and literature to illuminate "systemic violence," which is "the almost catastrophic consequences of the smooth functioning of our economic and political systems" (2–3).

The attacks on September 11, 2001 prompt some of Žižek's reflections, and America's subsequent wars in Iraq and Afghanistan gave many new occasions to consider the relationship between violence and representation. Many of these considerations, however, focus on visual rather than literary culture. As Judith Butler writes in her *Frames of War* (2009), we tend to assume that the materials of war are limited to guns, bombs, and other weapons, without realizing that "very often the one who uses the camera is positioned within the perspective of battle, and becomes a soldier-reporter who visually consecrates the destructive acts of war. As a result, we have to pose the question of the material of war waging, what counts as material, and whether cameras and their images are part of that extended materiality" (xi). Watching war in this way, Butler argues, can be a kind of recruitment.

The relationship of violence and the image has been a longstanding critical concern. In 1975, John Cawelti began a kind of taxonomy in his article "Myths of Violence in American Popular Culture," delineating the "Myth of Equality Through Violence," for instance, or "The Myth of the Hard-Boiled Hero and His Code." (Cawelti later published that piece as part of his broader study, *Mystery, Violence, and Popular Culture*, in 2004). Works like *Why We Watch: The Attractions of Violence Entertainment* (ed. Jeffrey Goldstein, 1998) and David Trend's *The Myth of Media Violence* (2007) interrogate the assumptions about social and psychological effects of violent representations, a particularly vexed issue after school shootings like the one at Columbine High School in 1999. Studies by Stephen Prince and James Kendrick have been significant contributions to these discussions as well.

Violence in literature, however, has generally been considered a different animal from violence in other media; the power of text is seen to be different, and usually less worrisome, than the power of the image, perhaps because it requires our own imaginative construction. There are any number of studies examining the workings of violence in the literature of a particular author or time period; my search in the MLA Bibliography for books on violence and literature turned up more than five hundred entries. A small sampling would include

R. A. Foakes' *Shakespeare and Violence* (2002), Garrett Stewart's *Novel Violence: A Narratography of Victorian Fiction* (2009), Chantal Kalisa's *Violence in Francophone African and Caribbean Women's Literature* (2009), or Hermann Herlinghaus' *Violence Without Guilt: Ethical Narratives from the Global South* (2009). Some studies do take a broader view, like John Fraser's *Violence in the Arts* (1974), which calls violence in all kinds of representations "the great sharpener of judgment" and "the cutting edge of ideas and ideologies" (156, 162). Terry Eagleton is more specific in his *Sweet Violence: The Idea of the Tragic* (2003), in which he reads everything from Sophocles and Seneca to Rousseau, Hegel, George Eliot, Fitzgerald, and Beckett to find the value of tragic suffering:

> . . . [It is] not that destruction is an inherent good, but that when humanity reaches its nadir it becomes a symbol of everything that cries out for transformation, and so a negative image of that renewal. "Am I made a man in this hour when I cease to be?" Oedipus wonders aloud when he arrives at Colonus. Such change can spring only from a full acknowledgement of the extremity of one's condition. If even *this* can be salvaged, then there is hope indeed; but unless the promise of redemption extends even to the flesh of those like Oedipus who are destitute and polluted, then it is ultimately worthless. In this sense, tragedy of this kind is itself a *pharmakos*, both gift and threat, power and weakness. (Eagleton 282)

For Eagleton, the destruction inherent in tragedy is made meaningful by the potential for not just reconstitution, but change. In the study of American literature—which is my own field, and thus the one I turn my attention to here, but also a body of scholarship that has considered the representation of violence a topic of significance— arguments often focus similarly on the ways that violence becomes meaningful, with the texts demanding, in this case, recognition of the workings of justice or its absence. W. M. Frohock provided the first real consideration in his *The Novel of Violence in America* (1946), in which he explains violence's aesthetic function in what he calls the "novel of destiny." In works like those by Steinbeck, Faulkner, and Hemingway, the hero confronts a problem that only an act of violence can solve, defeating others but also himself and leading the reader to experience "a feeling of enlightenment, realizing, always as if for the first time, what man's predicament is and how gravely awful it is to be human" (7). (Leslie Fiedler's better known and more canonical *Love and Death in the American Novel* [1960] deals with violence in a more abstract way, tracing the archetypes of Clarissa and Lovelace, doomed victim and seducer, though their many adaptations and changes in American literature: the anti-sentimental novel, the gothic novel, the historical romance, and finally Hemingway, Faulkner, Melville, and Hawthorne. Ultimately, the violence Fiedler examines is less visceral and more symbolic, although near the end of the study, he does mention the 1930s trends of the urbanization and ennobling of violence.)

Richard Slotkin then took up the subject in a trilogy of well-known works—*Regeneration Through Violence* (1973), *The Fatal Environment* (1985), and *Gunfighter Nation* (1992)—arguing that violence is often represented as a regenerative force for American civilization, and exploring how this myth functions as the "structuring metaphor of the American experience" (*Regeneration* 5). He shows how this myth has its origins in colonial-era captivity narratives like Mary Rowlandson's, where the stark opposition between the Native American and the Christian and between savagery and civilization eventually created the need for a kind of go-between, who could fight for civilization while existing outside of it, as Cooper's Leatherstocking does or, much later, Jack Schaefer's Shane. James Giles, who contributes an essay to this volume, shifted the focus from the frontier to the city in his *Violence in the Contemporary American Novel* (2000), which he followed with *The Spaces of Violence* (2006). In the former, he discusses eight "urban novels" by authors like Caleb Carr and Sandra Cisneros that emphasize an oppressive class structure and the resulting violence in urban America. He argues that texts like these "bear witness" to this kind of suffering and senseless violence and that the writers "have assumed a responsibility not only to record the plague of violence that so threatens the survival of children and indeed a redemptive national innocence, but to seek explanations for its origins" (Giles 3). And Marilyn Wesley considers how acts of violence intersect with conceptions of masculinity in her *Violent Adventure: Contemporary Fiction by American Men* (2003). She reads contemporary authors like Pinckney Benedict, Richard Ford, Walter Mosley, and Don DeLillo to argue that these books are revisions of the typical masculine adventure formula, which dictates that male violence creates masculine power. Instead, she argues that these authors write about violence not to make men more violent, but instead to "expose the destructive assumptions it generates" (xiv, 3).

In contrast to the approaches taken by scholars like Frohock, Slotkin, Giles, and Wesley, other critics have focused less on violence's connection to contextual issues and more on the ways that it is rendered into language. In *Deadly Musings: Violence and Verbal Form in American Fiction* (1993), Michael Kowalewski examines "the nature of the verbal conditions—the muses, if you will—that make violence 'possible' in certain American works" (4). Kowalewski wants to consider the ways violence is imagined or performed rather than the way it serves a theme or other textual purpose. To this end, he chooses works by Edgar Allan Poe, Stephen Crane, Flannery O'Connor, and Thomas Pynchon, among others, which include "extended depictions of violence, scenes that cannot be thought of as merely functional because their very length and energy outstrip whatever dramatic function they might have said to have initially served" (Kowalewski 5). The need to find interpretive significance in represented violence, he argues, gets in the way of describing what's there in the first place, which is the very task he intends to undertake. Kowalewski's claim is that one must examine the violent language before one discusses the cultural or historical conditions that may account for that violence, and he takes as his methodological model the "descriptive scrupulosity" of Wittgenstein's *Philosophical Investigations* (21).

In his book *The Modern American Novel of Violence* (2000), Patrick Shaw also addresses novels in which violence is "dramatically excessive," but not gratuitous, to use Kowalewski's terms. Shaw chooses novels written after 1930 in which violence is the "central focus or force," but not, he claims, where violence "operates in an aesthetic void" or is "an end in itself" (6). As counterpoint, he mentions Anne Rice and Stephen King and instead turns to Faulkner, Hemingway, Truman Capote, Cormac McCarthy, and Toni Morrison, among others. Shaw, however, draws no summative conclusions: "the fact [is] that no one theory can explain the origin or cause of human violence. Violence is a primal motivator, beyond language and absolute analysis. Past that one consensus opinion, no one view or philosophy of violence encompasses all the authors" (206). Elana Gomel goes further in her book *Bloodscripts: Writing the Violent Subject* (2003), in which she analyzes a wide range of popular fictions to show that violence may be a part of our identity, but not innately so: "And it is in the field of narrativity that the enigma of the violent subject may be approached as a cultural phenomenon and not a supposedly biological deviation" (xiv). Because in this view the propensity to kill is socially constructed, just like one's gender identity, Gomel sets her goal as showing how "violence interacts with narrative to create identity" (xiv). Gomel is particularly interested in what she calls the "violent sublime," or violence that is pragmatically motiveless and often characterized by extreme feelings, sometimes of ecstasy and sometimes of horror, and that ruptures the fabric of the discourse because it is, in many ways, unrepresentable. Echoing trauma theorists, she notes that it "exceeds language but provokes speech" (xxviii).

Telling stories about violence, and writing about stories about violence, is just about the oldest artistic and critical practice there is. It's a long history, involving modes of violence that range from the global to the interpersonal, from the abstract to the excruciatingly specific. The subject is old, but always—unfortunately—fresh, and a necessary one for any real consideration of the human place in the world.

Works Cited

Arendt, Hannah. *On Violence*. 1969. San Diego: Harvest, 1970.

Ashcroft, Bill, Gareth Griffiths, & Helen Tiffin. "General Introduction." *The Post-Colonial Studies Reader*. 2nd ed. Eds. Bill Ashcroft, Gareth Griffiths, & Helen Tiffin. New York: Routledge, 1995.

Butler, Judith. *Frames of War: When is Life Grievable?* 2009. London: Verso, 2010.

Caruth, Cathy. *Unclaimed Experience: Trauma, Narrative, and History.* Baltimore: The Johns Hopkins UP, 1996.

Cawelti, John G. *Mystery, Violence, and Popular Culture.* Madison: U of Wisconsin P, 2004.

_____. "Myths of Violence in American Popular Culture." *Critical Inquiry* 1.3 (1975): 521–41.

Clausewitz, Carl von. *On War.* 1832. Ed. Anatol Rapoport. New York: Penguin, 1982.

Eagleton, Terry. *Sweet Violence: The Idea of the Tragic.* Oxford: Blackwell, 2003.

Fiedler, Leslie. *Love and Death in the American Novel.* New York: Stein and Day, 1960.

Foakes, R. A. *Shakespeare and Violence.* Cambridge: Cambridge UP, 2003.

Foucault, Michel. *Discipline and Punish: The Birth of the Prison.* 1975. Trans. Alan Sheridan. New York: Vintage, 1995.

Fraser, John. *Violence in the Arts.* Cambridge: Cambridge UP, 1974.

Frohock, W. M. *The Novel of Violence in America.* Dallas: Southern Methodist UP, 1946.

Giles, James R. *Violence in the Contemporary American Novel: An End to Innocence.* Columbia, SC: U of South Carolina P, 2000.

Girard, René. *Violence and the Sacred.* 1972. Trans. Patrick Gregory. Baltimore: The Johns Hopkins UP, 1977.

Goldstein, Jeffrey H., ed. *Why We Watch: The Attractions of Violent Entertainment.* New York: Oxford UP, 1998.

Gomel, Elana. *Bloodscripts: Writing the Violent Subject.* Columbus: Ohio State UP, 2003.

Henke, Suzette. *Shattered Subjects: Trauma and Testimony in Women's Life Writing.* New York: Palgrave Macmillan, 2000.

Herlinghaus, Hermann. *Violence Without Guilt: Ethical Narratives from the Global South.* New York: Palgrave Macmillan, 2009.

Herman, Judith. *Trauma and Recovery.* 1992. New York: Basic Books, 1997.

Holmes, Richard. *Acts of War: The Behavior of Men in Battle*. New York: Free, 1985.

Homer. *Iliad*. Trans. Stanley Lombardo. Indianapolis: Hackett, 1997.

Horvitz, Deborah M. *Literary Trauma: Sadism, Memory, and Sexual Violence in American Women's Fiction*. Albany: State U of New York P, 2000.

Kalisa, Chantal. *Violence in Francophone African and Caribbean Women's Literature*. Lincoln, NE: U of Nebraska P, 2009.

Kendrick, James. *Film Violence: History, Ideology, Genre*. London: Wallflower P, 2009.

_____. *Hollywood Bloodshed: Violence in 1980s American Cinema*. Carbondale: Southern Illinois UP, 2009.

Kowalewski, Michael. *Deadly Musings: Violence and Verbal Form in American Fiction*. Princeton, NJ: Princeton UP, 1993.

Prince, Stephen. *Savage Cinema: Sam Peckinpah and the Rise of Ultraviolent Movies*. Austin: U of Texas P, 1998.

_____, ed. *Screening Violence*. New Brunswick: Rutgers UP, 2000.

Shaw, Patrick. *The Modern American Novel of Violence*. Troy, NY: Whitston, 2000.

Shay, Jonathan. *Achilles in Vietnam: Combat Trauma and the Undoing of Character*. New York:
Simon & Schuster, 1995.

_____. *Odysseus in America: Combat Trauma and the Trials of Homecoming*. New York: Scribner, 2002.

Slotkin, Richard. *The Fatal Environment: The Myth of the Frontier in the Age of Industrialization, 1800–1890*. New York: Atheneum, 1985.

_____. *Gunfighter Nation: The Myth of the Frontier in Twentieth-Century America*. New York: Atheneum, 1992.

_____. *Regeneration through Violence: The Mythology of the American Frontier, 1600–1860*. Middletown, CT: Wesleyan UP, 1973.

Stewart, Garrett. *Novel Violence: A Narratography of Victorian Fiction*. Chicago: U of Chicago P, 2009.

Sun Tzu. *The Art of War*. Trans. Samuel B. Griffith. London: Oxford UP, 1963.

Tal, Kalí. *Worlds of Hurt: Reading the Literatures of Trauma*. New York: Cambridge UP, 1996.

Thucydides. *Thucydides*. Trans. Benjamin Jowett. London: Oxford UP, 1881.

Trend, David. *The Myth of Media Violence: A Critical Introduction*. Malden, MA: Blackwell, 2007.

Tritle, Lawrence. *From Melos to My Lai: War and Survival*. London: Routledge, 2000.

Twitchell, James B. *Preposterous Violence: Fables of Aggression in Modern Culture*. New York: Oxford UP, 1989.

Weil, Simone. *The* Iliad, *or the Poem of Force*. Wallingford, PA: Pendle Hill Publications, 1956.

Wesley, Marilyn C. *Violence Adventure: Contemporary Fiction by American Men*. Charlottesville: U of Virginia P, 2003.

Žižek, Slavoj. *Violence*. New York: Picador, 2008.

The Thing and the Image: Violence in Chinua Achebe's *Things Fall Apart*

Aaron Bady

> The true hero, the true subject, the center of the *Iliad*, is force. Force employed by man, force that enslaves man, force before which man's flesh shrinks away. In this work at all times, the human spirit is shown as modified by its relation to force, as swept away, blinded, by the very force it imagined it could handle, as deformed by the weight of the force it submits to . . . .To define force—it is that x that turns anybody who is subjected to it into a thing.
> (Simone Weil, *The* Iliad, *or the Poem of Force* 45)

> My turn to state an equation: colonization = "thingification."
> (Aimé Césaire, *Discourse on Colonialism* 42)

> Whatever happens, we have got The Gatling gun, and they have not.
> (Hilaire Belloc, *The Modern Traveler* 41)

In a variety of essays and speeches, Chinua Achebe has made it clear that his first intention, as a writer, was to displace what he called "the image of Africa," an image that novels like Joseph Conrad's *Heart of Darkness* had helped to propagate, naturalize, and reproduce. "It was and is the dominant image of Africa in the Western imagination," Achebe famously wrote in "An Image of Africa: Racism in Conrad's *Heart of Darkness*," and he argued that "the West seems to suffer deep anxieties about the precariousness of its civilization and to have a need for constant reassurance by comparison with Africa" (Achebe, "Image" 18). As would Edward Said in works like *Orientalism* and *Imperialism and Culture*, Achebe drew a homology between imperialism and culture. Just as the precariousness of European civilization had been, in economic terms, bolstered and propped up by imperial empires in Africa and elsewhere, the coherence and stability of "the West" was supported and sustained by reference to the "Africa" of Conrad's fantasies, an existential absence and negation that helped to produce "Western Civilization" as thesis, by serving as its antithesis. Alongside the material violence of conquest, dispossession, and exploitation, there was the cultural violence through which "Africa" was rendered an image of negation.

Novelist Ngugi wa Thiong'o was more succinct, describing the "cultural bomb" that imperialism dropped on colonial cultures:

> The effect of a cultural bomb is to annihilate a people's belief in their names, in their languages, in their environment, in their heritage of struggle, in their unity, in their capacities and ultimately in themselves. It makes them see their past as one wasteland of non-achievement and it makes them want to distance themselves from that wasteland. (3)

For Achebe's generation of African writers, the analogy between culture and struggle was foundational: at the very least, "culture" was a parallel site of struggle to the political arena of decolonization, what Kwame Nkrumah named "the political kingdom." In publishing *Things Fall Apart* in 1958, in fact—almost two years before Nigeria would achieve independence—Achebe could be said to have sought the cultural kingdom first, making the problem of culture primary. But the continuity between cultural production and decolonial struggle was nearly always presumed. In essays like "The Role of the Writer in a New Nation," Achebe argued that "the fundamental theme" for African writers was to establish "that African peoples did not hear of culture for the first time from Europeans; that their societies were not mindless but frequently had a philosophy of great depth and value and beauty, that they had poetry and, above all, they had dignity" (8). Against the "image of Africa" that African students of his generation had imbibed from books like Conrad's *Heart of Darkness* and Joyce Cary's *Mister Johnson*, Achebe famously argued in "The Novelist as Teacher" that the African novelist's primary objective had to be to contest this image, to demonstrate its falsity: "I would be quite satisfied if my novels (especially the ones

I set in the past) did no more than teach my readers that their past—with all its imperfections—was not one long night of savagery from which the first Europeans acting on God's behalf delivered them" (205).

This sense of African culture's function, utility, and responsibility has become almost a truism, but even before Achebe wrote his famous essay on Conrad in 1973, the notion that "the image of Africa" was a prime arena for Africanist cultural struggle was well-established. The term itself was first and most influentially used by Es'kia Mphahlele—in his 1962 *The African Image*, and then at the influential 1962 Makerere conference, which Mphahlele convened—but it has grown to become an overwhelming critical touchstone, both for Achebe's own work and for the broader field of African literature (for which Achebe has long served as a kid of father-figure).[1] Indeed, while Simon Gikandi's declaration that Achebe "invented African culture" is intentionally hyperbolic, such hyperbole serves to spotlight the epoch-marking importance of Achebe's first novel, the central text—and Achebe the central author—of the "renaissance" of African literature, which occurred after decolonization, a narrative that Achebe elsewhere called the "Restoration of Celebration" necessitated by "Africa's Tarnished Name" ("African Literature as Restoration of Celebration" and "Africa's Tarnished Name"). If it was the primal trauma of colonialism that had tarnished Africa's name—the violation of sovereignty and cultural vitality from which "new nations" had to work to recover—then the emergence of African literature began with a stock-taking account of colonial violations. Achebe vigorously argued, therefore, that recovering dignity required coming to terms with the manner in which it had been violated:

> is this dignity that many African peoples all but lost in the colonial period, and it is this dignity that they must now regain. The worst thing that can happen to any people is the loss of their dignity and self-respect. The writer's duty is to help them regain it by showing them in human terms what happened to them, what they lost. There is a saying in Ibo that a man who can't tell where the rain began to beat him cannot know where he dried his body. ("Role" 157)

Critical Insights

This analysis begins with the above idea because this critical perspective has been the first and primary entry point for generations of readers, students, and scholars, and as *Things Fall Apart* has been canonized, this has been the principle of its canonization: the subjects of empire striking back against the empire of signs in which they have been interpellated, or the images by which their names had been "tarnished." As a result, it has often been difficult to read *Things Fall Apart* except through the text's struggle with the cultural politics associated with Joseph Conrad, and through an understanding of that struggle in binary, even martial terms. In British and American universities, for example, where Achebe's first novel is often used as a model "postcolonial" text, Conrad and Achebe are often taught together, placed in the kind of binary conversation that has characterized so much postcolonial theory: first, the empire speaks, and then the colonized retort (Ashcroft, et al). Especially in the 1990s, as the so-called "canon wars" raged, Achebe's complaint at being excluded from Conrad's Africa came to be construed (though not by Achebe) as the censorious demand that Conrad be eliminated from Achebe's Africa. Even though Achebe himself frequently insisted that he had no desire to ban the book—merely that he wanted his perspective to be included in the discussion—Conrad's "defenders" have repeatedly answered Achebe's charge as if he had demanded its abolition, producing a broad counter-literature disputing the "attack" they characterize Achebe having produced.[2] The result is a critical fantasy, in which Achebe and Conrad represent opposing champions, fighting for the soul of literature.

As the martial flavor of this meta-critical discourse indicates, this mode of framing the novel understands its significance through its relationship to Conrad and the image he created, construing its work as the essentially negative project of disproving what Conrad had written. Conrad remains primary for this line of interpretation, just as "colonialism" remains the first term, disputed by (but also presumed) by "post-colonial" theory's displacement of it. Achebe's intervention, especially as a figure for the entirety of postcolonial studies, is understood as revisionary, but essentially dependent on and inextricable from the field in which it intervened, which it revised: because Conrad wrote Africa as dark, static, and silent, Achebe must write it as bright, vital, and voiced.

This opposition has long been a critical cul-de-sac. No one would deny that Conrad is an important context for framing and appreciating Achebe's accomplishment (and readings of *Heart of Darkness* that do not incorporate an African perspective are impoverished by the absence of that present-absence, something even Achebe's critics tend to admit). But if the martial metaphor suggests an illuminating approach to this novel—and a way of staging its central place in the emergence of African literature—it also tends to obscure Achebe's essentially pluralist, liberal perspective, the context in which he used the term "image" and understood it to be a problem. After all, Achebe's argument was never that Conrad was simply *wrong*, even if "one long night of savagery" was a story that he sought to displace in its comprehensive ambition. For Achebe, Conrad's "image" of Africa was *not even wrong*: both the image of Africa that his novel produced and the violent project of literary image-making, of which the novel was a part, were culpable in the violation of African cultural history that he sought to contest. Yet it was the premise from which Conrad began—Africa's unitary, monolithic cultural identity—that was the real problem, the conversion of a continent's humanity into something so reified as "an image."

It is here that we find Achebe's basic insight into the symbolic economy of colonial culture: the original violation of Africa's "image" was its construction as the object of colonial violence, the reduction of "Africa" to the site upon which colonial violence exerted itself (and the occlusion of all else). It was not enough, therefore, to simply show Conrad's "image" of Africa to be a false one, or to displace that image with nostalgic visions of a pre-colonial Arcadia, in the way that many of Achebe's contemporaries have done. Indeed, while it was part of Achebe's achievement to evoke the vibrant, harmonious, and sophisticated African society whose vitality was ruptured by colonial invasion, *Things Fall Apart* does not succumb to what Wole Soyinka called the "poetics of neo-Tarzanism," in which Africa becomes "a landscape of elephants, beggars, calabashes, serpents, pumpkins, baskets, towncriers, iron bells, slit drums, iron masks, hares, snakes, squirrels" (38). Achebe does not idealize African traditional culture in response to Conrad's absolute negation of it, for to do so would merely transform Africa into a different set of images. Again, a human society would be reified into a "landscape" of objects and things, and this, too, would violate its humanity. Not only is Africa not the particular image that Conrad made of it; Africa is not an image at all.

In this way, Achebe's first novel far exceeds the context of its conventional framing and is much more subtle and insightful than the positive that Joseph Conrad negates (or which negates his negation). To understand the novel in those terms—to construe it as a photo-negative of Conrad's own vision—is to produce a *different* image of Africa, but also to reiterate and efface the violence of that form of image-making, to accede to the question of what image to make of Africa. Indeed, this framing of Achebe—in which illuminating proverbs and the rhetorical culture of the Igbo people disprove Conrad's vision of a voiceless, howling African darkness—is to reduce Africa "to the role of props for the break-up of one petty [African] mind," to demand a landscape of bells, calabashes, and serpents instead of jungle darkness, but not to establish the basis upon which humanity could be differentiated (and recovered) from its *thingification* as image-commodity (Achebe, "Image" 12).

Achebe's first novel is not simply the rather ahistorical argument that Africa never was a thing. Rather, it is a dramatization of the thingification of a single man and the cultural formation for which he was the living embodiment—all the better to imagine the possibility of his restoration to life. To understand *Things Fall Apart* as, itself, a violent act—a martial retort to the original colonial violation, and, therefore, an inverted repetition of that original trauma—is to misapprehend the novel's understanding of what Simone Weil called *force*: "that x that turns anybody who is subjected to it into a thing" (45). Colonization, as Aimé Césaire understood, was the violent exercise of that type of force, an enterprise not merely to exploit and govern African labor—nor merely to psychologically displace the discontents of European civilization—but to draw the boundary between human and thing according to the act of violent thingification. Just as Hilaire Belloc reduced the difference between the colonial "we" and the colonized "they" to the timeless possession of the Gatling gun, violence clarifies what other frames might obscure: the difference between self and other as fundamental.

To say that *Things Fall Apart* is a novel concerned with violence is not to say very much: conflict is a basic building block of narrative, and violence might be the most common theme in literature over the course of human history, especially if we give Greek epic its conventional pride of place. But *Things Fall Apart* is not only *concerned* with violence; as in Simone Weil's description of the *Iliad*, violence is its narrative vocabulary. Using Weil's formulation, one might say that in *Things Fall Apart*, the true hero, subject, and center of the story is violence: violence used by man, violence that enslaves man, violence that makes man's flesh shrink away. As in Homer, Achebe's novel shows how violence modifies the human spirit, how that spirit is swept away and blinded by the violence it thought it could handle, and how it is deformed by the violence to which it submits (Weil 45).

For Achebe, the violence of the colonial state is its effort to turn people into things, both the bodies of the colonized (bare life, which can be violated with impunity) and the commodities, whose production drives the colonial political economy. Since Weil's understanding of force is primarily a philosophical and literary account that abstracts it from any concrete historical conditions— rendering "force" an epic property of the divine—Césaire (as does Achebe) usefully links the violation of colonized bodies and society to the economies of global production:

> Between colonizer and colonized there is room only for forced labor, intimidation, pressure, the police, taxation, theft, rape, compulsory crops, contempt, mistrust, arrogance, self-complacency, swinishness, brainless elites, degraded masses. No human contact, but relations of domination and submission which turn the colonizing man into a classroom monitor, an army sergeant, a prison guard, a slave driver, and the indigenous man into an instrument of production. (42)

But in sharp contrast to the narrative moralization that makes Achebe the "good" version of Conrad's "bad" Africanist text, *Things Fall Apart* is like the *Iliad* in its relatively amoral vision of civilization's violence, or, like Walter Benjamin, in its willingness to see a document of civilization as a document of barbarity and vice versa. While functionally connecting the violence of the colonial state to the production of commodities for the global market, colonialism as a historically particular form of violating force is coextensive with the broad spectrum of violence out of which human society is constituted. Force is force, and it makes people into things regardless of the language in which it is spoken.

Colonial violence—and the struggle for full humanity on the part of colonial subjects—was a recurring theme among Achebe's generation of writers. But among this literary cohort, *Things Fall Apart* is exceptional for its refusal to give white people a monopoly on violence. As Weil puts it, force "petrifies the souls of those who undergo it and those who ply it" (61); Achebe's protagonist, Okonkwo, is no less of a "thing" when he is the subject of his own violence, but this violent force precedes colonialism itself. As the subject formed by his own self-understanding through violence— the subjectivity of fear and hostility, which defines his personality— Okonkwo was a "thing" well before his society was invaded and colonized by the British empire. His "thingification" is self-imposed, derived from his fear of becoming like his father; a hatred of his own weaknesses, which he projects upon his others and which manifests as misogynistic violence against his wives; filicidal violence against his children; and—eventually—suicidal violence against himself. Moreover, his violence—the violence that is already endemic to Igbo society long before the English arrive—is what prepares the field for colonial conquest, sowing the seeds of defeat in the jaws of victory.

In *Things Fall Apart,* violence is woven into the fabric of daily life. Indeed, there is a distinctly Conradian flavor to the narrator's bland observation that "on great occasions such as the funeral of a village celebrity [Okonkwo] drank his palm-wine from his first human head," a head he took in war (Achebe, *Things* 10). The reference is not discussed, but it raises the question of normative judgment: in this scene, are we seeing the violence of Igbo culture? Or are we are seeing a peaceful domestic tableau, a moment of quiet contemplation and sociability? *Things Fall Apart* is filled with moments like this, brief bursts of affective dissonance: the reader feels a startled sense of unease with such things (*to drink out of a skull?*), while observing the nonchalant ease with which Okonkwo does so. While the reader might regard such an act as a violation (or simply disgusting), Okonkwo does not regard it at all; for him and for his society, there is nothing to see.

This moment inevitably recalls a much more iconic moment in Conrad's *Heart of Darkness*, in which skulls affixed to posts surrounding Kurtz's compound are essentially self-explanatory, vivid signs of Kurtz's savage, atavistic decline from a cosmopolitan European modern into an animalistic jungle savage. As images of savagery and icons of violent force, the skulls speak for themselves: only a savage would decorate his home with skulls, and the sight of them, glimpsed through Marlowe's spyglass, demonstrates the horror and depth of Kurtz's fall. For Marlow, this revelation of what Kurtz has become is also homologous with the revelation of the skulls themselves, the demonstration that whatever the phrenological measurement of our heads may be, we are all skulls underneath, a truth exposed by death (or by killing). Indeed, if Kurtz can become a savage as the result of environmental conditions—if his white skin cannot protect him from the effect of the African jungle—then the novel implicitly demonstrates the failing of phrenological science: skull measurements cannot tell us anything useful about the line between savage and civilized.

By contrast, the grand piano in the study of Kurtz's intended— which "stood massively in a corner, with dark gleams on the flat surfaces like a sombre and polished sarcophagus"—is barely a grace note in Conrad's novel and, therefore, easily overlooked (120). It has been left to critics like Laura Chrisman to observe that the piano's ivory keys no doubt originated in a place like the Congo, and that Kurtz himself—whom Marlow is told "had been essentially a great musician"—not only played the piano, but used violence to acquire the ivory from which the keys were made (Chrisman 27; Conrad 114). Conrad's use of the figure—if the reading is apt—draws attention both to the violence through which "civilization" and culture are constructed as well as to the manner in which some forms of violence are emphasized while others are erased. Civilization can recognize the violence of ivory production in Africa; when it plays upon the skulls of African animals in European parlors, however, that violence fades into the background. Yet as Achebe observed, however apt this critique of European culture may be, it allows no sense of an outside, no trace of the possibility that there is any alternative perspective from Conrad's, in which all is dark and violent, and in which Marlow has no alternative but to close his eyes to the truth.

Is Okonkwo a savage and violent man? Achebe's novel is not interested in the question because it is not a question: Okonkwo's skull-cup is both a document of civilization and a document of barbarity, and violence is woven into the culture-work of basic domestic production. But while the novel's title suggests the timeless permanence of historical violence—a sense of human history that might, in Conradian terms, be seen to be as endless procession in and out of "darkness"—*Things Fall Apart* imagines a cycle of violence that, because it finds its origin in violent thingification, leaves room for a pathway out.

Okonkwo, after all, is a man of violence, and he is defined by his place as violent champion within Umuofia's social hierarchy; from the first lines of the book—"Okonkwo was well known throughout the nine villages and even beyond. His fame rested on solid personal achievements"—we are reminded that Okonkwo's identity is defined by his wrestling prowess and his warrior successes (Achebe, *Things* 8). As the narrator tells us, however, Okonkwo's propensity for violence is derived from weakness, his bravery a function of his fear. "[Okonkwo] was not afraid of war," the narrator explains; "He was a man of action, a man of war. Unlike his father he could stand the look of blood. In Umuofia's latest war he was the first to bring home a human head" (Achebe, *Things* 8). Okonkwo's *lack* of fear, however, is produced by his fear of fear:

his whole life was dominated by fear, the fear of failure and of weakness. It was deeper and more intimate than the fear of evil and capricious gods and of magic, the fear of the forest, and of nature, malevolent, red in tooth and claw. Okonkwo's fear was greater than these. It was not external, but lay deep within himself. It was the fear of himself, lest he should be found to resemble his father. Even as a little boy he had resented his father's failure and weakness, and even now he still remembered how he had suffered when a playmate had told him that his father was *agbala*. That was how Okonkwo first came to know that *agbala* was not only another name for a woman, it could also mean a man who had taken no title. And so Okonkwo was ruled by one passion—to hate everything that his father Unoka had loved. One of those things was gentleness and another was idleness. (Achebe, *Things* 10)

Here, with remarkable clarity, Achebe reveals what a psychoanalyst would call Okonkwo's "primal scene," in which the image of his father—the masculine model for his self-knowledge of himself as masculine—is destroyed by being declared to be "agbala," a word that means "woman." Okonkwo's ego is bruised by this event, even if, like all primal scenes, it is a retroactive condensation of a broader structural field into a single instant. He will, however, turn this violence on himself. It is himself that he fears: the fear that he will grow to resemble his father, that he will become the self-image that failed to reflect him as man. Put simply, he fears that he will become what he (as he) is not: a woman. And so, he proves that he is not a woman—not not-masculine—by doing violence to those that are not men: he beats his wives, he kills his son, he kills a court messenger. If violence makes a man into a thing—and for Okonkwo, man and "human" are co-extensive—then Okonkwo's violence is an effort to make others into things, by comparison to which he would remain a man. In this sense, Okonkwo's life—and the plot of the novel—are ruled by the logic of thingification. Because Okonkwo fears being a thing, like the image he inherits of his father, he must make his father into a thing, must dominate the things he makes of his family, and he must subject the earth to the force of his will, growing wealthy as a farmer as a measure of the crops (things) he has drawn forth from the earth.

Violence, however, does not reinforce the boundary lines of difference, which Okonkwo hopes to clarify: violent force, in making others into things, sends ripples of alarm across his community that reflect back on him. When Okonkwo is contradicted at a meeting over a trivial matter, for example, his first and instant reaction is "kill" the man's spirit, by un-manning him:

> Only a week ago a man had contradicted him at a kindred meeting which they held to discuss the next ancestral feast. Without looking at the man Okonkwo had said, 'This meeting is for men.' The man who had contradicted him had no titles. That was why he had called him a woman. Okonkwo knew how to kill a man's spirit. (Achebe, *Things* 24)

The community, however, unanimously sides with Osugo. As members of his community perceive—through him—that "they see their relations with other human beings as a kind of balance between unequal amounts of force," as Weil puts it, the communal spirit of his society identifies Okonkwo as the source of the thingification (10). Okonkwo is reprimanded, reminded of his dependence on others, both the "benevolent god" that has favored him and the fact that he, as human, once "sucked from his mother's breast." In moments like these, the violence of Okonkwo's individual force— the self-assertion of his ego—is reflected back onto him by the Igbo community, which he might otherwise represent, as in times of war when his violence turns *enemies* into things. But because there is no outside to Okonkwo's warrior image, his understanding of his own personhood, through and as violent masculinity, cuts him off from the community that might otherwise give him strength.

Moments like this are emblematic of the movement of the novel as a whole. While *Things Fall Apart* begins with Okonkwo's "solid personal achievements," its narrative swiftly charts his decline, as his violence turns inward. Or, put differently, as the violence of his original wound is reflected outward, the fabric of his society reflects it back onto him: again and again, Okonkwo's fear of himself leads to violent self-assertion, which results in the suppression of his self. Though *Things Fall Apart* is often considered an "anthropological" novel—and is sometimes treated as a compendium of ethnographic details—its ethnographic account of Igbo society charts this dynamic, describing how an individual's violence is contained and curbed; long before the English colonizers arrive, a cascading series of events tear apart the life that Okonkwo's violent masculinity allowed him to build.

Okonkwo's breaking point is his loss of family. As when Okonkwo's violence made a human being into a cup for drinking palm wine, Okonkwo participates in the thingification of his foster son, Ikemefua, who turns into a pot: "As the man who had cleared his throat drew up and raised his machete, Okonkwo looked away. He heard the blow. The pot fell and broke in the sand. He heard Ikemefuna cry, 'My father, they have killed me!' as he ran towards him. Dazed with fear, Okonkwo drew his machete and cut him down. He was afraid of being thought weak" (Achebe, *Things* 61). Okonkwo's transgression is not against his foster son, but against the community order that was to regulate him. As he had been warned and understood, Okonkwo was to be present when Ikemefuna was killed, but not to lift a hand in his death. In the event, Okonkwo cannot keep this social injunction: he fears being thought weak for the inability to murder his own son, and fears to be seen as such. This self-assertion demonstrates the incompatibility of his ego in the face of social injunction and sets him on a path to be punished by fate. When the elder dies who had warned Okonkwo not to take part in the killing of his son, he recalls the command he could not keep, and "[a] cold shiver ran down Okonkwo's back" (Achebe, *Things* 125). The implication of a divine hand in the proceedings is clear, and this event sets in motion the chain of events that will lead to Okonkwo's death.

With this chain of causality in mind, Okonkwo's death—his literal conversion into a thing—is the problem of the novel: who killed him, why, and what meaning is to be made of his corpse. His society will not bury him (as suicides are taboo), the district commissioner will not understand him (in the novel's critique of colonial discourse), and only his friends and family will remember him. To the very limited extent that his name survives, it is through those links of sociality he so despised and condemned. In their absence, he is dead, a thing.

To Achebe's readers, on the other hand, the question of genre structures how we answer the question. If it is strongly implied that "things fall apart" because Okonkwo's fate determines that he be punished for being who he was—and the implication is palpable, if not confirmed—then it would be possible to read the novel as tragedy, a reading that is certainly still available. If "things fall apart" because colonialists divide the Igbo people—pitting the strong against the weak, until the center cannot hold—then we can read the novel as a critique specifically of colonial violence; this reading, too, is still available to us.

However, it could be argued that there is a third reading possible, which an address to the novel's interest in "thingification" makes available: "things" fall apart because that simply is what things do. The novel functions, then, as an epic on the model of the *Iliad*: a poem whose structural center is not society or family or nation, but the human problem of force, the violence that makes things out of people. People hold together as a society; things do not. In rejecting what Achebe has called the "mother principle"—and any sense that he, too, once sucked at another's breast—Okonkwo emulated Kurtz and "kicked himself loose of the earth." He therefore dies when he realizes that his people have abandoned him. At the climax of the novel, Okonkwo cannot restrain his violence and kills an offending court messenger. But his people do not follow him into battle, do not understand his actions. At this point, the violence, which defines who he is, has nowhere else to go, so it turns inward, on himself, and he commits suicide.

In this sense, *Things Fall Apart* is about—as the district commissioner titles his book—"The Pacification of the Primitive Tribes of the Lower Niger," only in the way that the *Iliad* is a poem about the Trojan War (209). If colonization turns people into things, it does so only as part of a pattern much deeper and more elemental, the violence in the absence of which humans remain human.

Notes

1. As Edris Makward observed in his presidential address to the African Studies Association in 1977, "There is definitely in principle no need to argue at this time for the legitimacy of the Africanist's concern with the 'Image of Africa.' This concern is indeed very abundantly illustrated in the African Studies literature. There is for instance Ezekiel Mphahlele's *The African Image* first published in 1962. There are also the two volumes of Philip D. Curtin's *The Image of Africa* which first appeared in 1964 . . . 'Correcting the record,' 'unveiling the misconceptions,' 'reaching out for a better and more truthful understanding of Africa'—these were (and still are) the pressing preoccupations of all true Africanists—be they English, French, American or Africans."

2. For example: Edward Said wrote that "Some years ago Chinua Achebe attacked Conrad's racism in *Heart of Darkness*, and found direct links between that work and the dehumanisation and exploitation of Africa" (173); David Denby wrote that "In 1975, the distinguished Nigerian novelist and essayist Chinua Achebe attacked *Heart of Darkness* as racist and called for its elimination from the canon of Western classics" (409); and Patrick Brantlinger asserted that "In a 1975 lecture the Nigerian novelist Chinua Achebe attacked *Heart of Darkness* as 'racist'" (255).

Works Cited

Achebe, Chinua. "African Literature as Restoration of Celebration." *Chinua Achebe: A Celebration.* Eds. Kirsten Holst & Anna Rutherford. Portsmouth, NH: H.E.B., 1990. 1–10.

_____. "Africa's Tarnished Name." *Multiculturalism and Hybridity in African Literature.* Eds. Hal Wylie and Bernth Lindfors. Trenton, NJ: Africa World Press, 2000.

_____. "An Image of Africa: Racism in Conrad's *Heart of Darkness*." *Massachusetts Review* 18 (1977): 782–94.

_____. "The Novelist as Teacher." *Hopes and Impediments.* London: Heinemann International, 1988.

_____. "The Role of the Writer in a New Nation." *African Writers on African Writing.* Ed. G. D. Killam. Chicago: Northwestern UP, 1973.

_____. *Things Fall Apart*. London: Heinemann, 1958.

Ashcroft, Bill, Gareth Griffiths, & Helen Tiffin, eds. *The Empire Writes Back: Theory and Practice in Post-Colonial Literatures*. New York & London: Routledge, 1989.

Belloc, Hilaire. *The Modern Traveller*. London: Edward Arnold, 1898.

Brantlinger, Patrick. *Rule of Darkness: British Literature and Imperialism, 1830–1914*. Ithaca, NY: Cornell UP, 1988.

Césaire, Aimé. *Discourse on Colonialism*. Trans. J. Pinkham. New York: Monthly Review Press, 2000.

Conrad, Joseph. *Heart of Darkness, With The Congo Diary*. Ed. R. G. Hampson. NY: Penguin, 1995.

Denby, David. *Great Books*. New York: Simon & Schuster, 1997.

Makward, Edris. "Africans, Africanists, and the Image of Africa." *Issue: A Journal of Opinion*. 7.4 (1977): 1–5.

Ngugi wa Thiong'o. *Decolonizing the Mind: The Politics of Language in African Literature*. London: James Currey, 1986.

Said, Edward. "The Importance of Being Unfaithful to Wagner." *Music at the Limits*. New York: Columbia UP, 2008.

Soyinka, Wole. "Neo-Tarzanism: The Poetics of Pseudo-Tradition" *Transition* 48 (1975): 38–44.

Weil, Simone. *The* Iliad, *or a Poem of Force: A Critical Edition*. Ed. James P. Holoka. New York: Lang, 2003.

Modern War and American Literature: Ironic Realism, Satire, and Escape_____

Ty Hawkins

According to Joshua S. Goldstein, a scholar of international relations, little to no evidence exists of any human society in any historical period that has avoided war of its own volition. That is to say, there may not be a single society that truly has chosen pacifism, as opposed to being forced into nonviolence because a greater power subdued that community directly through conflict or indirectly by instilling the fear thereof. As Goldstein writes, "Some societies are far more (or less) warlike than others, in terms of frequency of war, its effect on mortality rates, and its place in the culture. But these are all differences of degree. In virtually no society is war unknown" (28). Given its centrality to human experience, it should not surprise us that war plays a crucial role in the development of literature, nor should it surprise us that we find in literature an attempt to derive war's meaning.

For the sake of clarity, this essay limits its investigation of the dynamic exchange between war and literature to American literature that is responding to modern war. In many ways, the United States is a nation created, sustained, and empowered by war. The Revolutionary War cemented the nation's birth, while wars against American Indians, a second round with the British, and a war with Mexico, among other conflicts, enabled its expansion. The US thwarted its greatest challenge—the South's secession—through a successful war to end slavery and preserve the Union. The US entered the international arena to become a superpower through its involvement in two world wars. The post-World War II era saw the country eliminate its greatest threat, the Soviet Union and international Communism, with a mixture of economic pressure, intelligence-gathering, the arms race, and "limited" engagements in the Third World (Korea, Vietnam, and so on). Today, the US, the world's lone superpower, fights a "war on terror" that has spawned two limited wars—one in Afghanistan and a second in Iraq.

Throughout the nation's history, the US' involvement in warfare has given rise to sense-making efforts on the part of writers and other artists. As literary and cultural critic Richard Slotkin explains, "War requires people to endure and inflict terrible suffering; and once the pressures of crisis have passed, individuals and societies alike experience a reaction against the war, against the things war has compelled them to do and endure" (326). Modern war increases not only the horror of conflict, as we will see, but also the degree to which participants and witnesses seem compelled to write about it. For scholars, the term "modern war" has a specific meaning. It refers to the emergence of a form of warfare in which states organize violence under the rubrics of nationalism and industrialization. That is, modern war becomes possible only when citizens understand their identities to be bound up with those of their nations. Only when people think in this way will they be willing to fight for their nations and be able to define a modern enemy in clear-cut terms.

Yet this alone is not enough for war to be "modern." Modern war also depends upon industrialization, such that nation-states couple the creative potential of an industrialized or industrializing economy with the destructive force that economy can mass produce. In addition, with modern war, the state applies the logics of industrialization—centralization, hierarchy, rationalization, and the rhetoric of efficiency—to conflict. With the emergence of modern war, which began in the US during the Civil War and remains with us today, the distinction between citizen and soldier—a distinction pre-modern societies often held firm—erodes dramatically. All members of the nation are called upon to aid the war effort in some way; thus, the logic of modernity moves toward "total war."

The effects of modern war are such that around 100 million people died in the twentieth century's two world wars alone, and most of these people were civilians, not soldiers. Carnage on that scale assaults meaning, positing a tremendous challenge to writers who wish to convey precisely that to their readers. Highlighted in what follows are three aesthetics that American authors employ, with considerable success, to make sense of modern war: the ironic *Bildungsroman*, rooted in realism; satire; and the "separate peace" narrative of pursuing escape from war. To frame these approaches, this essay offers canonical examples of each, which include, respectively, Stephen Crane's *The Red Badge of Courage* (1895), Joseph Heller's *Catch-22* (1961), and Ernest Hemingway's *A Farewell to Arms* (1929).

Realism and War's "sense-datum": *The Red Badge of Courage*

Early in what arguably stands as the most influential work of American war literature ever published, Stephen Crane depicts his terribly young and innocent protagonist, Henry Fleming, on the march to confront Confederate troops in 1863 during the US Civil War's Battle of Chancellorsville. At this point in Crane's novella, Henry has yet to see combat. Along with the rest of the Union soldiers who form his New York-based regiment, Henry is what American Vietnam War veterans a century later would have termed an "FNG"—a "fucking new guy." Crane's novella settles on a softer term for Henry, repeatedly calling him "the youth."

The Henry we meet at the beginning of Crane's narrative is an unworldly farm kid who has fantasized for much of his short life about the glory of war and war's ability to make a man out of him. Yet Henry also is a boy who believes, along with many of his countrymen, that modern man is too enlightened to do much in the way of bloodthirsty mass killing. As Crane tells us,

> He [Henry] had, of course, dreamed of battles all his life—of vague and bloody conflicts that had thrilled him with their sweep and fire. In visions he had seen himself in many struggles. He had imagined peoples secure in the shadow of his eagle-eyed prowess. But awake he had regarded battles as crimson blotches on the pages of the past. He had put them as things of the bygone with his thought-images of heavy crowns and high castles. There was a portion of the world's history which he had regarded as the time of wars, but it, he thought, had been long gone over the horizon and had disappeared forever. (5)

It is through his experiences in America's first modern war—through his confrontation with what *Red Badge* terms "war, the red animal—war, the blood-swollen god" (Crane 25)—that Henry will be disabused of both his innocence and his blind faith in man's "progress."

Crane's genius in *Red Badge* is to capture Henry's change by way of an ironic *Bildungsroman* (or coming-of-age tale) in which Henry's transition to adulthood figures as loss as much as it does growth. This *Bildungsroman* charts Henry's development from boy to man by way of the liminal period of battle. In short, war does "make a man" out of Henry in *Red Badge*. That said, the man Henry becomes is one cynical before his time, as well as one stripped of all his previous convictions about his place in the world. By the end of the novella, Crane writes,

> He [Henry] felt a quiet manhood, nonassertive but a sturdy and strong blood. He knew that he would no more quail before his guides wherever they should point. He had been to touch the great death, and found that, after all, it was but the great death. He was a man. (139)

Crane's success in portraying Henry's ironic, three-part journey from boy to man by way of combat is such that critics often credit *Red Badge* with nothing less than birthing the canon of modern war literature in America. For example, literary and cultural theorist Frederic Jameson lauds how *Red Badge* captures war's "sense-datum," thereby offering readers an invaluable window into "the existential experience of war" (1534). Moreover, war-literature scholar and World War II combat veteran Paul Fussell argues convincingly that the type of *Bildungsroman* Crane conveys has so influenced Western conceptions of modern war as to structure the very way we "know" industrialized combat. As Fussell writes of British soldier-writers of World War I who adopt strategies similar to those of Crane, "By applying to the past a paradigm of ironic action, a rememberer is enabled to locate, draw forth, and finally shape into significance an event or a moment which otherwise would merge without meaning into the general undifferentiated stream" (30).

To realize his goal of representing war's "sense-datum," as Jameson calls it, Crane's aesthetic for *Red Badge* combines myriad components, three of which are emphasized here. First, Crane breaks with much of classical war literature in choosing to center his examination of the Civil War on the often non-heroic actions of a typical infantryman. Henry is no Abraham Lincoln, Ulysses S. Grant, or Robert E. Lee. In fact, Henry runs from his first battle, and even when he does fight with great honor, *Red Badge* strongly suggests that his actions have as much to do with external stimuli (a fight-or-flight response) as they do with Henry's personal virtues or vices. Hence, we can say that Crane chooses for his protagonist a "representative character" from the war—an everyman—rather than an exemplar of military merit.

In addition, *Red Badge* commits itself to verisimilitude, producing a simulacrum, or copy, of war's sights, sounds, and smells through prose characterized by a high degree of mimetic precision. Crane combines verisimilitude with impressionistic renderings of the psychological experience of war, which he filters through Henry's consciousness. By doing this, Crane relates how war impacts the body and psyche of an individual soldier. For example, *Red Badge* likely stands as the first work of literature to capture a key component of the modern war experience many veterans report—that during battle, one feels so intense a bodily and mental "high" that one experiences a kind of transcendence, even while one is busy ceding total control over his or her fate to chance. Of this paradox, Crane writes,

> It seemed to the youth that he saw everything. Each blade of the green grass was bold and clear. He thought that he was aware of every change in the thin, transparent vapor that floated idly in sheets. The brown or gray trunks of the trees showed each roughness of their surfaces. And the men of the regiment, with their starting eyes and sweating faces, running madly, or falling, as if thrown headlong, to queer, heaped-up corpses—all were comprehended. His mind took a mechanical but firm impression, so that afterward everything was pictured and explained to him, save why he himself was there. (109)

By successfully portraying, and structuring ironically, the representative experiences of a representative character of the American Civil War, Crane finds a way to read the significance of modern war's mass slaughter. In doing so, he has spawned legions of protégés, who range from Hemingway, an enthusiastic reader of *Red Badge*, to filmmaker Oliver Stone, whose Academy Award–winning Vietnam War drama, *Platoon* (1986), could well be viewed as an extended reworking of Crane's novella. *Red Badge* has become the archetypal modern-war-as-ironic-journey tale in the American canon; moreover, this form—the ironic *Bildungsroman*, conveyed by way of realism—is itself the archetypal narrative into which we tend to fit the modern-war experience. However, while Crane's paradigm dominates how Americans specifically, and Westerners generally, conceive of modern war, it does not do so with exclusivity.

Satirizing "the military business": *Catch-22*

With *Catch-22* (1961), his first and greatest novel, Joseph Heller offers an approach to understanding and critiquing modern war that, at first glance, appears the polar opposite of *Red Badge*. *Red Badge* is a tightly controlled narrative that plunges readers into the mind and experiences of a Civil War infantryman. In turn, Henry finds himself plunged into the dark heart of modern war, a confusing, thrilling, and horrifying arena that *Red Badge* communicates to readers by way of a simulacrum of battle and its effects. The momentum of Crane's novella is ever forward, delivering Henry and the reader closer and closer to violence so that we can test—and so Crane can render ironic—Henry's desire to discover whether "the youth" can become "a man of traditional courage" (26).

By contrast, *Catch-22* centers on the experiences of an American bomber squadron stationed in Italy and tasked with attacking German targets almost a hundred years after Chancellorsville, during the waning days of World War II. Rather than a concise work of fewer than 150 pages, *Catch-22* checks in at triple the length of *Red Badge*. Heller's masterwork is a sprawling, heaving novel, most of whose action takes place away from the fighting. Moreover, the novel's protagonist, Yossarian, never actually comes face-to-face with a German adversary, and the vast majority of *Catch-22*'s plot unfolds in the rear. Likewise, those portions of the novel Heller does dedicate to directly conveying war's horrors mostly occur thousands of feet in the air, where combat seems at once an entirely abstract and a viscerally terrifying affair. The question that animates *Red Badge* is, *What is modern war like?* Conversely, the question driving *Catch-22* is, *What does modern war mean?* We discover Heller's answer over the course of his novel: for *Catch-22*, modern war signals the bureaucratic mind's triumph over morality, with the modern era devoting itself to questions of efficiency and subsuming questions of goodness to such a degree that mass killing on an industrial scale comes to seem "normal." By definition, anyone who would question this new normal stands as "abnormal," or degenerate. On the other hand, whoever fails to question the new normal necessarily acquiesces to and participates in it. In fact, that is the catch that is "Catch-22," a lesson Heller teaches us a thousand times over in his wildly funny and deeply moving satire of what the text at one point terms "the military business" (46).

Much to his credit, Crane also saw that modern war applies the techniques of modern industry to the problems of producing and deploying death machines. At one point in *Red Badge*, Henry spies from a distance a commanding officer that the text characterizes as follows: "Sometimes the general was surrounded by horsemen and at other times he was quite alone. He looked to be much harassed. He had the appearance of a business man whose market is swinging up and down" (Crane 45). This general is no Alexander the Great; for today's reader, *Red Badge*'s general likely calls to mind Mike Judge's wicked spoof of contemporary corporate life, *Office Space* (1999), and the character of Bill Lumbergh (Gary Cole). Later in *Red Badge*, Henry overhears a conversation between another general and a subordinate officer in which the general asks, "What troops can you spare?" for an attack on the Confederates that he knows is a suicide mission. In response to the general's question, the lower-ranking man indicates Henry's regiment, saying, "They fight like a lot 'a mule drivers. I can spare them best of any" (Crane 105). With passages such as these, Crane shows how well he grasps the single soldier's place in modern war: constituent part of a system of death-making much larger than him- or herself.

Catch-22 moves this insight to the center of its project. The novel aligns itself with Yossarian's desire to uncover what of human goodness can be saved or reborn amid a world that has become profoundly dehumanized. It is no accident that the opening lines of Heller's novel portray Yossarian, hospitalized while faking a liver problem to avoid flying, falling in "love at first sight" with a chaplain (Heller 15). Yossarian and the novel long for a day in which goodness, rather than efficiency, would stand as the key criterion (or "metric," in today's business-speak) by which we judge the efficacy of what we do—a world in which our work (or "deliverable") aims at the extension of love, not death, and of hope, not its abridgement. Beginning immediately with its first chapter, *Catch-22* establishes the aesthetic "rules" of its investigation into whether such a world might be possible. On the novel's surface, we find blisteringly precise and funny prose that conveys the madcap adventures of *Catch-22*'s enormous cast of colorful characters. This surface scalds the pretensions toward order and control of the modern military machine. However, just beneath this surface, we uncover horror, such as in the first chapter of *Catch-22*, when we meet a character called "the soldier in white." The novel introduces this character as so:

> The soldier in white was encased from head to toe in plaster and gauze. He had two useless legs and two useless arms. He had been smuggled into the ward during the night, and the men had no idea he was among them until they awoke in the morning and saw the two strange legs hoisted from the hips, the two strange arms anchored up perpendicularly, all four limbs pinioned strangely in air by lead weights suspended darkly above him that never moved. . . . A silent zinc pipe rose from the cement on his groin and was coupled to a slim rubber hose that carried waste from his kidneys and dripped it efficiently into a clear, stoppered jar on the floor. When the jar on the floor was full, the jar feeding his elbow was empty, and the two were simply switched quickly so that stuff could drip back into him. (18)

As the novel careens along, horror like this displaces the text's veneer of hilarity, such that the reader suspects he or she has been tricked: having started the novel laughing at the fate of Yossarian and his squadron mates, the reader becomes responsible to them. Hence, we can say that Heller's aesthetic is itself a Catch-22.

Furthermore, this aesthetic conjoins *Catch-22* to a picaresque tradition in Western literature that dates to Cervantes' *Don Quixote* (1605, 1615), a tradition Mark Twain's *The Adventures of Huckleberry Finn* (1884) perhaps best exemplifies in the American canon. Just as Cervantes works through his anti-hero, Don Quixote, to satirize early modern Europe's romantic ideas about knighthood and chivalry—and just as Twain works through anti-heroes Huck and Jim to satirize nineteenth-century America's ideas about equality in light of persistent classism and racism—so does Heller, through anti-hero Yossarian, lay bare a reality in which

> Men went mad and were rewarded with medals. All over the world, boys on every side of the bomb line were laying down their lives for what they had been told was their country, and no one seemed to mind, least of all the boys who were laying down their young lives. There was no end in sight. (25)

We learn that Yossarian, who by the end of the novel has seen more of war's killing and dying than anyone should have to see, commenced his tour of duty believing not only in the justice of the cause, but also in the rightness of those tasked with running it. By the end of the novel, he still believes in the justice of killing in order to combat fascism. As he tells Major Danby, who counsels Yossarian to stick to the mission and just keep flying his runs, "I earned that medal I got, no matter what their reasons were for giving it to me. I've flown seventy goddamn combat missions. Don't talk to me about fighting to save my country" (Heller 456). However, Yossarian's tour also makes him privy to the ineptitude and greed of not only the military commanders running the war, but also the nation-states and corporations producing it. In his conversation with Danby, Yossarian names several of the men who command his squadron, saying,

That's my trouble, you know . . . . Between me and every ideal I always find Scheisskopfs, Peckems, Korns, and Cathcarts. And that sort of changes the ideal . . . . When I look up, I see people cashing in. I don't see heaven or saints or angels. I see people cashing in on every decent impulse and every human tragedy. (Heller 455)

By *Catch-22*'s conclusion, Yossarian's attempt to reconcile his ideals with his reality has run aground, as it were. All Yossarian can salvage is his own skin. Given as much, Yossarian and *Catch-22* insert themselves into the third major tradition of modern American war literature taken up here. This tradition is the "separate peace" narrative, the key example of which is Hemingway's World War I novel, *A Farewell to Arms*. All the same, *Catch-22*'s satirical approach to portraying modern war stands as a precursor to the enormously popular television series M*A*S*H (1972–1983), as well as more recent texts that include David Abrams' adroit Iraq War novel *Fobbit* (2012). Even today, *Catch-22* remains the anchor text of American war satire.

Seeking "a separate peace": *A Farewell to Arms*

To this point, this essay has argued that the central question animating *Red Badge* is, *What is modern war like?* Conversely, the central question that drives *Catch-22* is, *What does modern war mean?* As we have seen, these questions are not mutually exclusive. Rather, they interpenetrate and, in many ways, are interdependent. Along this same vein, then, Hemingway's *Farewell* hones in on a query embedded in *Red Badge* and *Catch-22*, but *Farewell* moves this interrogative to its core. *Farewell* asks, *Is there life after modern war?* Hemingway poses this question in the context of a first-person narrative that protagonist Frederic Henry shares with readers.

Born into a wealthy American family, Henry has left his life of relative ease to join the Italian army well in advance of the US' 1917 declaration of war and the inception of the nation's direct participation in World War I. Henry is a low-ranking officer who oversees the transport of wounded infantrymen as the Italians battle on the side of the Allies against Austrian and German forces. He serves with honor and skill and barely survives his own "red badge of courage" during a bombardment, among several other close scrapes. That said, Hemingway does not make "men under fire" his main subject in *Farewell*, as Crane does in *Red Badge*. Nor is Hemingway primarily interested in "the military business" and its analogues, as Heller is in *Catch-22*. Rather, *Farewell* offers an intimate foray into the mind and actions of a man war has debased, who seeks an alternative to mass death. To read this novel well, one must push past pre-conceived notions we inherit about Hemingway, given stereotypes that paint him as obtuse, obsessed with proving his toughness, and misogynistic. *Farewell* is an empathic, tender novel that risks sentiment without devolving into sentimentality. It demands readers consider seriously that the logic of modern war and our commitment to it may prove inescapable. Inasmuch, *Farewell* looks forward to the oeuvre of America's most important living writer, Cormac McCarthy. It also forecasts the work of Kevin Powers, whose recently published first novel, *The Yellow Birds* (2012), is a fine study of the Iraq War that is deeply indebted to Hemingway.

Readers suspect that *Farewell* will end badly from the novel's outset. Yet it is not until roughly two-thirds of the way into the text that Henry tells us just that in a direct address to the reader. In what has become one of the most frequently cited passages in all of Hemingway, Henry states,

> If people bring so much courage to this world the world has to kill them to break them, so of course it kills them. The world breaks every one and afterward many are strong at the broken places. But those that will not break it kills. It kills the very good and the very gentle and the very brave impartially. If you are none of these you can be sure it will kill you too but there will be no special hurry. (267)

Over the course of the novel, we discover that Henry does indeed "bring so much courage to this world" and is "strong at the broken places." However, the character in the novel "that will not break" and stands as the true hero of the book is the Scottish nurse, Catherine Barkley, who also volunteers to serve the Allies. She and Henry strike up a romance that deepens while he recovers from wounds he sustains during the bombardment alluded to earlier. Barkley has suffered tremendously because of this war, losing her first love. Henry must leave her to return to the front, where, during a retreat, he narrowly escapes execution by his supposed brothers-in-arms, who wrongly label him a "deserter." Afterward, Barkley and Henry seek "a separate peace" from the war (Hemingway 260). He goes AWOL from the army, reconnects with her, and the two flee Italy in a daring maritime adventure to Switzerland.

That no such peace is possible is the crucial lesson and tragedy of *Farewell*. In the following selection, Henry muses on the idea of what we might call "permanent war." This selection stands as especially prescient, given that the United States has been at war or readying for war constantly over the last century. He states,

> It looked as though the war were going on for a long time. We [Americans] were in the war now but I thought it would take a year to get any great amount of troops over and train them for combat. Next year would be a bad year, or a good year maybe. The Italians were using up an awful amount of men. I did not see how it could go on . . . . Still nobody was whipping any one on the Western front. Perhaps wars weren't won any more. Maybe they went on forever. Maybe it was another Hundred Years' War. (Hemingway 126)

According to Fussell, "The idea of endless war as an inevitable condition of modern life would seem to have become seriously available to the imagination around 1916" (74)—about a year prior to the present action of *Farewell*. When he elaborates on this point, Fussell contextualizes the idea of "permanent war" in a way that will serve us here. He writes,

> Events, never far behindhand in fleshing out the nightmares of imagination, obliged with the Spanish War, the Second World War, the Greek War, the Korean War, the Arab-Israeli War, and the Vietnam War . . . .The 1916 image of never-ending war has about it, to be sure, a trace of the consciously whimsical and the witty hyperbolic. But there is nothing but the literal in this headline from the *New York Times* for September 1, 1972: U.S. AIDES IN VIETNAM SEE AN

UNENDING WAR. Thus the drift of modern history domesticates the fantastic and normalizes the unspeakable. (74)

Within the confines of *Farewell*, the "drift of modern history" overwhelms and subsumes the prospect of "a separate peace."

Almost from the moment we meet each of them, Henry and Barkley sense their own superfluity to the war effort. At one point, Henry even says, "Evidently it did not matter whether I was there or not" (Hemingway 16). Yet both push back at this nagging fear and continue doing the jobs for which they volunteered. For a while, they find in each other a reason and the ability to continue on, even while the horrors of World War I undermine all their ideas and beliefs. As Barkley tells Henry during a poignant exchange, "I haven't any religion . . . .You're my religion. You're all I've got" (Hemingway 123). Neither she nor he can believe in an ordered world or a higher purpose after the toll the war has taken on them. In another of Hemingway's most famous passages, Henry encapsulates this loss beautifully:

> I was always embarrassed by the words sacred, glorious, and sacrifice and the expression in vain. We had heard them . . . and had read them, on proclamations . . . now for a long time, and I had seen nothing sacred, and the things that were glorious had no glory and the sacrifices were like the stockyards at Chicago if nothing was done with the meat except to bury it. There were many words that you could not stand to hear and finally only the names of places had dignity . . . . Abstract words such as glory, honor, courage, or hallow were obscene beside the concrete names of villages, the numbers of roads, the names of rivers, the numbers of regiments and the dates. (196)

Once the war makes its final betrayal of these two in the "desertion" scene, Henry and Barkley try to become one another's "concrete names" to the total exclusion of all else.

The aesthetics of *Farewell* are such that Hemingway collapses the distance between text and protagonist by way of the novel's first-person point of view. In this, Hemingway pursues what the poet and literary critic Yvor Winters terms "imitative form," or, "a procedure in which the form succumbs to the raw material" (41). Winters is derisive in his characterization of imitative form, which is at the heart of American and European modernisms. He believes that such an aesthetic forces a writer or poet to cede his or her ability to comment on the morality of that which a text represents. For Winters, imitative form involves a writer or poet rejecting reason and judgment in the face of the power of the material world. However, Hemingway proves Winters wrongheaded, at least insofar as the workings of imitative form in *Farewell* are concerned. Rather than amorality, what readers find in the novel's remainder is a truly intimate, suspenseful work replete with dramatic irony—a work that humanizes the protagonist and Barkley, thereby pushing back at the war. He and she go to great lengths to create and preserve domestic harmony. They do nothing less than attempt to stop time while in Switzerland, boldly asserting their individuality and their commitment to one another against a fallen world's "progress."

This is a deeply courageous act. All the same, readers always feel war lurking in the shadows—so much so that war functions as a kind of specter for the last third of *Farewell*. Furthermore, readers know that, at some point, these characters will be doomed. By the end of the novel, our worst suspicions realize themselves, and when they do, Hemingway will have shown us both the fallacious nature of and beauty inherent in a quest for "a separate peace." Likewise, when we consider his work alongside that of Crane and Heller, readers are better positioned to engage a twenty-first-century world, in which war, for most Americans, is a ubiquitous white noise ever humming in the background of our lives. Readers also become better positioned to engage those Americans and others all over the planet for whom modern war comes to the foreground, bringing horror with it.

Works Cited

Crane, Stephen. *The Red Badge of Courage*. 1895. *The Red Badge of Courage and Other Stories*. By Stephen Crane. Ed. Gary Scharnhorst. New York: Penguin, 2005. 1–140.

Fussell, Paul. *The Great War and Modern Memory*. 1975. London: Oxford UP, 1977.

Goldstein, Joshua S. *War and Gender: How Gender Shapes the War System and Vice Versa*. Cambridge: Cambridge UP, 2001.

Heller, Joseph. *Catch-22*. 1961. New York: Simon & Schuster, 1994.

Hemingway, Ernest. *A Farewell to Arms*. 1929. Shelton, CT: The First Edition Library, n.d.

Jameson, Frederic. "War and Representation." *PMLA* 124.5 (2009): 1532–1547.

Slotkin, Richard. *Gunfighter Nation: The Myth of the Frontier in Twentieth-Century America*. Norman: U of Oklahoma P, 1992.

Winters, Yvor. *In Defense of Reason*. Denver: U of Denver P, 1947.

CRITICAL
READINGS

Violence in the Bible from Genesis to Job_____

David Mikics

The Hebrew Bible has often been seen by Christians as a document dripping in blood, exulting in barbarous and gruesome punishments. As I often point out to my students, though, Christianity has a serious advantage over Judaism when it comes to relishing bodily agonies. No Israelite ever imagined subjecting his enemies to the eternal, hellish torments so eagerly described by the author of Revelation. A sheer delight in torture, as Nietzsche reminds us, is also memorably expressed by Saint Thomas Aquinas, who tells us that one of the chief pleasures of the blessed will be looking down from heaven on the desperate writhings of their opponents in hell (Nietzsche 29). The Hebrew Bible describes ruthless violence frequently, but the Christian interest in the never-ending flaying of body and soul is thankfully absent. This division between the Hebrew and the Christian Bible is a basic one. The New Testament narratives about Jesus and his follower Paul make violence an internal matter, a psychic struggle between the drive towards vengeance and the drive towards peace and purity. The Gospels, unlike the Hebrew Bible, are not so much concerned with literal deeds of violence as with the rancorous impulse within us that makes us want to destroy others. Jesus asks how we might quiet or rise above that impulse, but there is a cost to this. Revelation, the endpoint of the New Testament, shows that the very stress of Jesus' effort at transcendence can lead to a relapse, a new multiplication of vengeful wishes.

For the Hebrew Bible, unlike the Christian one, violence is an ineradicable, strange, and permanently troubling part of human life. Isaiah's hopes that war and bloodshed will cease, like later rabbinical fantasies of the perfected *olam haba*, or world-to-come, are thought-experiments meant to be balanced against the evidence of our inclination to destroy one another so abundantly presented in the stories of the Tanakh. This essay will focus on Genesis, since it shows us how violence begins, virtually as an aftermath of the creation story. The episode of Cain and Abel implies that we cannot have the goodness of creation without the subsequent desire to tear it apart, to ruin the peaceful bonds between people that are God's greatest gift. By the time Genesis concludes, it has repaired these bonds, but only by exiling God from its culminating Joseph narrative. The looming question is God's own investment in violence, and it is addressed not only in Genesis, but in subsequent books of the Bible, like Exodus and Job.

Is the Bible too bloody? Does it endorse bloodshed, prefer violence to peace? The answer to both these questions is no: the Bible, taken as a whole (including the Christian Gospels, too), centers on the hope for peace. But the Bible, like any scripture, would be of little worth if it did not try to grasp the worst and most resistant things about us as well as the best, and try to comprehend how the best and the worst might be tied together. In its probing, uncertain approach to the question of why we are violent to each other, the Bible makes a demand that is absent in the Greek and Roman classics, for which violence is a simple fact of life. No classical author ever argued that murder, or any other violent act, is wrong. For the Greeks and Romans, violence, since it is tied so closely to anger, is potentially harmful to the soul of the one who commits it—and harmful in an obvious way to the one who suffers it. But there is nothing in any classical source to suggest that doing violence to other humans is basically unjust, that it shouldn't happen because it violates the point of creation. The Bible does, by contrast, emphasize the wrongness of violence, even as it knows that aggression in its worst forms remains, alas, a constant possibility.

"Death thou hast seen / In his first shape on man," the archangel Michael tells an appalled Adam in book eleven of Milton's *Paradise Lost* (11.466–67). Michael is projecting before Adam's eyes a lengthy, rather cinematic prophecy of future events. He has just shown Adam the very first thing that will happen in human history: a dreadful act of blood, Cain's killing of his brother Abel. Milton's Adam, like his Eve, "knew not eating death" (so the poem describes her taste of the forbidden fruit)—but now he knows. What Adam sees appalls him: his son Abel "rolling in dust and gore," after Cain, "as they talked, / Smote him into the midriff with a stone / That beat out life" (Milton, *Paradise Lost* 11.460, 444-46).

In the Genesis account of Cain and Abel that Milton drew on, the Bible gives us a haunting enigma: what can account for unjust, violent death? Cain, a farmer, brings God an offering of first fruits; Abel, a shepherd, sacrifices the firstlings of his flock. "The Lord paid heed [*vayisha*] to Abel and his offering, but to Cain and his offering he paid no heed [*lo shaa*]," we are told: there is no hint as to why God makes this decision.[1] Maybe it's not God's decision, but just a fact in God's universe, an accidental outcome. God does not pay attention to Cain's offering: this probably means that some mischance follows his sacrifice, for this is the clearest way that Cain's failure can become evident. But crucially, in this case, divine intention is in the eye of the beholder. God will not say whether he accidentally overlooked Cain or actively disdained him. But the words that God speaks to Cain, though they stop short of telling him he is at fault, cannot help but be felt by him as an accusation. God opens for Cain the path from enduring a misfortune to the feeling that he is to blame for it. Cain will invent, on his own, the next, fatal step: he imposes the final misfortune, death, on the person closest to him, his brother Abel.

Cain's face falls when his offering is not accepted, and God speaks to him a warning poem:

> Why are you distressed,
> And why is your face fallen?
> Surely, if you do right,
> There is uplift [*seet*].
> But if you do not do right
> Sin couches [*rovetz*] at the door;
> Its urge is toward you,
> Yet you can be its master [*timshol-bo*].

The encouraging reading of the poem's first two lines, by Shneur Zalman of Lyady (*Etz Hayim* 25), is bound to sail far above Cain's head: if the life you live is a just one, you will be able to bear any misfortune (like that of the rejected sacrifice), since you know you have done right. It's more likely that Cain thinks he is being blamed by God for letting his face fall and assumes that God sees his distress as evidence that he has done wrong. If you don't do right, God adds—implying that Cain has offered his sacrifice in the wrong spirit, perhaps—then sin awaits you (the verb used, *rvtz*, implies the resting posture of a predatory animal). But man can master the sin that lurks in readiness for him. The problem with this advice, for the inexperienced Cain, is twofold: first, it presents no practical guidance for the control of the evil impulse, what the rabbis will later call the *yetzer hara*. And second, Cain has, as yet, no idea of how or why he might have done wrong. If you do not do right, Cain is told, then sin is waiting. So Cain must assume that he has somehow not done right—why otherwise would his offering have been rejected? But how could he have done wrong?

Here, Cain's sense of wrongness is internal, mysterious, rather than evident in a deed. It's the kind of feeling that often follows a run of bad luck: you suspect that something in you must have been responsible. (This, of course, is the line that Job's comforters will take.) The son's offering of first fruits, intended to please God, stands in sharp contrast to his parents' eating of the forbidden fruit in the garden; yet he, too, seems to have made a mistake. Knowing that you are somehow, strangely, in the wrong and, therefore, liable to sin, is like an invitation to sin. And then to become the sinning one offers a kind of relief: having your experience and, therefore, your identity defined and explained, as by a curse.

Cain does not achieve, or even attempt, mastery over his violent impulse. In the field with Abel, he attacks and murders his brother. When God asks Cain "Where is your brother Abel?," this echoes the terrifying question he posed to the hiding Adam in 3:9, "Where are you?" What follows is Cain's wild lie and his fierce challenge: "I do not know: Am I my brother's keeper [*hashomer akhi*]?" And then God laments, "What have you done? Hark, your brother's blood cries out to me from the ground."

The most intriguing comment on this agonized conversation between Cain and God is the oldest one that has come down to us, from the Midrash Rabbah, a commentary on the Bible from the early centuries of the Common Era: "Your brother's blood cries out *against* me [i.e., God], accusing me of letting this injustice happen" (*Genesis Rabbah* 22:9). The Midrash Rabbah has it right, grammatically and otherwise: the preposition *el* can mean either "to" or " against." The cry of Abel's blood has never stopped echoing: to speak of human violence is to accuse God for letting it happen, allowing it to corrupt the creation.

Cain's question to God pretends ignorance: he falsely claims that he wasn't even there. It's not my role to keep watch over Abel, he says; perhaps, as Joseph's brothers will put it, a wild beast tore him. The murderer has a steady will toward denial: he manages the event by imagining it didn't occur.

The story of Cain suggests that not to be a keeper, a *shomer*, is to risk becoming the opposite, a slayer. Yet it seems beyond our human capacity to be the keepers of one another, to guard other people against violent attacks in the same way that we guard ourselves. Even worse, we are tempted to destroy others, not just because they are the objects of our envy or resentment, but because to do so feels, for a moment at least, desperately God-like. The most drastic way of lashing out against our feeling of guilt for our own suffering—playing God by depriving someone else of life—might lead to a brief delusive rush of power and freedom, but it only makes us infinitely more guilty.

Cain's deed of blood exiles him from history: "You will become a ceaseless wanderer upon the earth [*Na venad tehiye baaretz*]," God tells him. But the pathos of his defenselessness does not last. Eventually, Cain becomes the ancestor of that crude cartoon of a hero, Lamech, who boasts to his wives of his impressive slaughters (with the wives, the critic William Miller suggests, no doubt rolling their eyes [Miller 24]). The legacy of Abel's death is this slow descent of killing from trauma into caricature, even as Lamech prides himself on being far bigger and badder than his forefather Cain. Lamech is not doomed like Cain, but satisfied, his ego puffed up by easy acts of vengeance. Cain's sense that his act of murder has cut him off from humanity is only a passing feeling. Within a few generations after Cain, murder becomes normal and even desirable—something to brag about.

By the time of Noah, violence is epidemic. In the Noah story, Genesis gives us a portrait of the difficulty God faces in dealing with the masses of humanity, who have become so evil that there is nothing to do about them except kill them. "All flesh has corrupted [or destroyed, *hishkhit*] its ways on earth" (6:12), God announces to the lucky Noah, who will be spared along with his family. And so "I am about to destroy them [*mashkhitam*] with the earth," God says (6:13). It will escape no reader's notice that God uses the same verb for what he is about to do to his humans that he has just used for what those humans have done to themselves. Though such mimicry of human evil on God's part succeeds in clearing the slate, really a new system is needed: God can't solve the problem of humanity's destructive ways simply by destroying them. God needs to create again, not merely mirror his creation's bad impulses. And, in fact, God does create something new after the Flood: the law. If you spill someone's blood, your blood will be spilled, God decrees (9:6). This stands in contrast to the lenient punishment of exile given to Cain. Then, God even improvised a protection for Cain the wanderer, the divine mark designed to defend him against attackers. Like a parent moved by his mixed feelings and his sense of responsibility, God with Cain, as with Adam and Eve, both shields and punishes the ones he has created. But the law given to Noah and his descendants is meant to be impersonal, not parental. The law imposes a predictability that did not exist in the case of Cain and Abel or the masses killed in God's Flood. If you make blood flow, your blood will flow in return. The law's fixed penalties free us from the terror of what might be lurking within us, ready to spring out at any moment. If we know the punishment for murder, we will try to master our impulse to murder.

But the law must be enforced in order to work. In the tale of Sodom and Gomorrah, we see a lawless society, in which the basic rules have been turned upside down. In Sodom, it's considered *de rigueur* to rape one's guests. Mob rule presides over this baddest of all bad places, and the cry of its victims reaches God (18:20). But God, hearing the cry, does not instantly reach out and annihilate the cities of the plain: the law binds him, too, or so we are meant to think. God is now becoming a judge rather than the ruthless, large-scale destroyer he showed himself to be during the Flood. Rather than acting on the basis of the impression that has reached him from afar, as he did with the generation he ruined in the Flood, God sends a team to investigate, the two messengers (the *malachim*, traditionally translated "angels"), who seek lodging with Abraham's nephew Lot in Sodom.

Just before the turbulent scene with Lot and the messengers, God engages in a dialogue-cum-negotiation with Abraham. Suspecting that God is about to level Sodom, Abraham objects to the collateral damage that will result: how can God, the judge of all the world, he asks, destroy a good person (*tsadik*) along with an evil one (*rasha*)? After a lengthy and shrewd negotiation, in which Abraham more than holds his own, Abraham makes God accept his own human terms: if ten righteous people can be found in Sodom, then God will not destroy the city. By talking God down to ten people rather than one, Abraham tacitly abandons the idea he started with, that it is unjust to kill even one righteous individual. (Surely, the infants of Sodom are not culpable; but perhaps they do not count in the negotiation, as they are not mature enough to be just or righteous, rather than merely innocent.) The criterion is a political one: whether there is a sufficient critical mass of just people in Sodom to demonstrate that the city is not completely corrupt. Even if they are vastly outnumbered—only ten—this small group can still show itself, make its voice heard. (Not by accident, ten is the number required to make a Jewish *minyan*, the quorum needed for a full prayer service.)

As it turns out, not even one righteous man lives in Sodom. All the men of the city, down to the last one, surround Lot's door, demanding to "know" (i.e., rape) his guests. Sodom shows that a society can be so corrupt, so morally damaged, that no one dares to act justly; when, beyond this, every adult male joins the mob of rapists, this is sufficient public evidence for God's decision to annihilate. No such large-scale extermination has taken place since the Flood, and it, like the Flood, requires God to act directly from the heavens, rather than through human agents. The law God announced after the Flood, that death would be a punishment only for individual murderers, applies in cases when humans carry out the sentence. When God punishes, he reserves the right to kill on a larger than individual scale and without the evidence of already spilled blood, if he deems it morally or politically necessary. He kills the Sodomites in order to remove a standing danger to humanity, in addition to preventing the rape of his messengers. By crushing Sodom, God stamps out a corrupt, unsalvageable society.

Yet God, though he rains down fire on Sodom, goes beyond the terms he has offered Abraham: God interprets the law generously. Even though the ten just people have not been found, God spares Lot and his family. Lot is neither completely righteous nor completely evil: he offers the men of Sodom his daughter as a substitute for the messengers, and so upholds hospitality at a terrible cost (the daughter is saved when a blinding light stuns the Sodomites). As if he realizes that Lot has been put in an impossible position and that it is, therefore, impossible for him to act justly, God spares him, reserving destruction for the Sodomites, who actively choose evil. The collateral damage, the killing of women and children, goes unmentioned, either because their deaths cannot be helped or because they don't exist: Sodom could be an encampment consisting of men only, as in the American West.

In the Sodom story, God uses violence on a massive, terrifying scale, as he did in the Flood; and as in the Flood, he saves a single family from the devastation he has caused. Yet the ruin inflicted on Sodom is different from the mass death during the Flood, since God here subjects himself to a legal process that proves the guilt of the Sodomites before he proceeds to act against them.

The next instance of God's violence in Genesis, the sacrifice of Isaac, does not actually take place, but the implications of this quasi-event are far more troubling than those of Sodom. The *Akedah*, or binding of Isaac, is the enigmatic center of the book of Genesis. Why does God make his outrageous demand of Abraham, to sacrifice his son Isaac? If it is simply to assert a ruthless claim over all he has bestowed on Abraham, to remind him that God gives death as well as life (as the Book of Job puts it, the Lord gives, and the Lord takes away), then the near-death of Isaac seems too brutal a spectacle to make the point that Abraham should not rest too assured of God's protection. There are more fitting ways to crease Abraham's complacence than terrifying him by telling him to kill his son. The radical Protestant explanation made popular by Kierkegaard in *Fear and Trembling* also seems inadequate. If the point of the Akedah is God's assertion of an absolute authority beyond any possible morality, as Kierkegaard thought, then there is no difference between this God and the idol of the fanatic, and the Bible's statements about divine justice become mere camouflage for a brutal doctrine of God's absolute, unquestionable power.

Perhaps Abraham ought to realize all along, to know deep down, that God will not after all make him kill Isaac, despite all apparent evidence to the contrary: the wood, the hatchet, the cords around the son's body. The very senselessness of the event makes it impossible that it could come to pass. Then why not say this to God; why not ask the judge of the world to act justly, as Abraham did before Sodom? But Abraham, shocked by the senselessness of the order, is in no position to argue with God. He goes along not out of faith, but out of defeat. He resigns himself to the worst. What if this God turns out to be like the pagan idols, with their horrible demands for child sacrifice? In that case, what will be must be. Abraham, since his departure from Ur, has gone too far with God, he owes God too much, to back out now.

The angelic messenger's approval for Abraham's willingness to kill his son (22:15–18) is clearly a later addition to the text, as scholars have long recognized, and more than likely, it misses the original point: that Abraham's willingness was not a sign of steadfast loyalty, but a doomed indication that he has given up. Abraham has given in to a God whose true nature he could not possibly know, and this surrender is a betrayal on his part of the contract he made with that God, who has not been an unreasonable murderer, but instead has been careful to justify his destructive actions. The sparing of Isaac by God feels like a reprimand for Abraham that he did not dispute God's outrageous demand for child sacrifice, despite the speech of angelic approval added later on. The missing argument between Abraham and God over God's authority to command the most terrible deed of violence from his chosen patriarch haunts every reader. This absence will be filled in the Book of Job, in which God, through his operative Satan, inflicts violence on a favored follower, Job. Job disputes with God as Abraham did not and so raises the dreadful and inescapable prospect that God is merely a combined destroyer and preserver, who sees little difference between the two sides of the cosmos he has created, the violent and the peaceful. Genesis, confident that life outweighs death, does not approach Job's interrogation of God as a being who might base his authority on the sheer superiority of his power, rather than his capacity to care for the world he has created.

In light of the trauma that God imposes on Abraham during the Akedah, it is small wonder that the culminating story of Genesis, the career of Joseph, exiles God almost completely from its narrative (with the exception of God's brief cameo in Jacob's dream [46:2–4]). Instead, the adept and civilized Joseph speaks for the deity, making God over in his own image. Serious violence is alien to Joseph's God, who stands in contrast to the threatening deity who presides over earlier episodes in Genesis, from the Flood and the ruin of Sodom to the claim made to the life of Isaac in the Akedah.

Joseph's suave and redemptive brand of irony is opposed to his brothers' violent, crude irony. When the jealous brothers, savoring their evil intent, see Joseph approaching them, they murmur, "Behold, this dreamer cometh" (Norton, KJV 37:19). They plan to kill the precocious and self-assured young Jacob and throw him into a pit, exulting, "We can say, 'A savage beast devoured him.' We shall see what comes of his dreams!" (Norton, KJV 37:20). Joseph has naively told his brothers his dreams, which imply that he will rule over them; they retaliate by casting him down, and raising themselves up through violence. (Reuben will modify the plan so that the brothers throw Joseph into the pit without murdering him, but their ironic point remains the same.)

The brothers' brutal irony (think you're so high and mighty? See how we put you down!) yields, in the course of the Joseph story, to Joseph's triumph over them and to the sophisticated irony that he uses to make peace between himself and his brothers. In this way, Joseph reconciles himself to the brothers, as well as soothes their fear that he will take revenge on them. Don't reproach yourselves for what you did to me, he tells his brothers after he reveals himself to them at the Pharoah's court, because "it was to save life that God sent me ahead of you" (45:5). Violence in the Joseph story, as in the Akedah, is narrowly averted: the killing of Joseph, because of Reuben's intervention, is never carried out. But the difference from the Akedah is that here it is the Cain-like, all-too-human brothers, rather than God, who propose the murder. Even more crucially, in the Joseph story, an easy redemptive explanation is given for the threat made to Joseph (as it is not, or not convincingly, for the threat to Isaac in the Akedah): it was all staged by God so that he could make Joseph into a savior for the Israelites, solving their famine with Egyptian grain and resettling them in the rich land of Goshen. (As Tyndale marvelously puts it in his version, "God was with Joseph, and he was a lucky fellow.") Yet the redemptive fiction only extends so far. Joseph, by transporting his family to Egypt, has unknowingly set the stage for the slavery of the Israelites four hundred years later. At the end of Genesis, a future of greater violence, of persecution and struggle, looms for the people of Israel.

In Exodus, the violence of the plagues and the drowned Egyptians seems to be the necessary price for the deliverance of Israel from Egypt. Later on, in the Golden Calf episode, there is another price to pay as well for a new, equally necessary deliverance: Moses' determination to save the Israelites from idolatry. Only the Levites' slaughter of their fellow Israelites can stem the wild mob rule that attends the Golden Calf apostasy, and this use of killing to pacify rebellion forecasts later instances, like the deaths of Korach's band of rebels and Pinchas' slaying of Zimri and Cosbi (both in Numbers). In all these cases, the danger is internal, a threat to Israelite unity, and in all of them, a zealous and bloody prosecution is needed to still the revolt. The Talmud, especially in its tractate Sanhedrin (a section of the Talmud concerned with questions of judgment and justice), will pursue a troubling question that stems largely from this series of episodes in the wilderness: when is zeal that involves violence beyond the bounds of the law required to keep the law in place? The violence is most disturbing in the case of the Levites because, as Leslie Brisman and Christine Hayes have argued, they make no distinction between innocent and guilty, but simply do mayhem, taking lives at random. This is what Abraham feared God would do in the case of Sodom; now, unlike then, God endorses arbitrary killing, seemingly because a newly complex and vulnerable political structure requires the support provided by terror. The Levites are terrorists who do the equivalent of throwing a bomb in the crowd so that the ensuing shock and fear can tame the unruly mob and make it manageable. Moses leads his people not just out of Egypt, but into the realm of politics, and along with this transition, a new role for divinely sanctioned violence appears: to defend Moses' and God's authority.

In Exodus and Numbers, God makes an argument through violence about the need to aggressively shape a polity, to turn it from riff-raff (in Hebrew, *asafsuf*) to an obedient group of followers. Yet the deadly eruptions on the part of authority against a restive or rebellious community are not sufficient to make them take the law to heart. Instead, a fervent inward loyalty must be insisted on, most overtly in the passionate words of Deuteronomy. There is a difference between a merely obedient group and a loyal and responsible community, as the Torah, taken as a whole, insists; a community whose members are legally bound to one another and to God has little or no place for arbitrary violence, but instead follows the law willingly, even eagerly. Still, to remain convincing, the law must reiterate the disastrous consequences of disobeying it. If Israel ever forsakes the law, what follows will be the curse of violent upheaval in a dismaying variety of forms (Deuteronomy 28:15–68). The law keeps peace; in its absence comes Yeats' blood-dimmed tide. This equation makes sense in social terms: a lawless mass, like the Sodomites, in effect destroys itself, rendering God's fiery rain a mere recognition of the obvious corruption that ruins communal life. But in individual terms, the idea is more troubling. What benefit accrues to the individual for cleaving to the law, instead of becoming one of the prosperous wicked? A society of wicked connivers would fall apart instantly, thus proving the Torah's point about community. But since the wicked apparently prosper in law-abiding societies and the most responsible and honest often suffer, a new question arises about how God can ensure justice for individuals. The threat of violent breakdown is sufficient to convince a community as a whole to avoid becoming a Deadwood or a Sodom and, instead, adhere to the law. But can acting justly and lawfully benefit the individual, can it provide a shield against a person's violent suffering, as it does in the case of the community?

This is the overwhelming question of the Book of Job, the pinnacle of the Bible's books of wisdom. In Job, God, through his agent Satan, inflicts tremendous violence, first killing Job's family and his cattle and then afflicting Job himself with disease. Job rises to the challenge by insisting against his so-called friends that he is guilty of nothing, and so there is no reason for his suffering. The argument here is the overt version of what was concealed in the Akedah: God may choose an innocent person as well as a guilty one and for no reason at all.

The brutal trial of Job begins as a bet between God and Satan that Job will remain loyal to God's ways, and the stupendous irony of the book is that Job in fact does stay loyal, not by insisting that God will reward him, but by attacking God as a fundamentally unreasonable and unpredictable deity. God welcomes Job's attack because it allows him to unveil his true, uncanny nature, which has been kept hidden by the moralizing of Job's friends.

God, Job says, distributes good and evil arbitrarily, making ruin or giving reward as he pleases. The turbulent and savage things that please God will be unveiled at Job's conclusion, when God's voice from the storm extolls the fabulous sublime creatures that terrify mere humans, the burly Behemoth and the wild-eyed, fire-breathing Leviathan. God likes power, the ending of Job argues, and this power is, by its nature, violent. This is the only possible explanation for why human life is so bloody, so traumatic, so open to suffering.

Job is meant to recognize that to lament the violence inflicted on him, or on anybody, misses the real point: the sublime message that, according to the God of Job, is the inmost center of the Bible's teaching. God tells Job that it is shortsighted to measure suffering in terms of a single person's good or bad fortune; the stakes are not only much bigger, but utterly different. Creation is also and necessarily destruction. In the words of Isaiah 45:7, God creates light and darkness, good and evil together. The startling lesson of Job surpasses the more usual stances suggested elsewhere in the Tanakh and in later commentary: for example, that violence and the suffering it brings contribute in hidden fashion to the good ends of creation by adjusting us to reality and so giving us wisdom; or that violence places a hedge around goodness, as a sort of warning; or that violence marks an unavoidable limit to the creation's goodness. With deeply disturbing radicalism, the Book of Job embraces violence directly. In Job, violent destruction happens along with creation, and God invests equally in both, so that from God's viewpoint, it may be hard to tell the difference between the two. And from our human perspective, too, we are taught here that bloody aggression may feel like free and powerful creation.

God's lesson about the necessary violence of his cosmos at the end of Job feels almost inhuman. God refuses to offer consolation for the devastating effects of turmoil and aggression and, instead, displays a wild and strange cosmic perspective. The reader finds no comfort in the tremendous, deep darkness of this vista. In the Book of Job, God is uncannily intimate. He makes us share his enjoyment of his power and, therefore, does not give us the distance that would be needed for self-therapy. God here prevents any effort to heal human pain by putting it in perspective or seeing it as merely seasonal, as in Job's competitor for wisdom, Qohelet (Ecclesiastes). The God of Job makes us just as enthralled by his titanic creations as he is: we, too, thrill at seeing God's sublime monsters, as long as they are not threatening to devour us. Yet the gigantic horrors that God sets in motion cannot be kept at arm's length. God enthusiastically offers his sublimity not only to the reader, but also to Job, and it is Job who has been devoured. Certainly, there is no prospect here, as there is in the New Testament, of having your tears wiped forever from your eyes. The author of Job's tremendous confrontation with friends and then with God was, without doubt, the greatest poet of the Hebrew Bible; he seems to have worked from an oddly prosaic narrative frame, which gives its broken, persistent hero a new house and a new set of sons and daughters in the end. The text retains this Hollywood ending. And no wonder: we need some shield against God's violence, which threatens to strip Job and us of all our human defenses.

Note

1.   This essay cites the Jewish Publication Society (JPS) translation of the Bible.

Works Cited

Brisman, Leslie. "Sacred Butchery: Exodus 32: 25–29." *Theological Exegesis: Essays in Honors of Brevard S. Childs*. Eds. C. Seitz & K. Greene-McCreight. Grand Rapids: Eerdmans, 1999. 162–81.

Etz Hayim: Torah and Commentary. Philadelphia: Jewish Publication Society, 2004.

Genesis Rabbah. Ed. and trans. Jacob Neusner. Vol. 1. Providence, Rhode Island: Brown Judaic Studies, 1985.

Hayes, Christine E. "Golden Calf Stories: The Relationship of Exodus 32 and Deuteronomy 9.10." *The Idea of Biblical Interpretation: Essays in Honor of James L. Kugel*. Eds. James Kugel & Judith H. Newman. Leiden: Brill, 2004. 45–93.

Jewish Publication Society, ed. *JPS Tanakh: The Jewish Bible*. Philadelphia: Jewish Publication Society, 1985.

Kierkegaard, Søren. *Fear and Trembling*. Trans. Alastair Hannay. New York: Penguin, 1986.

Miller, William Ian. *Eye for an Eye*. Cambridge: Cambridge UP, 2005.

Milton, John. *Paradise Lost*. Eds. William Kerrigan, John Rumrich, & Stephen Fallon. New York: Modern Library, 2008.

Nietzsche, Friedrich. *On the Genealogy of Morality*. Ed. Keith Ansell-Pearson. Trans. Carol Diethe. New York: Cambridge UP, 2007.

Norton, David, ed. *Bible*. New York: Penguin, 2000. King James Version.

Talmud Bavli. Ed. Adin Steinsaltz. Vol. 15, Parts 1 and 2 (Tractate Sanhedrin). New York: Random House, 1986.

Tanakh (Hebrew-English). Philadelphia: Jewish Publication Society, 2001.

Tyndale's Old Testament. Ed. David Daniell. New Haven: Yale UP, 1992.

Street Violence and Youth in Shakespeare's *Romeo and Juliet*

Philip White

Violence is everywhere in Shakespeare, but the earliest plays are especially, even flamboyantly, sensationalistic. A. R. Foakes thinks this is because Shakespeare was competing with other dramatists to "invent more and stranger incidents of torture and murder," in order to attract to the new public theatres an audience that "enjoyed public spectacles of torture and violence in the execution of criminals and traitors staged as ceremonies validating state power, or in the punishment by whipping until blood flowed that could be inflicted on fornicators" (36). Shakespeare's first histories and tragedies seem made to order for such an audience, but they also register an insight Shakespeare would never abandon: that impulses toward violence and violation of supposedly natural bonds and feelings are inescapable in human life, if not actually fundamental to our nature.

Romeo and Juliet, his third or fourth tragedy, is perhaps the first to successfully integrate its acts of violence into an unfolding of tragic character and fate, and it is also the first to present human impulses toward violence in a rounded and coherent picture of human motivation. Youth, particularly male youth, is at the center of that picture, as males were thought to be physiologically more disposed toward violence than women, and youth considered the time when natural urges manifest themselves more vividly and are less moderated, shaped, controlled, and settled than later in life. Or, more precisely, youth was the time when that moderation, shaping, controlling, and settling was expected to occur. There is, of course, the ubiquitous imagery of violence in the love language of Romeo and Juliet, and Juliet herself commits the play's last act of tragic violence. But the act that turns the play toward the tragic is Romeo's killing of Tybalt, and this essay's focus will be how Shakespeare's depiction of the violence in the play's young men illuminates

Romeo's mindset and thus clarifies what is at stake in the play's turn toward tragedy.

Recent critics who deal with violence in the play tend to view it as an expression of the parental feud, which they in turn see as a function of the ideology of patriarchy (Cohen; Kahn; Snyder; Applebaum). Ideological analyses are rightly leery of the concept of human nature, considering how pervasively it has served to reinforce and perpetuate structures of power. But notions of nature are inevitable, and we should judge each for how adequately or powerfully it gives us access to some part of our reality, while remaining alert to its political implications. Underplaying a natural component in the analysis of violence in effect elides the aggression inherent in our "evolved genetic program" and our "animal past," to use one scientist's phrase (Archer 204), and it fails to register the way violence is construed as part of our animal nature in the Aristotelian and Galenic thought of Shakespeare's day. That the parents' feud has shaped the youth of the play is clear, but with or without a theory of ideology, it can't fully explain the acts of violence as Shakespeare depicts them without a certain amount of reduction and without obscuring much of the motivational and psychological specificity that Shakespeare writes into these young characters. Even when depicted as expressions of nature, their acts of violence take their specific dramatic power and carry their individual part of the tragic burden only when recognized in their particularity.

The reasons the feud seems so central are, however, built into the play and even given a quasi-authorial heft in the two choral prologues, with their emphasis on the "parents' rage" (Shakespeare, *Romeo and Juliet* 1.pro.10) as the problematic violence. The prologues imply that the final self-violence of the lovers, their "misadventured piteous overthrows" (Shakespeare, *R&J* 1.pro.7), may, within a larger perspective, be seen as a cure for the violence of the feud, as if a kind of providential fate raised their love up for that very purpose. Attended to more closely, the densely packed imagery of the two prologues gives an image of that fate as the processes of nature itself, at the same time suggesting that something much like ideological transmission is in fact one of those natural processes (see Snyder). In effect, an "ancient grudge" in one generation may come to define an object of visceral hatred—a "foe supposed"—in the next generation, and that grudge may thus "break" forth from a period of dormancy, not as itself exactly, but as a "*new* mutiny," a new fact and form in a new generation (Shakespeare, *R&J* 1.pro.3; 2.pro.7; emphasis added). Natural energies of grudges and "desire"— the "power," more broadly, of felt "passion"—may thus, if "time" affords the opportunity, be born, propagate themselves in new, "young affections" (meaning, here, passions), and die, in families and societies as in individuals (Shakespeare, *R&J* 2.pro.1–2, 13–4).

The emphasis on generations *and* on generation—on the "fatal loins" from which the lovers "take their life" (Shakespeare, *R&J* 1.pro.6)—suggests the process by which the new "takes" its life from the "loins," the bodily seat of procreative impulse, of two specific people in specific families propagating specific grudges in a specific town and a specific age, and so on. The phrase "from forth" implies both origin and a movement away, so that all of the ways the lovers seek to "take their lives" in the play—from the simple fact of their experiential being, to the names and language and airy words (see Shakespeare, *R&J* 1.1.88) and idioms of "steerage" and "conduct" (terms Romeo is fond of; 1. 4.112, 3.1.123, and 5.3.116) they find at hand, to the ways their own desires and grudges are formed out of and in opposition to inherited and ambient grudges and family bonds, to their frustrated attempts at self-definition within that matrix, to their final acts of self-violence—seem wrapped in the fatality of generation and generations. Birth, sexuality, and death collapse into each other in the temporal process of nature propagating and regulating itself.

On its face, the providential viewpoint of the prologues suggests that nature, in the deaths of the lovers and the parents' attempts at reconciliation, regains its balance between, say, Empedoclean internal forces of strife and love or what the Friar calls "opposed kings" of "grace and rude will" that perpetually battle ("encamp them still") for dominance in human nature (Shakespeare, *R&J* 2.3.27–8). But if we fully register the implications of the generational imagery, this can give little solace or justification. The feud ends because the process of generation is cut off. There will be no more of these two families. A truly terrible purgation, indeed, if that is what it is. But, of course, the real woe of the conclusion lies in the loss of the lovers sacrificed in that reassertion of natural equilibrium. The chorus itself recognizes that what we "miss" in the natural philosophy of its viewpoint (Shakespeare, *R&J* 1.pro.14), what in effect has been left out in its interpretive reductions, is the enacted specificities of the characters working out their destinies in the matrix of natural forces and conditions. In short, what the viewpoint of the prologue leaves out is our experience of the tragedy itself.

The prologue and the Prince speak of the feud as the mutual "rage" of the fathers (Shakespeare, *R&J* 1.pro.10 and 1.1.3), but we do not see that in the play, at least not as the initiating impulse of any of the acts of violence. What we see is particular young men experiencing youth with the energies and existential imperatives or concerns of young men (see Levenson). The fathers' "ancient grudge" is behind them, and we are right to see its still-powerful forms framing what is felt and done in these scenes, but the prologue is also right that what breaks from the old grudge in the two scenes of street violence is in important ways "new." In the recurrent figure of explosion (see Shakespeare, *R&J* 2.6.10, 3.3.132, 5.1.54) that the prologues' word "break" and Montague's "abroach" introduce, the "ancient quarrel" of the fathers has put casked gunpowder everywhere, but, of course, after the brawling of the first scene, neither Montague nor Capulet know who "set" it this time (meaning to break open the cask or to ignite the powder; see Shakespeare, *R&J* 1.5.103).

The men who start the fight, Samson and Gregory, are not for that matter actual kin, only servants in the respective houses, and they are hardly developed as characters beyond their vivid expressions of impulses associated with youth as a physiological condition. We moderns sloppily ascribe such moods and behaviors to "testosterone" or "adrenaline" without intending much clear science. But the Galenic medical theory of Shakespeare's period was based precisely on what we would think of as body chemistry. Moods and passions, for animals as for men, were physiological events, dependent on the specific blends of the four fluids called humors—blood, choler, phlegm, and melancholy—in the body at a given time. The humors in turn were materially associated with the elements that make up the world—air, fire, water, and earth, respectively—and so conditions, like hot or cold weather, could interact with the humors in the body. Even particular stars were associated with the humors and could thus materially influence one's feelings. The particular mix—the *temper* or simply the *humor*—of the fluids in a person was believed to vary with sex and age and was also thought to determine one's emotional disposition or the physiological aspect of character. A healthy balance of the humors indicates a good *temperament*, and that, by definition, means a disposition governable by reason. Similarly, the Aristotelian tradition located character and the emotional life in what it called the animal soul, implying that we are no better than animals if that soul is not cultivated and trained to obey the rational soul in us, the possession of which separates us from the beasts. The humoral model makes our character seem very vulnerable to physiological and environmental fluctuations, and the Aristotelian model suggests that the rationality of human nature is always only partially and precariously achieved out of our basically animal nature. When the humors are not well balanced or tempered, one's emotions, even when well-trained and developed in the Aristotelian sense, may override the injunctions of reason, and when they are very imbalanced, all kinds of madness may ensue.

The proportional balance of the humors also defined differences between the sexes. A predominance of blood and choler was considered the natural condition of males, and the same predominance was thought especially prominent, and problematic, in the young. Young males, then, are particularly driven by blood and choler, and the natural humoral imbalance of youth makes them prone to act impulsively rather than obey reason. The behavior of Sampson and Gregory in the first scene seems exactly what would be expected with excesses of these humors. Their desired state is explicitly "choler" (Shakespeare, *R&J* 1.1.3). That humor, related to fire, drives their obvious emotional heat: the self-assertion, the testiness, the belligerence, the anger, and ultimately the violence.

Similarly, the youthful male preponderance of blood, related to air and associated with life and vitality, issues in their high energy and elevated mood, their boldness, their spirited sociality, their pursuit of transgressive thrill and pleasure, and their sexual edge.

Blood and choler in interaction might also be seen as physiological drives toward interpersonal bonding and group definition on one hand and assertion of individual identity on the other, crucial and developmentally natural preoccupations of youth, then as now—hence Sampson and Gregory's pairing off and their demarcation of their group from the Montagues. The group dynamic pushes both toward more risk and creates the heady sense of being carried along, a little high on a shared prospect of action. Though there are just two, they act as a group, and are not really friends in a serious way. As for the impulses toward assertion of individual identity, we see these in the aggressive bravado and insult, puffing one's self up and deflating the other. The viciously playful give and take in their wit-play also seems responsive to the youthful humors. Under the pressure of urges toward violence (choler) and sexuality (blood), almost any common phrase occasions sexual and violent innuendo. An idiom of street courtesy, "taking the wall," eventually underwrites a fantasy of sexual assault and ruination: "women, being the weaker vessels, are ever thrust to the wall" (Shakespeare, *R&J* 1.1.14–5). Predictably, the conversation of these young men ends in genital bragging. "Standing" signifies standing one's ground *and* erection, the penis focusing bodily both of the drives. It becomes a weapon with which to "cut off" women's maidenheads. Meanwhile, actual weapons are spoken of as if they were extensions of one's physical virility—"Draw thy tool!" "My naked weapon is out" (Shakespeare, *R&J* 1.1.31–3). Biting one's thumb, a gesture with obvious sexual and violent implications, provokes the interaction with the Montague men.

In the humoral model, Sampson and Gregory are simply being, one might say, young men. Not that the model would sanction it, youth being so much like a disease. Still, the model sees aggression (choler) and boldness (blood) themselves as integral parts of human nature. They are necessary for any human action, but they are in need of balance with the other humors and, most of all, should be brought under control by reason and made responsive to the external counsel of parents and friends, who are themselves balanced and reasonable. Thus the two characters present, at the beginning of the play, almost a caricature of ungoverned male youth. But not only are these two ungoverned, they actively give themselves over to the humors, as they give themselves over to the dynamics of the brawl, refusing to be tempered or moderated by the self-awareness and lawfulness Benvolio urges on them: "Part, fools! / Put up your swords. You know not what you do" (Shakespeare, *R&J* 1.1. 62–3). The prologue's word "mutiny" for this outbreak of the feud thus seems particularly apt. We witness both a mutiny against civil order and authority and a psychological mutiny of impulse over higher faculties. More seriously, the two servants' vague code of manliness seems positively to embrace such a mutiny. If one is "in a choler" one must draw (Shakespeare, *R&J* 1.1.3) and thus show "if you be men" (Shakespeare, *R&J* 1.1.59). To suppress and bear psychological heat, to "carry coals" (Shakespeare, *R&J* 1.1.1), would not only make one a "collier" (Shakespeare, *R&J* 1.1.2)— a shameful debasement in status—it would also make him not a man. Finally, it is actually important in this code of being a man to be easily or "quickly moved" (Shakespeare, *R&J* 1.1.5) rather than slow and thoughtful in taking action. This rough code seems more like a development from the youthful humors and the youthful problem of identification and group formation among young males than it does from patriarchy per se. Insofar as it is natural, it is a code felt by the young in their interactions with the young, something like impulses of the schoolyard. It is not hard to imagine that an earlier version of it provoked the parental feud in the youths of the fathers.

Of course, this code of manhood is really a rejection of manhood, since in the humoral and Aristotelian models reason sets us apart from other animals. When the Prince calls the fathers "beasts," he implies that they are acting on impulse (Shakespeare, *R&J* 1.1.82). But it isn't their impulses that started the new mutiny. It's true that once the fighting begins, the old fathers are pretty quickly moved. But it's comical, too, partly because old men *as such* should not exist in a stew of blood and choler as young men do and partly because, for the same reasons, they really aren't in a condition to wield their weapons. Judging from Capulet's still-fearsome browbeating of Tybalt in the feast scene and his treatment of Juliet when she refuses to marry Paris, what is left of these humors in him may have been put into use countering, though clearly not effectively correcting or channeling, the energies of the young. At any rate, the play never shows either parent initiating conflict, and we are led to believe that the feud was not actively violent for some time, long enough for a new generation capable of fighting to grow up, long enough that the quarrel comes to feel "ancient" even to Montague (Shakespeare, *R&J* 1.1.103). As Capulet says, "'tis not hard, I think, / For men so old as we to keep the peace" (Shakespeare, *R&J* 1.2.3). From the generational view of nature, it is a new phenomenon, however much it has been conditioned by the old and drags the old into it.

What drives the violence in the first scene, then, as Shakespeare carefully highlights, is the condition of youthful masculinity, a condition which, by humoral nature, causes young men to engage in self-assertion, heady risk-taking, bold action, and a period of life in which individual and social identification occurs. The father's feud is important to these two youths, first as a way to help them do the work of identification and then as a way to justify indulging destructive and violent impulses, but the impulses and energies themselves are natural to their sex and age. Clearly, the real energies of the feud have shifted to the next generation. Though it is the parental feud that has drawn the lines, their behaviors and emotions are worked out in engagement with those of their own age and status. We can't picture Sampson picking a fight with Romeo, much less with Montague himself. If we are thinking about what generational nature, at the level of the humors and elements, is doing here, it isn't renewing the feud, but pushing a new set of the young to do what the young do. The presence of the feud and the failure of the fathers to counter the youthful code of masculinity simply reduce the chances, already slight in any circumstances, that it will turn out well.

But the play gives us a more balanced view of youth in the four young men involved in the second street fight, in which

Mercutio and Tybalt are killed and Romeo's fate turns tragic. The same humoral language informs the depiction of these young men. In Benvolio's first words of the scene, humoral chemistry is aggravated by hot weather: "now, these hot days, is the mad blood stirring" (Shakespeare, *R&J* 3.1.4). But there is more individuation among these youths than there is in Gregory and Samson. The latter two are distinct in character, but push toward violence *as a pair*, egging each other on to the point that it's hard to say which really is responsible for starting the fight. Such, the scene might suggest, are the group dynamics of young men itching for action and out to prove themselves. But the dynamics among Romeo, Benvolio, Mercutio, and Tybalt are much more complex. Tybalt and Mercutio share with Gregory and Samson the humoral disposition toward aggression and also their code of manliness, but with somewhat more sophistication of mindset and motive. Benvolio and Romeo represent more serious and reflective young men, less definable by physiological urges or the options for social identification their situations offer them than any of the other youths in the play.

Of the two aggressive-spirited characters, Tybalt seems the most clearly defined by the feud. When he finds Benvolio using the sword to part the fighters in the first scene, Tybalt suggests such peacekeeping is somehow vile: "What, drawn and talk of peace? I hate the word / As I hate hell, all Montagues and thee. / Have at thee, coward!" (Shakespeare, *R&J* 1.1.68–70) To Tybalt, peace itself is contemptible. Once fighting has begun, any ceasing would be unmanly cowardice. Tybalt is not only confessedly choleric, but willfully so. Under his uncle's correction, Tybalt can scarcely contain his bodily rage: "Patience perforce with willful choler meeting / Makes my flesh tremble in their different greeting" (Shakespeare, *R&J* 1.5.90–1). His hate couples with a strong identification as a Capulet that guides even his moral sense: "Now, by the stock and honor of my kin, / To strike him dead I hold it not a sin" (Shakespeare, *R&J* 1.5.59–60). Conversely, his identification of himself against "all Montagues" carries moral overtones as well, making the mere the presence of a Montague at a Capulet party admiring a Capulet girl seem to him a personal affront, a "shame"

(Shakespeare, *R&J* 1.5.83) and a grievous "intrusion" (Shakespeare, *R&J* 1.5.92), multiplying in his mind into plural "injuries" worthy of death (Shakespeare, *R&J* 3.1.65). Moreover, Tybalt refuses to be mollified by Capulet or by the Prince's injunction against fighting. He actively seeks to extend the feeling of offense into the future. It is his challenge of Romeo, then, that sets up the acts of violence of 3.1.

But for all Tybalt's visceral hatred, there is something formal in his identifications and his aggression, something we didn't see in Sampson and Gregory. To him, the Capulet party is a family rite, a "solemnity" (Shakespeare, *R&J* 1.5.58) that Romeo is violating by his presence. Further, if Mercutio's description of Tybalt as a fighter isn't mere Mercutian fanatasy, Tybalt is also punctilious in his style of fighting, adopting faddishly named swordstrokes and adhering to the new rules of dueling. Sampson and Gregory had to consult with each other about the laws of fighting, but Tybalt has apparently read the books. The fact that he fights Benvolio, a cousin to Romeo, but does not respond at first to the provocations of Mercutio, a kinsman to the Prince and neither Montague nor Capulet, suggests that the feud identification has given his fire a focus. And he demonstrates a sort of restraint when Romeo refuses to fight him. He is apparently walking away from Romeo when Mercutio steps in. Tybalt's violence is guided strictly by family, with a possible hint of respect for the Prince's kin though not for the Prince's authority. He is beloved of Lady Capulet and even Juliet, but he has no friends that we see. His group is his family. His youthful identification is given to the Capulet identity, if not to Capulet himself. He is defined by that version of patriarchy, even when he resists the patriarch's correction. If we are looking for the spirit of youth, as represented by Sampson and Gregory, but fully shaped and defined—and given a degree of real meaning—by the feud mentality or ideology, Tybalt seems our best candidate.

By contrast, Mercutio's aggressiveness seems more driven by mood. His attitude toward fighting, like Tybalt's, is basically that of Samson and Gregory. In 3.1, anticipating action, he engages in florid boasting, revealing an impulse to fight and a feeling that not to rise to a fight, no matter the circumstance, would be shameful.

As much as we can tell, it is partly a kind of vicarious shame for his friend Romeo's unflappability in the face of Tybalt's insults and challenge that makes him fight Tybalt: "O calm, dishonorable, vile submission!" (Shakespeare, *R&J* 3.1.72) But it is also contempt for what he sees as Tybalt's bookish and overly formal new style of fighting. Dying, he is horrified to have been killed by a "braggart, a rogue, a villain, that fights by the book of arithmetic" (Shakespeare, *R&J* 3.1.100–1). But where Tybalt shows no sign of intelligence or wittiness, Mercutio takes the kind of wordplay we saw in the servants' first dialogue to heights—and depths—not seen perhaps anywhere else in Shakespeare. Even so, it is as true of his wordplay as it is of theirs that it seems driven by the sexual and aggressive energies of youth. He has more blood than Tybalt, as evidenced by his manic wit and absurd bravado and brashness, and as suggested by Benvolio's comment on his death: "His gallant spirit aspired the clouds, / Which too untimely here did scorn the earth" (Shakespeare, *R&J* 3.1.115–7). But even his famous fantasia on Queen Mab ends in the servants' style of degraded genital and sexual humor; the sexual position here is not a woman thrust to the wall, but on her back and ridden like an animal. Benvolio and Romeo both try repeatedly—and unsuccessfully—to divert Mercutio's verbal momentum toward those subjects.

Wit plays a more complex social role for Mercutio than it does for the serving men. Mostly, it establishes and expresses his bond with Romeo, the only one smart enough and quick enough to hold his own with Mercutio in their amazing verbal riffing and pun-matches. It is a kind of sparring—"Come between us, good Benvolio! My wits faint" (Shakespeare, *R&J* 2.4.66)—but it is also a real meeting of two very bright minds, the only thing in the play that resembles the different, but equally witty, improvisational and collaborative meeting of minds between Romeo and Juliet. Mercutio is clearly jealous of Romeo's loves, though it is telling that he knows so little about them. After their last mental wrestle, he castigates Romeo, "Why, is not this better now than groaning for love? Now art thou sociable, now art thou Romeo; now art thou what thou art, by art as well as by nature" (Shakespeare, *R&J* 2.4.87). The bond between

Mercutio and Romeo is not equal, but it is mutual. They are friends, and the feeling might be more than that on Mercutio's part.

In general, Mercutio's irrepressibly spirited conversation and his interlocutors define him. He is kinsman to the Prince, but mostly, he is friend to Romeo. The feud doesn't define him, though the young code of masculinity does. As we've seen, the shame by association that he feels at Romeo's "vile submission" seems part of what makes him mysteriously fight Tybalt and thus send the play into tragedy. It might also be what makes him lash out against "both houses" (Shakespeare, *R&J* 3.1.90)—the Capulets because it is Tybalt he despises and who has given him the mortal wound and the Montagues because Romeo has shamed him. But the fight, for Mercutio, isn't about the houses; it seems more about being a man, answering the challenge, rising to the moment of action (see Shakespeare, *R&J* 3.1.58)—in short, about what Sampson and Gregory call "standing." And it's about being a friend. Mercutio thinks love for a woman has sapped Romeo's nerve, and so there could also be a touch of betrayed jealousy in the shame that pushes him to fight. By not fighting Tybalt, Romeo has proven that he is a lover of women, not of male (that is, his own) sociability (see Shakespeare, *R&J* 2.4.13–6). It is the same logic, of course, that makes Romeo say that loving Juliet has made him "effeminate" and softened his "temper" (Shakespeare, *R&J* 3.1.113), though Romeo seems trenchantly ambivalent about that change.

Benvolio is, in many ways, the good angel—"good heart" as Romeo roughly translates his name (Shakespeare, *R&J* 1.1.184)—to Mercutio's bad angel (*his* name suggests the mercurial spirit of youthful blood). Virtually everything we know about Benvolio serves to illuminate Romeo's character. Benvolio's good will makes him the one to break up fights, while Mercutio is driven to start them. Romeo shares Benvolio's disposition toward violence. Whereas all the other young men feel shame for *not* fighting, Benvolio and Romeo seem, by disposition, to feel it shameful and foolish to fight for lawless and stupid causes (Shakespeare, *R&J* 1.1.62–7 and 3.1.88); they are not driven by the code. Both value civil peace and want to obey the Prince (see Shakespeare, *R&J* 1.1.67 and 3.1.86), and both seek

---

out the guidance of adults, though for that, Romeo has turned from his father to the Friar in an apparent move away from feud-based identification. Finally, Benvolio at first seems more similar in humor to Romeo than Mercutio is, both sharing the pensive withdrawal of the melancholic (Shakespeare, *R&J* 1.1.127–8, 140).

On the other hand, Benvolio seems excitable when relating what happens in both brawls, narratives which he embellishes with flourishes of gallant imagery and bias. His bias is familial and friendly, and that shows his identifications. He diverts the blame for the brawl in 3.1 from his friend Mercutio to his enemy Tybalt and, unwittingly, may worsen Romeo's sentence by making the Prince see the action as a part of the paternal feud rather than an act of friendship, which Montague himself recognizes it as (Shakespeare, *R&J* 3.1.3). For his part, Romeo has reservoirs of Mercutio's high energy, though he manifests them very differently. Where blood drives Mercutio to outrageously lurid sexual wittiness and spirited contention, the same humor makes Romeo a lover. In fact, with Juliet, he seems elevated, energized, joyful, at ease, making his melancholy in 1.1 appear less dispositional than situational. Likewise, blood—but restrained by good "reason"—might be behind the courageous but calm rationality of Romeo's response to Tybalt's insults (Shakespeare, *R&J* 3.1.61). That rational, restrained boldness may be seen at the end of the play, too, when he grimly and composedly moves toward his suicide, and it helps us see his actions in the decisive act of killing Tybalt more clearly.

But before we turn to that, we should acknowledge that Romeo's humoral disposition is, in fact, hard to pin down. It is not so much that he is emotionally fickle or volatile, though he can be both. It is more that his emotions are based on emergent and changing situations as he understands them and tries to guide his energies appropriately, arousing and curbing them, as he comes to think it right, and collapsing into them only when they are too much for him. His character is more developed, in the Aristotelian sense, and less reducible to a humoral mix than that of any of the other young men. On the other hand, he is not a rationalist or stoic moralist, positions toward which the Friar directs him. He values and gives himself over to strong feeling, spontaneity, responsiveness, and impulse, especially in love and friendship. Those guiding values, rather than family as defined by the old feud, identify him. And he seems to have thoughtfully arrived at those values for himself.

Many have commented on the conventionality of his love language, but he consistently gives that language his own spin. Even the much-mocked oxymoronic passage of Petrarchan clichés of 1.1 is, in context, a description of the feud as much as, or more than, his own feelings, which it is usually taken to express. "I have heard it all," he says, knowing exactly what has happened in the brawl even before it is reported to him. "Here's," he says, meaning in the brawl, "much to do with hate, but more with love. / Why then, O brawling love, O loving hate, / O anything of nothing first create!" (Shakespeare, *R&J* 1.1.173–6). Each phrase here and in the lines that follow manifests a thoughtful recognition of the perverse intertwining of love and hate that drive the feud—kin love as it were participating in and energizing feud hatred and vice versa. And it also marks how petty its origins, how seriously those pettinesses are taken, and with what grave consequences. The end of his exclamation may suggest that he has set himself apart from the feud's loves: "This love feel I, that feel no love in this" (Shakespeare, *R&J* 1.1.182). In the passage, Romeo thus simultaneously recognizes the unnatural contradictions of the feud mentality *and* of Rosaline's rejection of love out of hand. His assessment of the latter situation, too, sets him at a distance from conventional thought. While his love language throughout is Petrarchan and focused on a conventionally moralized "beauty," what he clearly wants is Shakespearean: reciprocation, relationship, natural responsiveness to another and to the nature of love, a commitment to the power, we recognize, of the generational imagery of the prologues, the drive toward "posterity" (see Shakespeare, *R&J* 1.1.216-21).

Similarly, in the violence of 3.1, Romeo, alone among the others, knows what the situation really is. He registers and continually reorients himself to the changing scene in a way that is both rational and responsive to the complex of feelings that have identified him— his love for Juliet, his friendship with Mercutio, his new relation to

Tybalt, and ultimately, too, his personal sense of what it is to be a man. This entails not the parental feud or the code the others follow, which would dictate fighting merely because someone else does, but a personal sense of when violence is called for (see Shakespeare, *R&J* 3.1.107–114). Reason alone, for Romeo, cannot decide that last question, since reason for him, while important, is in the service of felt values; that is, its aims are determined by the bonds and identifications that define him. He follows, in Hamlet's terms, "excitements of my reason and my blood" (Shakespeare, *Hamlet* 4.4.58). The main excitement of Romeo's blood is not, as I've suggested, the parental feud, about which he expresses no feeling other than ironic recognition. Rather, it is the death of his "very friend" (Shakespeare, *R&J* 3.1.109), which cannot go unrevenged, even when revenge means killing the man his love for Juliet has made family. So he sends his achieved "respective lenity" to heaven, the only place, implicitly, it can be maintained; here, in Verona, in the tragic complications of this moment, "fire-eyed fury" must be his conduct (Shakespeare, *R&J* 3.1.122–3).

Even before he knows Mercutio is dead, Romeo senses "This day's black fate" has changed everything (Shakespeare, *R&J* 3.1.118). Then, when he stands over Tybalt's dead body, he registers the intricate tissue of mischances and flukes and ironies that have moved the scene toward that fate. To cite a few: Mercutio's strange provoking of the fight; Romeo's inadvertent role in Mercutios' killing; Mercutio's rejection of Romeo ("A plague a both your houses" Shakespeare, *R&J* 3.1.90), then his absurdly dying of a "scratch" (Shakespeare, *R&J* 3.1.98); and Tybalt's unaccountable return to the scene, giving Romeo occasion to fight. However, we understand those moments, if they are not mere accidents beyond our understanding, can only go back to our sense of each character's natural disposition. The play is, then, a tragedy of character rather than fate alone. Stepping back from this moment to the viewpoint of the prologue, we might say that the loves Romeo commits himself to— for Juliet and for Mercutio—are those formed in him by nature in its generational impulses and youthful urgings toward self-definition in interactions with others, in just such microscopic twists. He must, by his nature, love Juliet; he must, by his nature, kill Juliet's cousin. So there's a bitter eloquence in the pause and in the brevity of his tragic recognition: "O, I am fortune's fool" (Shakespeare, *R&J* 3.1.135). Whatever the big picture is—the eventual end to the parents' feud or a new equilibrium in nature's conflicting energies—closer in, where Romeo lives, in the minute workings of impulse and character and choice and time, is tragedy.

Works Cited

Applebaum, Robert. "'Standing to the Wall': The Pressures of Masculinity in *Romeo and Juliet*." *Shakespeare Quarterly 48.3* (Autumn 1997): 251–72.

Archer, John. "The nature of human aggression." *International Journal of Law and Psychiatry* 32.4 (July–August 2009): 202–8.

Cohen, Derek. *Shakespeare's Culture of Violence*. New York: St Martin, 1993.

Foakes, A. R. *Shakespeare and Violence*. New York: Cambridge, 2003.

Kahn, Coppelia. "Coming of Age in Verona." *The Woman's Part: Feminist Criticism of Shakespeare*. Eds. Carolyn Ruth Swift Lenz, Gayle Greene, & Carol Thomas Neely. Urbana: U of Illinois P: 1980. 171–93.

Levenson, Jill L. Introduction. *Romeo and Juliet*. By William Shakespeare. Oxford: Oxford UP, 2000.

Shakespeare, William. *The Complete Pelican Shakespeare*. Eds. Stephen Orgel & A. R. Braunmuller. New York: Penguin, 2002.

Snyder, Susan. "Ideology and the Feud in *Romeo and Juliet*." *Shakespeare Survey* 49 (1996):87-96.

Grappling with Violence in Latin American Literature

Núria Sabaté Llobera

"To say that violence is the fundamental problem of America and of the world is only to note a fact. That the Spanish-American novel reflects this preoccupation is advertised on each page written on our continent, those pages that are like the skin of our towns, the *witnesses of an always present condition*" (Dorfman 9, translation mine). Violence—and how one lives and dies with it—has been the central theme of Latin American literature since the continent's "discovery" in 1492.

Indeed, the fundamental tension driving Latin American thought and writing has remained unchanged for five hundred years: "Latin America was born in blood and fire, in conquest and slavery [and it] . . . is precisely conquest and its sequel, colonization, that created the fundamental conflict in Latin American history" (Chasteen 15). And from colonization, of course, came post-colonialism, neo-colonialism, and so on. Violence is thus both at the root and in the very warp and woof of Latin American life (as it is also perhaps elsewhere). The centrality of violence permeates Latin American history and literature, and each, in turn, bleeds into the other. With violence as the running theme, the relationship of "history" to "literature" (or art, more generally) is one of fluid dialogue rather than strict separation.

This essay is chiefly interested in organizing this dialogue into categories, so that it is possible to better understand the relationship, over time, between history and literature about violence. The essay's main purpose is to make an initial effort to break down the topic of violence, over the course of five centuries, into more comprehensible, digestible pieces. What are the constituent elements, the sub-sets within the focus on violence? Yet, the breadth and depth of violence in Latin American literature make even this seemingly modest goal a significant challenge.

I would divide the literature on the topic of violence into two broad categories: "fictionalized history" and "counter-narratives of violence." By "fictionalized history," I mean writing that claims to relate facts, including facts of violence, but that, in truth, contains strong strains of bias and fictionalization—a bias that underlies the very violence the work describes. And "counter-narratives of violence" are the texts that attempt to rectify a distorted view of a situation by telling a story of fiction, which is intended to better reflect reality than the image presented by "history." It is necessary to emphasize, however, that these works of fiction do not claim to substitute for history, since they use fiction-writing techniques distinguishable from historical writing. The writers lack even the basic building blocks of historical writing—archives, documents, and access to individuals able or willing to speak freely. Yet, as Frederick M. Nunn explains, "Fictional histories are interpretations, vehicles for reflection and revision. This is especially valuable in places where the historian's profession is not well developed and where consensus on the past is shaky" (2). An understanding of violence—the inescapable, ever-present legacy of Latin American life—emerges, then, by seeing fiction in history and history in fiction.

Fictionalized Histories

"The Chronicles," the group of texts written by Europeans who arrived in the New World in 1492 and shortly afterwards, offer first-person, eyewitness narratives of the author's experience. One overriding theme is the manipulation of information with the aim of satisfying the voyage's sponsoring patron and the justification for violence implicit in the writers' language and perspective. Take, for example, the *Cartas de Relación* [*Letters from Mexico*], written by Hernán Cortés to the Spanish king Carlos V between 1519 and 1526. In his First Letter (1519), following a description of human sacrifices by the Indians (which have been either witnessed or imagined by Cortés—it is unclear), he writes:

It is believed that not without cause our Lord has been served that these parts be discovered in the name of Your Royal Highnesses so that such great fruit and worthiness of God reach your Majesties sending reports and being by your hand brought to the barbarians the faith that according to what we have learned of them, we believe that having translators and people that made them understand the truth about the faith and the error that they are in, many of them and even all of them would separate very briefly from that error that they have and would come to the true knowledge. (Cortés 125, translation by Lynn Celdrán,)

On a textual level, the language of the passage—"by his own hand brought to the faith these barbarian people"—conveys a sense of superiority that condones previous acts of violence, such as the assassination of the Aztec leader Montezuma. This hardly comes as a surprise since, like Cortés, virtually all the writers were either soldiers or priests; the civilian voice is entirely absent.

Beyond the language of superiority, parts of the "The Chronicles" are simply pure fiction. Strikingly, the New World is often just as the European mind of the time would have imagined it to be—it was as if we, upon landing on Mars, found creatures that looked exactly like E.T.! Columbus, for example, writes in his letters to the Spanish Crown of men with tails and of finding islands inhabited solely by females "who engage in no female occupation, but use bows and arrows of cane . . . and they arm and protect themselves with plates of copper, of which they have much"—a description remarkably in line with the classical legend of the Amazons (Columbus 10, 14).

The fictionalization of reality by official eyewitnesses was sometimes ostensibly positive, casting the New World in an idealized light. Columbus wrote back to Spain:

The breezes [are] most temperate, the trees and fruits and grasses are extremely beautiful and very different from ours; the rivers and harbors are so abundant and of such extreme excellence when compared to those of Christian lands that it is a marvel. All these islands are densely populated with the best people under the sun; they have neither ill-will nor treachery. All of them, women and men alike, go about naked like their mothers bore them, although some of the women wear a small piece of cotton or a patch of grass with which they cover themselves. (Zamora 125)

This constituted a paradisiac vision of the New World where Indians and land were untouched and, thus, it was precisely the indigenous people's need for "civilization" that would justify the imposition of European systems, values, and exploitation. Like the fanciful tales of El Dorado and ignorant, animal-like natives, the Edenic world likewise reinforced the interest of the financiers in winning unchecked access to natural and human resources in the explored lands. The language in the "histories" of Columbus and others undergirded the Europeans' approach to the Americas, and when the reality failed to match the European imagery, they employed violence to impose the imagined life. If the natives were not conveniently pacific, then they would be pacified.

"The Chronicles" were written in the context of what critic Mary Louise Pratt calls "contact zones"—"social spaces where disparate cultures meet, clash and grapple with each other, often in highly asymmetrical relations of domination and subordination— like colonization and slavery, or their aftermaths as they are lived out across the globe today" (4). For Pratt, expedition literature (or what today we often call travel literature) was and is the form Europeans use to imagine the "rest of the world." Filled with exotic descriptions, rich in "material and semantic substance," and where the "landscape is estheticized" (Pratt 204), exploration literature suggests an empty, mostly uncivilized world, ripe for exploration and development. The texts offer readers a sense of superiority—they can improve the places (and people) observed . . . but to improve, they must first possess.

While the fictionalization of space and people—and the connection to violence—is unmistakable in the colonial exploration histories, a key feature of Latin American literature is the continuity of (distorted) visions of an empty and wild continent in contrast with "civilization." Perhaps the most illustrative case is *Facundo, civilización y barbarie* [*Facundo: Or, Civilization and Barbarism,* 1845] by the Argentine writer Domingo Faustino Sarmiento. Written four centuries after the arrival of the conquistadors and thirty years after Argentina's independence (1816), in this essay Sarmiento replicates within Argentina the divisions the Europeans saw in the New World. For Sarmiento, Argentina was divided into two parts—the civilized urban spaces (primarily Buenos Aires) and the uncivilized, barbaric *pampa*, including the remote jungles, forests, rivers, mountains, and flatlands resistant to civilization. The untamed hinterland—as it was imagined—likewise required civilizing and the force to make that happen.

The first chapter—"Aspecto físico de la República Argentina, y caracteres, hábitos e ideas que engendra" ["Physical Aspect of the Argentine Republic, and Characters, Behaviors and Ideas that it Engenders"]—is particularly important because in it, the narrator describes the geography of his own country:

> The evil that afflicts the Republic of Argentina is the extension; the desert surrounding it from all sides, the inner parts insinuate; the solitude, the desertedness without human habitation, are in general the unquestionable limits between provinces . . . to the south and to the north ambushes from the savages who keep watch at nights by the moonlight to attack, like swarms of hyenas, on cattle grazing on the fields and the defenseless people. (27–28, translation mine)

As in the works of Columbus and Cortés, Sarmiento's paragraph inverts reality because the Native American is portrayed as the foreigner (even as an invader) in his own land while the settlers (principally Europeans) are "defenseless people." Note, too, the author's emphasis on language of emptiness: "expanse," "desert," "loneliness," "deserted," "unquestionable limits."

If, for Sarmiento, the provinces represent "the authority without limits and without responsibilities from those who govern them, justice administered without education or dialogue" (33, translation mine), Buenos Aires, on the contrary, "alone, in the vast Argentinian expanse, stays in contact with the European nations, only this city exploits the advantages of foreign exchange; only this city has the power and the income. In vain have the provinces asked the capital to lend them a little bit of civilization, industry and European population" (30, translation mine). Thus, the conflict between European civilization and native barbarism in the conquistadors' histories is paralleled in Sarmiento's vision of the fissures in nineteenth-century Argentina. The people of the city are "dressed in European costumes, [living] a civilized life as we know it everywhere" and are depicted as superior to "the people in the countryside, who far from aspiring to resemble that from the city, reject with disdain their comfort and polite manners" (Sarmiento 36, translation mine).

Facundo, civilizacion y barbarie presents an even a further paradox, however. If the territory is empty, as Sarmiento maintains, then there would be no conflict—and indeed could not be, for there would be no "other side" with which to fight. Like the conquistadors, Sarmiento's imagination of space contorts and distorts the violent reality of what happens in the borderlands—the confrontation and extermination of the natives to gain control of the land. Civilization once again justifies conquest and violence.

The fictionalization of space and history continued in twentieth-century Latin American writing. In 1953, Jorge Luis Borges published, in the newspaper *La Nación*, the short story "El Sur" [*The South*]. Although the short story does not represent an intent to portray history, it still shares some common traits with the fictionalized histories previously mentioned. The "south" of the story represents the vast plains of South America, where the protagonist, delirious and hospitalized, retreats after suffering an accident. In the very first line of the story, Borges carefully describes the lineage of the main character, Juan Dahlmann: "The man who landed in Buenos Aires in 1871 bore the name of Johannes Dahlmann and he was a minister in the Evangelical Church. In 1939, one of his grandchildren, Juan Dahlmann, was secretary of a municipal library on Calle Córdoba, and he considered himself profoundly Argentinian" (167). Thus, the protagonist is a man of letters, of German origin, from Buenos Aires and works at the municipal library.

Dahlmann's trip south is not simply a trip in space, however, but also a trip in time. The reader is unsure even if the move is real or imagined, a part of his delirium. The "south" is wild and savage, and Dahlmann, after being challenged by a "compadrito de cara achinada," dies in a knife fight. The word "compadrito," used in Argentina and Uruguay, refers to a young man from a lower class who behaves provocatively. "Cara achinada" refers to a "Chinese-looking face"—that is, to an Indian. As in the imaginary of Sarmiento, the rural, barbaric native murders the man of culture and civilization.

Counter-Narratives of Violence

The previous section outlined depictions of violence originating in colonialism and labeled this type of literature "fictionalized history" because it claims to tell objective history while in truth introducing important distortions. By contrast, the second part of the essay will trace the theme of violence not from the view of dominant forces, but rather from the perspective of the victimized. This type of writing offers an alternative version to that proposed by official and/ or authoritative voices.

In the colonial period, there are a number of writers challenging the abuses committed with the complicity of the existing power structure. The most well-known is Bartolomé de las Casas, a Dominican priest who, in 1552, wrote *Brevísima historia de la destrucción de las Indias* [*A Short Account of the Destruction of the Indies*], in which he "describes the initial peaceful overtures made by the Indians, followed by the treachery of the Spaniards (torture, forced slavery, rape, murder, etc.)" (Hart 20). After reading a manuscript of Las Casas' work, the king of Spain, Carlos I, was prompted in 1542 to issue the *New Laws*, which aimed to protect the indigenous people of the Americas by limiting the power of Spanish landowners over the natives captured and transferred to Crown land grants, known as an *encomiendas*.

Las Casas' campaign against the harsh treatment of the natives countered the dominant idea that it was necessary to impose civilization on them. Yet, at the same time, Las Casas' own writing contains many of the same "fictionalizations" used by writers from the dominant perspective. Like Columbus, Las Casas idealized the Indians as ingenuous, child-like creatures:

God made all the peoples of this area, many and varied as they are, as open and as innocent as can be imagined. The simplest people in the world—unassuming, long-suffering, unassertive, and submissive—they are without malice or guile, and are utterly faithful and obedient both to their own native lords and to the Spaniards in whose service they now find themselves. Never quarrelsome or belligerent or boisterous, they harbor no grudges and do not seek to settle old scores; indeed, the notions of revenge, rancor, and hatred are quite foreign to them. (9–10)

Las Casas' purpose in emphasizing the innate goodness of the Indians is, however, the precise opposite of Columbus'. Rather than justifying the imposition of Christian "civilization" and commerce on the "undeveloped" New World, as the conquistadors do, Las Casas instead highlights the innocence of the Indians in order to underline the cruelty of the Spaniards.

Las Casas is consciously rhetorical in rendering the Indians' suffering in brutal detail. The *Brevísima historia* is organized by region or native kingdom and describes the atrocities witnessed in each place. For example:

The fifth kingdom was known as Higuey and its queen, a lady already advanced in years, went by the name of Higuanama. They strung her up and I saw with my own eyes how the Spaniards burned countless local inhabitants alive or hacked them to pieces, or devised novel ways of torturing them to death, enslaving those they took alive. Indeed, they invented so many new methods of murder that it would be quite impossible to set them all down on paper and, however hard one tried to chronicle them, one could probably never list a thousandth part of what actually took place . . . . After the fighting was over and all the men had been killed, the surviving natives—usually, that is, the young boys, the women, and the children—were shared out between the victors . . . . The pretext under which the victims were parceled out in this way was that their new masters would then be in a position to teach them the truths of the Christian faith. (Las Casas 22–24)

By stressing that the queen is an old woman, Las Casas draws a vivid picture of the Spanish murderers' wanton brutality. And by claiming to have witnessed the abuses "with my own eyes" he invites the reader to sympathize with the horrors he saw. Yet Las Casas also says he saw only a fraction of abuses. "They [the Spaniards] invented so many new methods of murder that it would be quite impossible to set them all down on paper," he writes. Las Casas' sympathy for the plight of the Indians—who, after all, have Christian souls—is palpable. Less evident than that counter-narrative, but equally important, is that Las Casas himself—in seeing the Indians as innocent babes and potential converts—is himself fictionalizing what he presents as fact.

If Columbus and Cortés presented European accounts of their encounter with the indigenous peoples of the Americas, and Las Casas presented a European counter-narrative, then the Quechua Indian Felipe Guamán Poma de Ayala offered the first view from the native side. In his *El primer nueva corónica y buen gobierno* [*The First New Chronicle and Good Government*] published around 1518, Poma de Ayala describes how the "West imposed on the inhabitants of newly discovered lands a creed they did not live up to themselves" (Hart 21). Unlike Las Casas, who attempted to reform the *encomienda* system, Poma de Ayala sees in it the very root of violence in the Americas. Again and again, he reminds the reader that prior to the Europeans' arrival, land in the Andes was attributed to a child at birth: In the Quechua saying, the "moment the child crawls from her mother's uterus she receives land" (Poma de Ayala 207, translation mine). The *encomienda* system disrupted and uprooted Indian life—Poma de Ayala illustrated the consequent suffering in 400 sketches—and a right considered fundamental was lost. As early as the sixteenth-century, the *Nueva corónica* turned the conquistador "eyewitness" narrative on its head.

That land is central to eruptions of violence is a continual theme in Latin American writing. And over the centuries, the connection between the two has often been related through a familiar literary form known as the *testimonio*, or testimonial. Without going into detail about the scholarly controversies regarding this genre—some scholars consider it history, others literature, and still others a genre of its own—testimonies are important for two reasons: first, because of their relationship with the theme of violence and, second, because they often correspond to what I call counter-narratives of violence, that is, texts that challenge the official versions received from the spheres of power. In *Me llamo Rigoberta Menchú y así me nació la conciencia* [*I, Rigoberta Menchu: An Indian Woman in Guatemala,* 1983], Rigoberta Menchú,[2] a Guatamalan peasant woman recounts, like Las Casas and Poma de Ayala, an endless series of abuses, including the inhuman working conditions under which the indigenous people labor in the fields and the constant assaults of the army—paid by the landowners—on the Indian communities. The central aspect of the violence is, as it was in Las Casas, Poma de Ayala, Colón, and Cortés, the expropriation of the lands that the Indians have lived on and worked for centuries. The violence behind the territorial dispute in Guatemala is inseparable from ethnic/racial and class issues, a dynamic often encountered in Latin American writing, with the victims (indigenous, poor, marginal) on one side and the abusers (landowners, rich, army, government) on the other.

The account given by Rigoberta Menchú, whose story and political activism would win her the Nobel Peace Prize in 1992, is embedded in the historical frame of the Guatemalan Civil War (1960–1996) and is told in the first person. Yet her voice is a representation of the voices of her community and that is why, from the beginning of her narration, she emphasizes that:

> what has happened to me has happened to many other people too. This is my testimony. I didn't learn it from a book and I didn't learn it alone. I'd like to stress that it's not only my life, it's also the testimony of my people . . . . My story is the story of all poor Guatemalans. My personal experience is the reality of a whole people. (Menchú 1)

Yet also like Las Casas, Cortés, and Columbus, Menchú mixes her "factual" narrative with evident fictionalization by narrating events that did not occur or that she invented or transformed. This was recognized by the critic David Stoll and became one of the most important debates of this academic area. One example of Mechú's possible fictionalization of her narrative occurs when she describes the assassination of one of her brothers who, according to her

---

testimony, dies after being brutally tortured and set on fire by the army. The soldiers

> lined up the tortured and poured petrol on them; and then the soldiers set fire to each one of them. Many of them begged for mercy. They looked half dead when they were lined up there, but when the bodies began to burn they began to plead for mercy. Some of them screamed, many of them leapt but uttered no sound—of course, that was because their breathing was cut off. (Mechú 179)

Menchú narrates the event in great detail, as if she had witnessed the killing. However, after interviewing Menchú's relatives in Guatelama, Stoll discovered that her brother had indeed been killed, but not set on fire, "only" shot by the army. According to Stoll, Rigoberta Menchú did not witness the killing (although her mother did), and this inconsistency raises questions about the truthfulness of her testimony. But what difference does it make if Rigoberta Menchú witnessed the killing of her brother or not? From this reader's point of view, this controversy does not nullify the long-term consequences of a war. Does changing the perspective of Menchú's story nullify the brutality of the crimes committed against the indigenous people of Guatemala? Does Menchú's story need to be based on particular historical facts at all? After all, we have seen that no single discipline or genre guarantees absolute truth and objectivity.

Menchú's depiction of violence is significant because her voice resonates not only with the colonial texts of the past, but with much of Latin American literature during and after her time. Twentieth-century Latin American literatures abound in stories set in a context of political distress. As in the case of Guatemala during the second half of the twentieth century, national Latin American armies, backed by the United States, seized control of most of the governments in Latin America, establishing durable dictatorships through what is known as the *guerra sucia,* or dirty war. Indeed, around this same time, we find works that engage the reccuring themes of political violence—kidnappings, tortures, disappearances, exiles, social control, and fear. While these stories are fiction, they originate in historical events. Take, for example, the Argentine novel *El beso de la mujer araña* [*Kiss of the Spider Woman*, 1976], written by Manuel Puig, which develops through a dialogue between Valentín, a tortured political prisoner, and Molina, his cell mate arrested for homosexuality. The characters are victims of the dictatorship, but represent all people who would be considered subversive—that is, every person who disagrees with the government's ideology. The political militancy and the torture of Valentín makes him easily identifiable as a "subversive," while Molina's homosexuality represents another threat to the dictatorship's power structures and definition of manhood. Puig sets political and sexual orientation on the same level in order to erase the boundaries between marginalization and political victimization.

In literature set in periods of dictatorship, the dichotomy between victim and aggressor seems clear (state versus civilians), but that distinction becomes problematic in democratic contexts. In a democracy, who is the aggressor and who are the victims? And what circumstances cause the criminal to commit the crimes? These questions lead us to a reality anchored once more in historical fact: the class differences in Latin America. In the classic Brazilian work *O Cobrador* [*The Taker and Other Stories*, 1979], Rubem Fonseca examines these questions. In the title story "O Cobrador," the opposition between murderer and victim is confused; the protagonist is an assassin from a very low class who kills because he is tired of having to survive in an environment fundamentally hostile to the poor. The story begins *in medias res*, when the protagonist goes to the dentist. After waiting for half an hour, the dentist looks at his mouth, takes out a few teeth and wants to charge him four hundred *cruzeiros,* which he does not have. When he wishes to leave without paying, the dentist tries to stop him. The protagonist reacts by shooting him in the knee and screaming: "I'm not paying for anything else, I'm tired of paying! . . . From now on I only collect debts" (Fonseca 8, translation mine). While the reader does not know the name of the protagonist, the setting, Rio de Janeiro, is indirectly revealed in the descriptions of the spaces of the city, mainly rich communities, to which the protagonist goes to "collect" what the elite owe him: "I say inside my head and sometimes out loud, they all owe me! They owe me food, sex, covers, shoes, home, car, watch, teeth, they owe me" (Fonseca 8, translation mine).

Space is as important in contemporary Latin American fiction as it was to Las Casas, Poma, or Menchú, as the predominantly urban environment turns out to be as hostile to the lower classes as were the rural places/scenes described by earlier writers. This literature reflects the migration from rural to urban areas experienced by the majority of Latin American countries in the twentieth century. But as we see in *O Cobrador*, the search for opportunities in the cities does not provide the hoped-for results, and many migrants end up stuck in outlying impoverished ghettos (*favelas*) with limited access to resources that would permit them a better quality of life. In *O Cobrador*, we see the division of Rio into neighborhoods that represent the socio-economic stratification of the city and, by extension, Brazil as a whole. This theme likewise appears in texts from other countries, such as the Colombian novels *La virgen de los sicarios* [*Our Lady of the Assasins*] (1994) by Fernando Vallejo and *Rosario Tijeras* (1999) by Jorge Franco. These works feature a protagonist who is a young male *sicario* (hitman), or in the case of *Rosario Tijeras*, a *sicaria* (hitwoman). Both protagonists live in an outlying barrio of Medellín, and they walk the city, like the protagonist of *O Cobrador*, to "clean" the street by assassinating the society's privileged.

The cities in these contemporary novels are not the Buenos Aires that Sarmiento —and sometimes Borges—idealized. Here, the city appears as another protagonist, ready to devour the people who inhabit it. These works criticize an urban system that creates characters who must kill in order to survive, and thus are both aggressors and victims. These counter-narratives of violence offer an unusual perspective, but, like Las Casas, Poma, and Menchú, they work to give voice to those negatively affected by violence.

Conclusion

In reviewing the topic of violence in Latin American literature, this essay has proposed two categories of literature: "fictionalized histories" and "counter-narratives of violence." The fictionalized histories include texts that see Latin America from a Eurocentric perspective, which creates a distorted view of the native cultures and peoples who are often described as inferior by the first explorers and conquerors to arrive in the Americas. These fictionalized histories date back to the period of the discovery of America and the beginnings of colonization, but not exclusively. Some texts of the post-colonial period—and even some contemporary works—repeat the same pattern, in which the natives are objectified, deprived of humanity, and seen as savages that need to be civilized. Violence is considered a necessary tool to transform the indigenous into "proper" citizens. For the purposes of this essay, this category is referred to as "fictionalized histories" because, although these texts provide information that has proven useful to interpret the New World from a historical perspective, they are dominated by both their writers' subjectivity and a lack of understanding of the different cultural dynamics they encounter and attempt to describe.

On the other hand, in the second category—the "counter-narratives of violence"—are texts that offer a counter-discourse to the ones offered by the fictionalized histories. Counter-narratives question the official stories and authoritative voices of the colonial and postcolonial period. They provide insights into the violence suffered by marginalized peoples, most often the indigenous, as experienced in Central America and the Andes, or by the Afro-Latin Americans in Brazil and the Caribbean. In the latter, class and race are clearly interconnected. On the other hand, in other countries such as Argentina—with a smaller indigenous populations and virtually no Afro-Latin Americans—authors still focus on the topic of violence and address similar themes: social justice, political repression, and class inequalities. Contemporary works often go even further and explore the direct interaction between violence and urban space, where the cityscape itself becomes yet another fictionalized character, one that either enables or disables the potential of the characters who inhabit it.

There are three final points that are, arguably, key to understanding how depictions of violence function in a Latin

American context. First, violence is a prevalent topic and reflects certain socio-historical aspects peculiar to the continent. However, it is important to note that any study of Latin America as a whole necessarily implies that one must deal in generalizations. Yet Latin America contains many different realities. Therefore, the literary realities examined in these pages cannot be taken and applied automatically to all its political and geographical regions. Second, this essay focuses on the topic of violence in connection to power dynamics (within colonial and postcolonial political systems), but this approach by no means exhausts the many possible ways to consider violence. Violence can also be studied through lenses of gender inequality, domestic abuse, or drug trafficking, all common themes in contemporary Latin American literature. Third, the literary representation of violence in Latin America cannot be taken as the only perspective for interpreting the history and social realities of the continent as a whole. Again, this would signify a reliance on stereotypes, an approach most of us and especially students of language and culture, wish to overcome.

Notes

1. I would like to thank Phyllis Bellver, Lynn Celdrán, and John J. Goodman for their assistance with the English version of this article and the translations.

2. Menchú's testimony is a transcription of several conversations that took place during a week between anthopologist Elizabeth Burgos-Debray and Menchú.

Works Cited

Borges, Jorge Luis. *Ficciones*. Trans. Anthony Kerrigan. New York: Grove Press, 1962.

Chasteen, John Charles. *Born in Blood and Fire. A Concise History of Latin America*. New York & London: W. W. Norton & Co., 2006.

Columbus, Christopher. "Columbus, Letter to Santangel." *Early Americas Digital Archive*. Department of English, University of Maryland, n.d. Web. 12 Jan. 2014.

Cortés, Hernán. *"Carta enviada a la Reina Doña Juana y al emperador Carlos V, su hijo, por la justicia y regimiento de la Rica Villa de la*

Veracruz, a 10 de julio de 1519." *Ibero-American Electronic Text Series.* University of Wisconsin, 2011. Web. 11 Jan. 2014.

Dorfman, Ariel. *Imaginación y violencia en América.* 2nd ed. Barcelona: Anagrama, 1972.

Fonseca, Rubem. *El Cobrador.* Trans. John O'Kuinghttons. Santiago: Tajamar, 2009.

Hart, Stephen M. *A Companion to Spanish American Literature.* London: Tamesis, 1999.

Las Casas, Bartolomé. *A Short Account of the Destruction of the Indies.* *Virtual Reading Room.* Columbia University, n.d. Web. 20 Jan. 2014.

Menchú, Rigoberta, and Elizabeth Burgos-Debray. *I, Rigoberta Menchú. An Indian Woman in Guatemala.* Trans. Ann Wright. London & New York: Verso, 1992.

Nunn, Frederick M. *Collisions with History. Latin American Fiction and Social Science from El Boom to the New World Order.* Ohio: Ohio University Centre for International Studies, 2001.

Pratt, Mary Louise. *Travel Writing and Transculturation.* London & New York: Routledge, 1992.

Poma de Ayala, Guamán. *El primer nueva corónica y buen gobierno.* Mexico: Siglo Veintiuno, 1992.

Sarmiento, Faustino Domingo. *Facundo.* Boston: Ginn & Co.,1960.

Zamora, Margarita. *Reading Columbus.* U of California Press, n.d. Web. 14 Dec. 2013.

Kill Lists: Sade, Cinema, and the Language of the Torturer_____

Lindsay Hallam

The Marquis de Sade was primarily an author of novels, and it is within these works he espoused his individual philosophy. What preoccupies this philosophy most of all is, of course, the human experience, but for Sade this experience was a wholly physical one. The human condition is an embodied condition, and therefore, the exploration of the possibilities and the limitations of the bodily form was his main project. Specifically, it was the extremes of bodily expression—sex and violence—that become the main driving force of his narratives and the subject of his characters' endless philosophical debates.

In cinema, too, there is a focus on the body and its participation in sexual and violent acts. Examples of extreme cinema, such as the recent "torture porn" trend and films from The New French Extremity, continue Sade's exploration of all possible perversions and atrocities. Recently, there has been an increase in representations of torture, of showing the body undergoing torture, as well as considering the motivations of those who commit torture and the place of the spectator in relation to what they are seeing on screen. Bringing the works of Sade into the discussion of these contemporary films helps illuminate further the relationship between images of violence and those who consume them. The use of Sade is apt, as he also used fiction in order to create a language of violence, revealing how violence is a fundamental aspect of humanity—even within civilized society, which often seeks to deny or explain away violence.

In the next section, Sade's main philosophical ideas are explained, as well as how he utilized language and narrative structure to articulate violence in a new and different form. Subsequently, the essay examines Georges Bataille's claim that Sade's language of violence was actually "the language of the victim," as it expressed violence in a way that did not rely on state-sanctioned excuses and explanations. Finally, the essay explores how Sade's expression of violence in literary form can be applied to the analysis of violence and audience reception in cinema.

Sade's Violent Philosophy

The combination of sex and violence in Sade's works is what led Richard von Krafft-Ebing to coin the term "sadism" to describe a pathological condition in his book *Psychopathia Sexualis*. A sadist is someone who experiences sexual pleasure from inflicting pain and humiliation on another person, and certainly, Sade's libertine characters do gain sexual pleasure from such behavior (while a "masochist"—named after the author Leopold von Sacher-Masoch—is someone who feels pleasure when receiving pain or being humiliated). As well as violence, though, the Sadean libertine also experiences sexual pleasure from other activities and objects, some of which may be viewed as non-sexual, such as filth and bodily waste. The telling of stories as primers to sexual activity and the discussion and analysis of these acts are also important aspects of the sexual scene. As Sade states: "There's more to it than just experiencing sensations, they must also be analyzed. Sometimes it is as pleasant to discuss as to undergo them" (*Juliette* 60).

What is being emphasised here is the place of order within transgression. Although Sade's libertines commit all manner of criminal and lustful acts, they do this within an organized system. They do not give into any desire or urge that comes to them spontaneously; they feel that urge and then subject it to much thought and planning. In *Philosophy in the Bedroom*, the young Eugenie is schooled by older libertines, Dolmance and Madame de Saint-Ange, in the ways of sex, which also involves participating in acts of violence, climaxing with her committing atrocities against her own mother. Yet, these events occur as lessons, as ordered and organized scenarios: "let us put a little order in these revels; measure is required even in the depths of infamy and delirium" (*Justine* 240). Similarly, in *Juliette* the eponymous heroine is reprimanded by her mentor, Clairwil, for getting too carried away in the heat of her passions. In response, Juliette devises an elaborate process that she carefully and methodically goes through before each of her crimes, which incorporates periods of abstinence and contemplation. Juliette later admits that this process produces greater pleasure: "execute it and you will find that this is the species of viciousness that suits you best and which you will carry out with the greatest delight" (*Juliette* 641) What is highlighted in this statement is that "viciousness" leads to "delight"—violence results in sexual pleasure.

For Sade, violence comes from nature and is bound up with nature's constant cycles of fornication and reproduction. Hence, the sexual and violent instincts are not separate; they are fundamentally connected. Sade feels that we should follow these "natural" instincts: "Absurd to say the mania offends nature; can it be so, when 'tis she who puts it in our head? Can she dictate what degrades her?" (*Justine* 230). However, despite the fact that Sade positions his libertines as followers of nature's urges, there is also the need to overcome nature's control, which is why systems of order are put into place when the libertines commit their crimes. By doing this, the libertine is asserting his or her superiority over nature, over society and its restrictive laws, and most obviously over the powerless victim. These crimes are expressions of the libertines' "sovereignty," a term used by both Maurice Blanchot and Georges Bataille to describe the state that the Sadean libertine strived to attain. Sade's libertines gathered together in small groups of likeminded individuals (both male and female), placing themselves above all others. Therefore, in order to assert this sovereignty, there must be within the sexual scene "victims, not partners," who are "denied any rights at all" (Bataille 167). Activities are meticulously organized and operate with a strict hierarchy in place. Those at the bottom of the hierarchy are abused and violated, with no remorse felt by their captors.

The libertine feels no remorse because in his or her view, they are merely following nature. Juliette joins a group called The Sodality of the Friends of Crime, who meet in order to commit crimes for purpose of sexual pleasure. This group "considers itself above the law because the law is of mortal and artificial contrivance, whereas the Sodality, natural in its origin and obediences, heeds and respects Nature only" (*Juliette* 418). Just as a natural force has no "feelings" about any devastation or disaster that it causes, so too does the Sadean libertine. In fact, there is a lack of feeling altogether, with the libertine becoming quite apathetic and numb to the violence committed. It is this apathy that leads to the more extreme and violent measures that the libertine is driven to in the midst of their pleasures. They are titillated primarily by the thought of what they are doing, about how their actions are transgressing social and moral laws:

> [B]elieve me when I tell you that the delights born of apathy are worth much more than those you get out of your sensibility; the latter can only touch the heart in one sense, the other titillates and overwhelms all of one's being. In a word, is it possible to compare permissible pleasures with pleasures which, to far more piquant delights, join those inestimable joys that come of bursting socially imposed restraints and of the violation of every law? (*Justine* 342)

As this quote illustrates, the acts themselves are almost irrelevant, as is the other person involved; it is more about what they represent in relation to societal laws and taboos. The notion of "evil" is important, as it is tied to Christian ideals, to which Sade was vehemently opposed. To show his complete disdain, Sade often incorporated Christian symbols into his sexual scenes in order to blaspheme them. Even though Sade's libertines were atheist, they found pleasure in blasphemy because of what it represented, as an act that was taboo and went against the foundations of Western Christian society: "It is not the object of libertine intentions which fires us, but the idea of evil, and that consequently it is thanks only to evil and only in the name of evil one stiffens, not thanks to the object" (*120 Days* 364). Again, we see that it is the idea, the thought, behind the action that is most important and leads to pleasurable sensations. The victim in the scenario is perceived as nothing but an "object," a thing to be exploited and then discarded, hence the prevalence of violence within the sexual scene and the most controversial aspect of Sade's novels and philosophy.

Sade and the Language of Violence

Sade's novel *The 120 Days of Sodom* in particular highlights the place of violence within Sade's quest to explore all possible permutations of sexual activity. The book itself is unfinished, as his manuscript was lost during the events of The French Revolution. Sade, at the time, was imprisoned in the Bastille, but during his transfer to an insane asylum at Charenton, his manuscript was misplaced and he never saw it again. As the novel is unfinished, it begins with a narrative, but then diminishes into a list of atrocities, concluding with a mathematical table showing who died and who survived. The story is about four libertines who kidnap eight young girls and eight young boys and hide themselves away in a remote chateau along with servants and four prostitutes, who serve as storytellers. They tell of their past exploits, which are meant to serve as inspiration for proceeding events. What then occurs is the rape, degradation, and violation of their young captives, as well as the libertines' own daughters.

What is most shocking about this novel, and Sade's work in general, is not just the violence that takes place, but the fact that the violence takes place in order to provide sexual satisfaction. Added to these scenes describing rape and torture are long dialogues between the libertines as they discuss and analyze their actions within the context of history and their philosophical conceptions of nature, society, and their place within (or should I say, "above"?) them. These interminably long conversations break up the descriptions of sex and violence, which problematizes the status of these novels as mere pornography. Gilles Deleuze explains in his study of Sade and Leopold von Sacher Masoch: "the work of Sade and Masoch cannot be regarded as pornography; it merits the more exalted title of 'pornology' because its erotic language cannot be reduced to the elementary functions of ordering and describing" (Deleuze 18). Instead, Deleuze places Sade and Masoch as "'patients' or clinicians or both" as well as "great anthropologists" and "great artists as they discovered new forms of expression, new ways of thinking and feeling and an entirely original language" (Deleuze 16). Situating Sade and Masoch as creators of "pornology" emphasizes how these authors combined a pornographic approach with a more scientific one and, as a result, employ language in a new and different way to describe both sex and violence, the two most taboo areas of Western culture.

Although Deleuze regards Sade as a "great artist," many have regarded Sade a "bad" writer. To actually sit down and read his novels can be quite an arduous task, not just due to their length (*Juliette* runs over a thousand pages; *The 120 Days of Sodom*, although incomplete, is almost five hundred pages long), but also because of their structure. Consisting of descriptions of physical sexual and violent activities and long philosophical treatises, his works involve a lot of repetition. Acts are repeated over and over with slight variations. For example, in *The 120 Days of Sodom*, a large section of the novel is dedicated to discussing and enacting the eating of feces. Karmen MacKendrick states that: "One could quite legitimately call both Sade and Masoch very bad writers. Sade's grammar book clarity is placed alternately in the service of grotesque anatomical detail and of numbing political rhetoric" (MacKendrick 30). Yet, MacKendrick then admits that it is these very factors that make Sade and Masoch significant literary figures: "Their works are important not because of the acts or scenes they depict, but, once more, because of their use of language . . . and their narrative structures" (31)

What Sade created was a language of violence. Despite his very clinical approach (or possibly because of it) Sade expressed violence through language in a way that had not been attempted before. As aforementioned, violence in Sade was not conducted in a chaotic frenzy; it was the result of thought and premeditation. According to Deleuze, in Sade, "reasoning itself is a form of violence . . . he [Sade] is on the side of violence, however calm and logical he may be" (Deleuze 118). The apathy and lack of feeling of the libertine characters is expressed through the way their actions and conversations are described. This language is not an expression of emotion but of rational thought, which would seem, superficially, to be in opposition to the forces of violence.

Violence in Sade is part of a grander scheme, part of an exploration of the possibilities and limits of the body, but which is expressed through thought and text. Although his works are fiction, there are elements of science and mathematics in how stories are structured, hence Deleuze's designation of Sade's novels as works of "pornology." MacKendrick states that "the Sadistic text often takes on the character of a mathematics textbook" (MacKendrick 42). There is an obsession with numbers in Sade's work, from the number of people involved in a scenario to the number of whip lashes, the measurements of body parts, the scheduling of events. This is related to the systems of order that are put in place, establishing balance and symmetry—to an almost absurd degree. The violence is so unrelenting and repetitive, and described so matter-of-factly, that it almost takes on the character of a farce. That there is humor amongst the horror and violence again emphasises the difficulty and discomfort that Sade's work evokes. It could thus be argued, then, that Sade's work places us, the readers, in the position of his "hero" libertines, and like them, we come to view the victims as objects also. Yet, as this essay also goes on to explore, Georges Bataille sees the language that Sade employs as not the language of a sadistic perpetrator, but as "that of a victim" (190).

Bataille on Sade

In his book *Eroticism*, Georges Bataille states that in Western culture, two extremes are constructed—those of civilization and barbarism. Yet, Bataille believes that "the use of these words is misleading, for they imply that there are barbarians on the one hand and civilized men on the other. The distinction is that civilized men speak and barbarians are silent . . . " (Bataille 186). Therefore, since the civilized man has the power of language, violence—which is the expression of barbarism—is "silent." The primary misconception here, though, is that there is a separation between the barbarians and the civilized. What Sade's works show us (and also what we see take place in the real world every day) is that all people are capable of being both civilized and savage. Sade's libertines commit the most atrocious crimes, but within a "civilized" and ordered structure.

Furthermore, the language that Sade uses to express this predicament is also different, as Bataille asserts that "Common language will not express violence. It treats it as a guilty and importunate thing and disallows it by denying it any function or excuse" (Bataille 186). In other words, within Western society, violence is often treated as a "mistake," the result of "something going wrong," which is explained away and excused (Bataille 187).

Bataille cites the example of the state torturer to further demonstrate his claims:

> As a general rule the torturer does not use the language of the violence exerted by him in the name of an established authority; he uses the language of the authority, and that gives him what looks like an excuse, a lofty justification. (Bataille 187)

The state torturer will hide behind the excuses provided to them through civilized language, which is the language of those who are in power. Alternatively, the state torturer can choose not to speak at all, thus avoiding responsibility and accountability, and again echoing Bataille's claim that violence is inherently "silent," or without language. Sade, therefore, presents a new form of language, which is able to articulate violence. Sade's writing is in "complete contrast with the torturer's hypocritical utterances," as the "language is that of a victim" (Bataille 190). Taking Bataille's point, Deleuze explains: "Only the victim can describe torture; the torturer necessarily uses the hypocritical language of established order and power" (Deleuze 17). Sade's work, although brutal, is not hypocritical; it "refuses to cheat" (Bataille 188) as the actions of his libertines are not excused or explained, and they do not deny what they do or the reasons why they do it. For Bataille, only someone who has experienced pain and violence could articulate it so precisely, and he cites Sade's instances of imprisonment as examples of his own victimization (Bataille 190). What Sade, then, did in his writing is use the language of the victim, but he did that in order to explore all aspects of violence and reveal that it is an integral part of the "civilized" human, no matter how much we try to silence these aspects.

Given that Sade developed this new use of language in literature, what are the implications for how violence and torture is portrayed in other art forms, specifically cinema? Cinema has its own form and "language," utilizing sound, vision, and movement, with the portrayal of violence being common throughout many genres. Like Sade, cinema as a medium has been criticized for incorporating images of violence that appear to revel in sadism and invite the spectator to enjoy the same pleasures as those who perpetrate violent actions on screen. Famously, Laura Mulvey characterized the "gaze" in classic Hollywood cinema as one that is inherently male and, important when discussing Sade, inherently sadistic. Carol Clover, in her book *Men, Women and Chainsaws,* examined audience identification in slasher films made in the 1970s and 1980s, positing that (the primarily male adolescent) viewers did identify with the killer through the employment of first person camera shots, but then there is a switch in identification to the "Final Girl," who is the sole survivor of the mass murders. Since these publications, there has been a rise in the portrayal of graphic violence in cinema, specifically in scenes of torture, but there has been little discussion of these films in relation to how Sade depicted violence and torture. Given Bataille's claim that Sade wrote literature in the "language of the victim," what are the implications regarding visual representations of violence in cinema?

Sade and Cinema Violence

Just as Sade's works focus on depictions of the body being violated, torn open, and probed, his language itself can create a bodily affect in the reader. Alistair Welchman explains: "this is a language that is directly transcribed on bodies, that is exhausted in production, distribution and consumption of affects" (Welchman 163). The experience of reading Sade can incite a bodily response, similar to that of seeing an extreme image on screen. One of Sade's many transgressions is the transgression of the boundary separating the work of art from the body of the person consuming it. Explaining further, Welchman states that:

Sade activates an artistic "disorder of all the senses" that, by giving words a specifically visual function, produces an entirely new effect capable of rendering in a geometrical instant the affective movement that instantaneously combines the spatial element of the posture and the temporal element of its activity. (Welchman 170)

What Welchman describes here in Sade's writing is what the cinematic image can also achieve, a *visual* representation that provokes the senses and produces bodily effects. It is primarily the movement in cinema, along with the visual, that unifies all these elements, the time and space in which these actions are portrayed. Welchman cites a statement from Sade: "It is not easy for art, which has no movement at all, to realize an action whose whole soul is movement" (Welchman 170). Obviously, since cinema was invented after Sade's death, he did not know that there was to be an art form that did incorporate movement in the depiction of physical action— *motion* pictures. But unlike theater, which also involves movement, this movement is captured on a camera and then projected as its own separate two-dimensional visual.

Writing additionally on this point, Welchman describes Sade's "scopic writing" in rather cinematic terms: "Within each combination, the voluminous body part arrangements must be projected onto a flat visual surface. . . . The visual mechanism that performs this function is the mirror, or rather, mirrors in the plural" (Welchman 167). Sade details sexual tableaux, precise combinations of bodies and perversions, creating elaborate pictures of libertine activity. The idea of the "ensemble of mirrors" is significant, and cinematic, in that everything is seen, but the depth is "crushed," the image is laid out "on a flat plane on which everything is visible" (Welchman 168). The "flat plane" that Welchman describes here can be likened to the cinema screen. The notion of everything being seen in multiple mirrors is comparable to the use of different camera angles, which show action from all sides and perspectives, allowing viewers to see all the permutations of transgression and perversion.

This idea of *seeing* everything is just as important as saying everything and doing everything within the libertine project. In cinema, this is also often the case, with certain films becoming notorious because they show something so shocking and extreme that has never been seen before. While many classic horror films trade on shadow and suggestion by not showing, there has always been a thread of horror that instead strives to show violence in a way that is as graphic as possible.

In one of the only studies of Sade and audience reception of cinema, "The Chaotic Text and the Sadean Audience: Narrative Transgressions of a Contemporary Cult Film," Graeme Harper and Xavier Mendik analyze Robert Rodriguez's 1996 film *From Dusk Till Dawn*, citing how the primary audience for the film, referred to as "Film Avids," were young and "hedonistic," with an appetite for extreme images and metatextual references (Harper and Mendik 241). This "Film Avid" audience, who appreciated the films of the likes of Rodriguez and Quentin Tarantino in the 1990s, can be seen as precursors to the next generation of film fans who consume "torture porn" horror films, such as the *Saw* and *Hostel* series. Similarly, this audience enjoys images of graphic violence as well as references to earlier horror classics. Earlier "rules" of the horror genre, such as the characteristics of the "Final Girl" and the mass murderer, or the order that certain characters are killed and why, are subverted in these new horror films. Whereas in the past, the sole survivor of the killer's rampage was usually a virginal, tomboyish girl, in torture porn films such as *Borderland* (Zev Berman 2007) and *Hostel: Part II* (Eli Roth 2007), the virgins are the first characters to get killed and in a much slower and more graphic way. They are not stabbed or chainsawed by a masked, almost supernatural monster; they are tortured by unmasked, seemingly "ordinary" people. Like Sade's libertines, the torturers in most of these films are rich and upper class, joining together with other likeminded individuals in order to explore their darkest desires and fantasies, such as The Elite Hunting Club in the *Hostel* series. Violence and torture are organized and ordered events.

Many of these films, such as the first *Hostel* (Eli Roth, 2005), *Martyrs* (Pascal Laugier 2008), and *Wolf Creek* (Greg Mclean, 2005), begin as one kind of narrative and then turn into something else, with the final acts of the film becoming a series of violent episodes depicting heinous torture—much like the genre switch in *From Dusk Till Dawn* and also mirroring the structure of Sade's *The 120 Days of Sodom*, which shifts from a narrative to a list of brutalities. Moreover, this emphasis on scenes that focus completely on depicting physical acts rather than plot development is similar to the structure of pornography, as Hyland and Shorey maintain:

> Structurally, torture porn borrows the vignette structure of pornography, with the acts of violence becoming increasingly explicit as the (usually) thin plot develops . . . instead of a focus on the victim-hero, we, the viewers, become invested in the killers, while the victims are flat and interchangeable. (Hyland & Shorey 177)

In many ways, this echoes the structure of some of Sade's works (not *Justine*, however, which focuses entirely on the victim figure) with their endless repetition of scenes of sexual violence. *Hostel: Part II* includes two scenes of torture that can be viewed as digressions away from the main narrative, becoming almost self-contained scenes of violent spectacle. The first scene of torture in the film is also the most controversial, leading to a ban in New Zealand ("A Brief History") and cuts to the scene when released in Germany (Rüdiger). Lorna, the only character in the set of three main girls who is a virgin, has been captured and wakes up to find that she is naked and suspended upside down. A woman enters, removes her clothes and lies underneath Lorna in a tub. She then takes a scythe and cuts Lorna's throat and slashes at her body as Lorna's blood rains over her, creating a literal bloodbath.

The second scene involves an older man who has a male character, Miroslav, tied to a slab in the foreground of the shot. The man goes over to Miroslav, slices off some flesh from his leg, then walks to a table in the background and eats it. What is most striking about this scene is how well staged and composed in the frame it is, utilizing deep-focus cinematography and scored by Bizet's *Carmen*. It is presented quite matter-of-factly, like Sade's scenes of violence, but also quite elegantly, in one take and in wide shot. Going back to Harper and Mendik's article about the Film Avid audience, what also "adds" to this scene is the fact that the older man is played by Ruggero Deodato, the director of the cult exploitation film *Cannibal Holocaust* (1980). Like Quentin Tarantino, Eli Roth, director of *Hostel* and *Hostel: Part II*, is also an unabashed horror fan and knowledgeable cinephile. For Harper and Mendik, this "encyclopaedic" knowledge aligns these filmmakers with Sade as "disciples of the encyclopaedia . . . Sade's *The 120 Days of Sodom* is nothing if it is not a gigantic catalogue; Tarantino's work is nothing if not an encyclopaedia of references to 1970s film culture" (Harper and Mendik 240). Roth also incorporates many references to previous horror films in his works, with Lorna's naked torturer referencing Elizabeth Bathory, a historical figure who has inspired characters in horror films such as *Countess Dracula* (Peter Sasdy 1971) and *Les lèvres rouges/Daughters of Darkness* (Harry Kumel 1971).

Outside Hollywood, other national cinemas have produced works of graphic violence, pushing the envelope even further than Hollywood allows. Since the late 1990s, France in particular has produced many films that employ graphic scenes, with several of these films grouped together into what has been termed The New French Extremity, headed by filmmakers such as Catherine Breillat and Gaspar Noé. There has also been an increase in the number of horror films being made, for example, *Haute tension/High Tension* (Alexandre Aja, 2003); *Ils/Them* (David Moreau and Xavier Palud, 2006); *Frontiére(s)/Frontier(s)* (Xavier Gens, 2007); *À l'intérieur/Inside* (Alexandre Bustillo and Julien Maury, 2007); and *Martyrs* (Pascal Laugier, 2008). The specific films cited here have become notorious for their incorporation of extreme representations of torture and sadism.

What is interesting about the rise in horror film production in France is that there is not a strong horror film tradition there (especially in comparison to other European countries, such as Italy or Great Britain). Although there are past examples, such as Georges Franju's *Les yeux sans visage/Eyes Without a Face* (1960), Roger Vadim's *Et mourir de plaisir/Blood and Roses* (1960), and the female vampire films of Jean Rollin, these films often employed a poetic and sensual approach to horror, quite different from the newer films, which are much dirtier and more graphic and extreme. Similar to other torture porn films, there are no supernatural elements in contemporary French horror; instead there is a focus on scenes involving prolonged torture perpetrated by French citizens. Going back to Georges Bataille's comment that Sade exposed how violence was inherent in all humanity, especially "civilized" humanity, torture porn films express this same idea. The torturers in these films are often pillars of the community who are using their place in society as a way to commit atrocities for their own selfish reasons.

Pascal Laugier's *Martyrs* is somewhat different from other examples of torture porn, as there is a total focus on the victim, Anna, with her torturers often partially obscured in the frame. In the second half of the film, Anna is imprisoned in an underground facility, where she is subjected to a series of almost unimaginable horrors in a succession of scenes that always open with a fade up from black, which serves to separate each act. The fades establish a rhythm and repetition, creating the feeling that Anna's suffering is never ending. Then following the fade up we see the next form of torture and physical degradation Anna must endure, such as vicious beatings, forced feeding, and head shaving. Anna has been kidnapped by well organized, and seemingly upper-class, members of a group who want to know the secrets of the afterlife by creating a "martyr," who will suffer so much that she will transcend her physical self. Although this group differs from Sade's libertines in that they do not inflict torture for sexual pleasure and have a belief in a higher plane, the clinical and methodical manner in which they carry out their plan is similar to the ordered experiments of Sade's characters. The members of the group obviously have no feeling for their victims, perceiving them solely as a means to reach their own aims.

This process of destroying Anna physically is the focus of the film's entire final act. As Hyland and Shorey point out, most torture porn films have a "vignette" structure like that of pornography, with the emphasis completely on depicting a series of explicit and graphic activities rather than developing plot and character. There is also the increase in explicitness and transgression, again similar to pornography, as Anna is told that there is a "final stage" that she must go through. She is taken into a room that looks like a surgery and fastened onto a metal frame. As with most of the scenes there are primarily close-ups, with one long shot showing the contraption flipping her over so she is facing the floor. Then it cuts back to a close-up of Anna's face, and we cannot see what is being done to her. The next scene does reveal it, however, as she is wheeled into her room with a bloodied sheet around her. The torturer then lifts her off the wheelchair and raises her to standing to show that, except for her face, all of Anna's skin has been removed. She has been flayed alive.

Compared to the scene of Lorna's murder in *Hostel: Part II*, where torture is presented as an elaborate visual spectacle, Anna's torture becomes repetitive, almost numbing. Much like in Sade's works, an excess of violence can produce an anaesthetizing effect. The outcome of this deadening of feeling, though, is the opening up of thought and contemplation of our own culpability and responsibility within the violent scenario. Considering Bataille's claim that Sade wrote in the "language of the victim," can the same be said for these cinematic images? Employing Sade to examine audience reception of violence in cinema, Mendik and Harper state that:

Sade's theories and experiments are paradigms of active rather than passive creation and reception. Here, the text's audience is both enticed into its celebrations of evil and perversity before being shocked, misled or violently forced to reflect on their gratifications from the narrative proceedings. (Mendik & Harper 238)

Just as Bataille claimed that Sade's works are written in the language of the victim, as it "refused to cheat" by not falling back on the language and excuses of the State, these images also confront the audience by seemingly revelling in and celebrating the acts of violence, but their extreme and graphic nature then serves to shock the spectator into reflecting on and analyzing their reactions. Violence is not presented as a "mistake"—it is presented as a desire that is within all of us.

The Marquis de Sade is a significant figure in the history of literature due to his exploration of how violence can be articulated in written language. Not only did he express how violence is an inherent part of humanity, he subverted forms of civilized behavior (language and art) to reveal the fundamental hypocrisies, inequalities, and perversions of organized, civilized society. Applying Sade to the analysis of violence in cinema similarly uncovers how graphic violence, expressed in scene after scene of prolonged torture, seeks to confront the viewer and invite them to contemplate their own place and responsibility in relation to such images and expressions of violence.

Works Cited

"A Brief History of Censorship in New Zealand." *Office of Film and Literature Classification*. newzealand.govt.nz, n.d. Web. 11 Feb. 2014.

Bataille, Georges. *Eroticism*. London: Penguin, 2001.

Clover, Carol J. *Men, Women and Chainsaws: Gender in the Modern Horror Film*. London: British Film Institute, 1992.

Deleuze, Gilles. *Coldness and Cruelty*. New York: Zone Books, 1989.

Frappier-Mazur, Lucienne. *Writing the Orgy: Power and Parody in Sade*. Philadelphia: U of Pennsylvania P, 1996.

Hyland, Jenn & Eric Shorey. "You Had Me at 'I'm Dead': Porn, Horror, and the Fragmented Body." *Transnational Horror Across Visual Media: Fragmented Nightmares*. Eds. Dana Och & Kirsten Strayer. New York: Routledge, 2014. 176–90.

Krafft-Ebing, Richard von. *Psychopathia Sexualis: The Case Histories*. London: Creation, 2001.

Le Brun, Annie. *Sade: A Sudden Abyss*. San Fransisco: City Light Books, 1990.

MacKendrick, Karmen. *Counterpleasures*. Albany: State U of New York P, 1999.

Mendik, Xavier, & Graeme Harper. "The Chaotic Text and the Sadean Audience: Narrative Transgressions of a Contemporary Cult Film." *Unruly Pleasures: The Cult Film and Its Critics*. Eds. Xavier Mendik & Graeme Harper. Surrey: FAB Press, 2000. 235–49.

Mulvey, Laura. *Visual and Other Pleasures*. Bloomington: Indiana UP, 1989.

Rüdiger. "Hostel: Part II". *Movie-Censorship.com*. 23 Oct. 2012. Web. 11 Feb. 2014.

Sade, Marquis de. *Justine, Philosophy in the Bedroom, and Other Writings*. Eds. Austryn Wainhouse & Richard Seaver. New York: Grove Press, 1965.

_____. *Juliette*. New York: Grove Press, 1968.

_____. *The 120 Days of Sodom and Other Writings*. Eds. Austryn Wainhouse & Richard Seaver. New York: Grove Press, 1987.

Welchman, Alistair. "Differential Practices." *Must We Burn Sade?* Ed. Deepak Narang Sawhney. Amherst: Humanity Books, 1999. 159–81.

Intimate Subject(ivitie)s: Race, Gender, and Violence in Toni Morrison's *Beloved*_____

Aretha Phiri

African Americanism and the Pain of Being Black

In an interview featured in *Time* Magazine in 1989, Toni Morrison argued that "black people have always been used as a buffer in this country . . . becoming an American is based on an attitude: an exclusion of me" (Angelo 255). As a pariah community, black national and cultural inclusivity has been consistently thwarted in a racialized and fundamentally racist America. More specifically, their subjectivity—that which asserts a legitimate sense of existential being and belonging and the means by which one affirms one's humanity or socio-politically/socio-culturally-recognized and participatory human self—has been continuously violated. Contrary to Jean-Paul Sartre's thesis in *Existentialism and Humanism* that "*existence* comes before *essence*" (26), in the black situation, *essence* has historically preceded *existence*; that is, the African American does not in fact "begin from the subjective" as Sartre asserts (26), because s/he has historically been subjected to an *a priori*, white process of de-subjectivity that precedes and negates black subjectivity. In that they inhabit a reality and specific contextual positionality that is incommensurate with universalized theories of subjectivity, Morrison has theorized the existential state of blacks in America as categorically grotesque: "quiet as it's kept much of our business, our existence here, has been grotesque . . . I don't mean as individuals but as a race" (Jones and Vinson 181).

In her fiction and in the allusion here to Wolfgang Kayser's model of the grotesque as the expression of the disorder and chaos that underlies life, Morrison implies this as a condition germane to the subjective history of African Americans, a situation demonstrated in the arrival of the first black slaves to the state of Virginia in 1617. Physically different and differentiated from white Americans, Winthrop D. Jordan notes that the "the 'Negro's' color attained greatest significance not as a scientific problem but as a social fact" (20), so that, as Reginald Horsman explains, Americans proceeded legally and customarily as though blacks were "essentially different" (102). Through a simple racist syllogism, the white mind concluded that all blacks were "degraded and contemptible" (Elkins 61).

Orlando Patterson maintains that because the slave had no socially recognized existence outside of his white master, slavery was concomitant with social death. The slave was a "nonperson" who "ceased to belong in his own right to any legitimate social order" (Patternson 5). The obvious and sinister violence of slavery meant that the slave lived "on the margins between community and chaos, life and death" (Patterson 51), in a liminal, in-between existence. It is instructive, then, that the American Constitution, which ruled African Americans "three fifths of all other Persons" was incompatible with the 1776 Declaration of Independence, which states that "all men are created equal and independent; that from that equal creation they derive rights inherent and inalienable."

In fact, V.G. Kiernan maintains that independence ironically reinvigorated thoughts on race and racial inequality, with the result that America "now became 'a consciously racist society'" (24). This was premised, Thomas F. Gossett observes, on the Darwinian principle of "a struggle among races" (174–75). In this respect, the Fugitive Slave Act of 1850, which made it illegal for anti-slavery supporters to aid runaway slaves, is revelatory as an expedient compromise between North and South in the attempt to head off the secession that led to the Civil War from 1861–1865. Tellingly, after the Emancipation Proclamation of 1863, black Americans were actually subjected to increased and more overt forms of racism. The "Black Codes," designed to curtail the rights of newly liberated slaves, were instituted in the South immediately after the War. The Reconstruction period from 1865–1877—characterized by institutionalized violence against blacks and legalized, "Jim Crow" segregation—constituted the "most elaborate and formal expression of sovereign white opinion," in which the African American "was made painfully and constantly aware that he lived in a society

dedicated to the doctrine of white supremacy and Negro inferiority"
(Vann Woodward 7, 17–18).

Toni Morrison: Re-Imagining Blackness

As a result of a historically imposed invidious group identity,
African Americans ironically became an "inescapable part of the
general social fabric" (Baldwin 125), a symbolically "easy and
reliable gauge for determining to what extent one was or was not
American" (Ellison 583). Indeed, in *Playing in the Dark: Whiteness
and the Literary Imagination*, Morrison notes that black Americans
have been fundamentally offered up as "surrogate selves for
meditation on problems of human freedom" (37–38). Her observation
intimates her own literary endeavor of ripping apart "that veil drawn
over 'over proceedings too terrible to relate'" (Morrison, "The Site
of Memory" 70) about the unspoken trauma of African American
existence. Her analysis of whiteness as a sinister, violent ideology
with persistent psychosocial/cultural repercussions for blacks
extends and challenges the limited tradition of slave narratives.
Premised on her belief that "the reclamation of the history of black
people in this country is paramount in its importance . . . and the
job of recovery is ours" (Davis 413), Morrison's assertion in her
fiction of black visibility (and voice) is rooted in her conviction in a
meaningful and viable black subjectivity.

In her 1989 essay, "Unspeakable things Unspoken," Morrison
asserts that "[i]t is no longer acceptable merely to imagine us and
imagine for us. We have always been imagining ourselves . . . . We
are the subjects of our own narrative, witnesses to and participants
in our own experience" (9). Some critics have consequently read
into her work racial militancy and cultural essentialism, so much
so, Betty Fussell notes, that many "accuse her of a racist agenda
that interferes with both scholarship and art" (295). Yet Morrison's
delineation and politicization of the African American experience
is not to be read as merely oppositional, but as an attempt to pursue
subjective and narrative possibilities not previously realized in
fiction (Peach 2). In an interview with Bill Moyers, she explains
that her fiction attempts to fill in the "extraordinary gaps and

evasions and destabilizations" that typify the narrow, stereotypical representations of African Americans (264).

Still, while she is concerned with examining the African American experience and exposing the systemic violence of white America, a kind of crisis of representation is played out and underpins in her fiction the tenuous processes of (black) subjectivity, evidenced in the fact that whiteness is often complexly mirrored in black subjectivity. Morrison's reference to black existence as "grotesque" is thus not limited to white violent racism, but includes black violence and highlights the problematics of achieving (autonomous) black subjectivity. In her fiction, violence is constitutive of ánd embodies the subjective process; that is, in considering how "the felt interior experience of the person that includes his or her positions in a field of relational power—is produced through the experience of violence" (Das and Kleinman 1), Morrison's novels propose that violence and subjectivity are mutually implicated in a lived, material, rather than abstract, theoretical paradigm of existence.

This chapter is concerned with the violation and violence of African American subjectivity, particularly that of the black female. *Beloved* reveals intricate and intimate links between violence, race and gender. In this novel, the poverty—the physical and psychosocial/cultural violation and disempowerment—of black subjectivity is figured as a consequence of metonymic, structural rape by white America, which in turn manifests in gendered violence in the community. That is, while whiteness is highlighted as an aggressive institution and ideology that works to dispossess African Americans, it does not nullify black complicity in perpetuating violence. With violence seemingly pervasive, *Beloved* unveils (the potential for and attempt at) black subjectivity as an inevitably dialectical and incongruous process that situates the mechanisms of subjectivity itself within a volatile, but profoundly experiential, lived paradigm.

"Unspeakable Things Unspoken": Slavery in *Beloved*
Published in 1987 and earning her the Pulitzer Prize for fiction, *Beloved* is indubitably Morrison's most critically read novel. Ironically, because of its sensitive subject matter—the horror of

African American slavery—Morrison assumed it would be the least read of all her work. Indeed, the novel was removed from a senior advanced placement English course at Louisville, Kentucky's Eastern High School in 2008 after parents complained about its difficult content, and in 2012, it was challenged but retained in Salem (MI) High School's advanced placement English. According to the American Literature Association (ALA), *Beloved* ranks seventh on the list of the top one hundred novels that have most often been the target of censorship.

To Bonnie Angelo, Morrison explains public anxiety about slavery as rooted in "national amnesia": it is "about something that the characters don't want to remember, I don't want to remember, white people won't want to remember" (Morrison, "Unspeakable Things" 257). Lonnie Bunch, director of the Smithsonian's National Museum of African American History and Culture, concurs. In a discussion of Steve McQueen's 2013 cinematic rendition of Solomon Northup's *Twelve Years a Slave*, the autobiography of a free black man kidnapped into slavery in the 1800s, Bunch maintains that "slavery is still in many ways the last great unmentionable in public discourse. It today is seen as an exotic story, something that ended a long time ago and is an example of the progressive nature of America—we were once bad, but now we are good" (Bunch 45). In spite of talk of a post-racial society initiated by the inauguration in 2008 of America's first African American president, Barak Obama, Morrison evokes history as a living, violent memory—"rememory"—in her novel; that is, she dispels the exoticism of slavery by suggesting the inextricably constitutive role violent (slave) history plays in (modern) identity formation, thus making, or "re-membering" the "historical past a part of our own experience" (Michaels 6).

Beloved's effectiveness is evidenced the varied critical responses it garnered in the year of its publication. Ann Snitow in *The Village Voice Literary Supplement* largely discredited the novel as melodramatic, and Stanley Crouch's *New Republic* review proclaimed it "a blackface holocaust novel [which] seems to have been written in order to enter American slavery into the big-time martyr ratings contest." Margaret Atwood in the *New York Times*, however, pronounced *Beloved* "a hair-raising triumph," and A. S. Byatt, in *The Guardian*, described it a "generous, humane and gripping novel." Morrison explains that the novel "was not about the institution—Slavery with a capital S. It was about these anonymous people called slaves" Angelo 257), evinced in the novel's dedication to an estimated "sixty million and more" who suffered the trauma of slavery, and in its biblical epigraph, which reads, "I will call them my people, / which were not my people; / and her beloved, / which was not beloved." Unveiling the subjects of an historical epoch frequently reduced to rhetorical abstraction and specifically highlighting the violation and violence towards African American women, *Beloved* bespeaks Morrison's narrative burden and concern: illuminating race as a troublesome, violent fixture that continues to haunt the (African-) American psyche and socio-political existence.

Grotesque Subjectivity: Freedom, Responsibility, and Women's Place in *Beloved*

Set in 1873, during the Reconstruction period, *Beloved* revisits and reworks the documented story of Margaret Garner, an escaped slave who, when caught, attempted to kill her own children rather than see them returned to an institution that denied black humanity. The "red ribbon knotted around a curl of wet woolly hair, clinging still to its bit of scalp" (Morrison, *Beloved* 213) encountered by Stamp Paid on the Ohio River tellingly alludes to the violence of whiteness. In that there "was no bad luck in the world but whitepeople" (Morrison, *Beloved* 123), the existential "jungle" (Morrison, *Beloved* 234) that black people are perceived to inhabit is subverted; Morrison posits whiteness itself as terror, revealing slavery as a haunting, gothic mode of existence for black people and stressing the grotesquery of the experience through the specific lens of the African American female slave. As that which underscores the chaos of life, Morrison's use of the grotesque here extends and simultaneously problematizes the conventional theme of female innocence by articulating the unimaginably and incomprehensibly murky terrain of black womanhood.

In the unintelligible mutterings and "roaring" (Morrison, *Beloved* 213) of the women housed in *Beloved*'s personified 124 Bluestone Road is the vocalization of a legacy of violated innocence, "of the broken necks, of fire-cooked blood and black girls who had lost their ribbons" (Morrison, *Beloved* 213). The women here have a "speech" that, as Stamp Paid witnesses, "wasn't nonsensical, exactly, nor was it tongues," but pronounces the "interior sounds," the "eternal, private conversation that takes place between women and their tasks" (Morrison, *Beloved* 202–3). In privileging female interiority and articulating generational black female violation, the novel intimates the possibility of "feminine" language in response to racial and gendered violation. But where female slaves are raped as a matter of course, disallowed familial relations, separated from their children/mothers and treated like animals, the novel centralizes the socially grotesque and unspeakable—women's own violence—to explore the grotesquery, that is, incongruous character, of black female subjectivity. *Beloved* contemplates female violence as both an affirmation of and struggle against the "nonsensical" conditions of their existence. Here, the protagonist Sethe's infanticide ironically, but ultimately, embodies violence as a woman's "task," an unenviable but inevitable responsive undertaking that attempts to restore subjective dignity. In this way, the novel compels meditations on the inextricability of violence in the articulation and assertion of a limited black female subjectivity.

Womanhood in/as Slavery: Black Female Violation and Violence

Contemporary feminist theory maintains that woman has pervaded Western thought as "devalued difference" (Braidotti 64) and that motherhood as an institution has "ghettoized and degraded female potentialities" (Rich 13). Womanhood and motherhood are seen as enforced identities that reinforce and reproduce the socio-political parameters of patriarchy. While this is historically true of white women, it also reveals the way in which whiteness pervades and is unquestionably viewed as constitutive of all female subjectivity. Black women have typically been exploited by and excluded from dominant codes of female subjectivity. This is historically acknowledged in the nineteenth-century "cult of true womanhood" which, dramatized in Harriet Beecher Stowe's *Uncle Tom's Cabin* (1852), is interrogated in Harriet Jacob's autobiographical *Incidents in the Life of a Slave Girl* (1861), a novel in which conventional mores of sexual and moral purity are unveiled as incompatible with black women's lived experience. Both biological "right" and enforced identity, black womanhood/motherhood bespeaks an "impossible contradiction" under slavery (Keenan 60–1) and emerges in a grotesque void, suspended between existential absence and presence, between being and not being.

Ann DuCille notes that "[w]here gender and racial differences meet in the bodies of black women, the result is the invention of an other Otherness, a hyperstatic alterity" (22) that testifies to the unconventional, even abnormal, character of black female subjectivity. Morrison has thus maintained that black women are fundamentally different from white women. Insisting that black women consistently "defied classification" ("What the Black Woman Thinks" 18) by virtue of their varied and often extreme lived experiences, she asserts elsewhere that black women bear and are on "the cross" of existence (Stepto 384) and occupy a "special place in this culture" (Koenen 72) premised on an incongruous, fragile subjectivity. In *Beloved* the "nastiness of life" is the tension between losing a child to slavery and being consistently raped by "the lowest yet" (Morrison, *Beloved* 301), and Sethe's violence against the institution of slavery is key to unlocking and (physically) enunciating this subjective and moral void. In a context in which subjectivity is characterized by violation and violence, infanticide is presented as both an extreme form of resistance and as an ultimate mode of mothering.

Significantly, Sethe's infanticide is precipitated and underpinned by an act of maternal violation, in which she is forcibly milked by Schoolteacher's nephews. Having herself been denied her mother's milk as a child, she describes their action as "theft" (20–1), a crime against her maternal, subjective autonomy. As an act that is concomitant with rape, it is also a "perversion of the primal scene," which lays bare white "impulse to reject black subjectivity in order to eradicate the black roots of the white imaginary" (Moglen 208). The white men's violence against Sethe's sense of self underscores their and Schoolteacher's sense of her as a social "nonperson," of her existential liminality—somewhere between human and animal (Morrison, *Beloved* 228). But her explanation to Paul D of the significance of her milk to her "baby girl" realigns her maternally with the subjective: "Nobody was going to nurse her like me . . . nobody had her milk but me" (Morrison, *Beloved* 19). As a metaphor for "nonspeech, of a 'semiotics' that linguistic communication does not account for" (Kristeva 312), Sethe's milk, which Denver later drinks "right along with the blood of her sister" (Morrison, *Beloved* 179) when she is killed, signifies a cultural, intergenerational subjectivity premised on responsibility for the other. Thus, while the repetitive emphasis on "nobody" in her explanation suggests, as her whipping by Schoolteacher attests, slavery's disavowal of subjectivity, it also indicates that Sethe's (sense of and opportunity for) subjectivity lies in her very corporeality. In claiming her physical right to motherhood, Sethe arrives at freedom and a place of desire—"where you could love anything you chose" (Morrison, *Beloved* 191). On seeing Schoolteacher approach to take her children, Sethe "just flew. Collected every bit of life she had made, all the parts of her that were precious and fine and beautiful, and carried, pushed, dragged them through the veil, out, away, over there, where no one could hurt them" (Morrison, *Beloved* 192). Traversing the life-and-death veil of slavery she purposively cuts her daughter's throat and enacts a "democratic violence" (Rapport 53) that, expanding Baby Suggs' gospel of "[f]lesh that needs to be loved" (Morrison, *Beloved* 104), is rooted in both self- and mother-love and levels the negating structure of slavery by itself negating white racist negation.

This violent repossession, the physical countering and reclaiming of historical dispossession, proposes a corporeal discourse in which Sethe's brutal action can be read as a "narrative of self" that "enables the projection of desire and intention" (Worthington 13) in and beyond the present moment of slavery. In a world in which linguistic and existential "definitions belonged to the definers—not

---

144   Critical Insights

the defined" (Morrison, *Beloved* 225), Naomi Mandel concurs that it is "Sethe's *act*, rather than anything else she can *say*, that disrupts the discourse that authorized the power balance between herself and Schoolteacher" (189). The performative efficiency of the act simultaneously annuls and enunciates, that is, "gives body" to the trauma of slavery. In this regard, the gaps in Sethe's explanatory narrative bear witness to the inability of language to re-present her violent past reality and the ways in which it consequently violates or unmakes the self or the subjective enterprise. Described as "spinning . . . . Circling, circling, now she was gnawing something else instead of getting to the point" (Morrison, *Beloved* 189), she could "never close in, pin it down for anybody who had to ask. If they didn't get it right off—she could never explain" (Morrison, *Beloved* 192). Kristin Boudreau here notes that Sethe's "momentary attempts to recuperate a violent past for the sake of transcendence are met with the implied accusation that such interpretive gestures occlude the moment of slavery" (454). As with the circuitous narrative technique of temporally segueing from present to past and between different narrative perspectives, *Beloved* emphasizes how slavery and the maternal project therein defy narrative articulation/coherency and engender, instead, the hysteria of history—the subversive rather than pathological expression of that which is repressed.

Kalí Tal maintains that bearing witness is "an aggressive act" born out of a "refusal to bow to outside pressure to revise or to repress experience" (7), and Shoshana Felman and Dori Laub suggest that, in testifying, it is language that is "in process and in trial" because to testify is to "accomplish a *speech act*, rather than to simply formulate a statement" (5). *Beloved* and Sethe's act function similarly because they are experiential rather than referential— vivid testimonies to and survivalist resurrections of the violence of slavery. That is, the novel and her act of violence do not present a conclusive statement of fact but engender the lived, inexplicable reality of slavery's trauma as "*not* directly available to experience" (Caruth 61). In her foreword to the novel, Morrison maintains that "[t]o render enslavement a personal experience language must get out the way" (*Beloved* xiii). In a further attempt to give body to the phenomenological, Morrison has Beloved, Sethe's slaughtered baby girl, return in palpable, bodily form in which actual flesh functions as a narrative bridge. In the appropriation of the text by her living body, Beloved permits "*history* to arise where *immediate understanding* may not" (Caruth 11) and articulates the peculiarity of slavery. Her disturbing corporeality, as Mandel highlights, "forces materiality back into language—a materiality that the unspeakable deliberately works to exclude—and challenges the assumption that that which is excluded from 'speech' is excluded from the world in which speech functions" (28–9). Not unlike Sethe's infanticide, Beloved's bodily form becomes the ground for political (black, female) self-placement, effectively embodying, in her terrorizing of her mother and the community, the subjective horror of slavery and pronouncing it a hauntingly historical presence.

Ambiguous Freedom, Rough Choices

Sartre posits that because we are *a priori* free beings, we "are unable ever to choose the worse [but] always the better" (*Existentialism and Humanism* 29). But as Patterson asserts and as Morrison's novel shows, slavery as social death or non-being problematizes and negates the opportunity for moral choice. Frederick Nietzsche has argued for the historicization and contextualization, rather than naturalization or normalization, of morality, and in *Beloved*, where "anybody white" could "[d]irty you so bad you couldn't like yourself anymore" (Morrison, *Beloved* 295), Sethe's is a "rough choice" that parallels her incongruous existential condition (Morrison, *Beloved* 212). Her ambivalent idea of "safety with a handsaw" (Morrison, *Beloved* 193) invokes a "too thick" (Morrison, *Beloved* 192) love, which is, like Baby Suggs' ostentatious generosity, read by the community as "reckless" (Morrison, *Beloved* 162), irresponsible to the survivalist, communal cultural narrative that underpins African American subjectivity. To Moyers, Morrison herself states that Sethe's infanticide "was the right thing to do but she had no right to do it" (272), and her violence is criminal because it carries "the paradoxical qualities of an existential victory and moral offense" (Otten 83). Her violent act is both transgressive and regressive, and she becomes, as Raphael Perez-Torres observes, "subject to the tyranny of history" (191), a position underscored by the macabre scene that Schoolteacher and his men encounter when they arrive to capture Sethe: "a nigger woman holding a blood-soaked child to her chest with one hand and an infant by the heels in the other" (Morrison, *Beloved* 175).

The twin imagery of Sethe as a bird, which initially elicits the notion of maternal nurturance and protection and registers as a metaphor for a kind of transcendental existential freedom, thus assumes a sinister tenor grounded in the excessive, material reality of slavery and Sethe's actions. The hummingbirds sticking "their needle beaks right through her headcloth and into her hair and beat their wings" (Morrison, *Beloved* 192) signal a frenzied yet fragile, violent subjectivity, while the ominous hawk inverts the idealized (psychoanalytic) maternal image of the "Great Mother" (Eckard 34). Sethe's maternal violence becomes indicative of "arrested development" (Wyatt 130) because it memorializes an original, originary violence and violation. Her version of motherhood, rooted in racism and realized in violence, is excessive in that it paradoxically undermines her own humanity and exceeds the individual and communal attempt at subjectivity. In violating her self and the other's sense of self, Sethe effectively disrupts the African American subjective enterprise premised on mutual reverence for the historically denied self. That this is a morbid existential condition is suggested in Beloved's metaphoric cannibalism, in which—in her attempt to make Sethe "pay" for her own subjective loss—she "ate up her life, took it, swelled up with it, grew taller on it. And the older woman yielded it up without a murmur" (Morrison, *Beloved* 295). In Sethe claiming and "yielding" her self, she becomes, by grotesque inversion, a "slave by choice" (Morrison, *A Mercy* 139).

Sethe's violence repeats the self-violating premise of slavery and threatens to erode a communal narrative of survival invoked in the novel generally and by Baby Suggs in the Clearing in particular. In the tension between individual and communal subjectivity, Morrison gestures at an intersubjective space—a space for self within community—characterized by a communicative, relational interdependency, in which the individual female "self" "lies in blackness" (Rigney 38). This is evidenced in the fact that Sethe is saved by the very community of women that initially rejects her. Their communal hollering—a "song" of individuated suffering and survival—signals the community as a powerful "psycho-political" resource (Kella 24) and articulates a pre-discursive, pre-symbolic genesis that is, at the same time, future-oriented: "In the beginning there were no words. In the beginning was the sound, and they all knew what that sound sounded like" (Morrison, *Beloved* 305). In preceding their horrific, violent existence, they go beyond it to envisage what Paul D calls "some kind of tomorrow" (Morrison, *Beloved* 322), a future subjectivity dramatized in Sethe's rejuvenating "baptism" (Morrison, *Beloved* 308) and in her redirected violence against the original (white) violence, symbolized by Mr. Bodwin.

Conclusion: "Not a story to pass on"
While this suggests an "attempt to combine hope and development" (Raphael-Hernandez 15), the refrain at the novel's end— "It was not a story to pass on" (Morrison, *Beloved* 323)—warns against and undercuts a concrete utopian vision of blackness. The refrain ambivalently suggests that, although the violence to and of African American female existence is not a narrative to be ignored for risk of repetition, it is also not a narrative to be continuously dwelled upon for similar risk of repetition. Morrison's narrative ambiguity suggests that she recognizes black female subjectivity as rooted in the experiential fragility of a violent, lived existence, not in an anesthetized, abstract ideal. Tellingly, in the end, Beloved's "footprints come and go" as she becomes "[d]isremembered and unaccounted for" (Morrison, *Beloved* 324). While necessarily disruptive of and providing significant intervention in conventional meditations on African American (subjective) violence, Morrison's novel finally re-registers a place of absence, a persistent subjective vacuum and space of unbelonging and testifies to its own inability to recuperate a black female subjectivity that exceeds the violence of race and gender.

Works Cited

Angelo, Bonnie. "The Pain of Being Black: An Interview with Toni Morrison." *Time*. 22 May 1989. Web. 10 May 2009.

Atwood, Margaret. "Jaunted by their Nightmares." *New York Times*. 13 Sep 1987. Web. 24 Sept. 2013.

Baldwin, James. *Collected Essays*. New York: Library of America, 1998.

Boudreau, Kristin. "Pain and the Unmaking of Self in Toni Morrison's *Beloved*." *Contemporary Literature* 36.3 (1995): 447–65.

Braidotti, Rosi. "Mothers, Monsters, and Machines." *Writing on the Body: Female Embodiment and Feminist Theory*. Eds. Katie Conboy, Nadia Medina, & Sarah Stanbury. New York: Columbia UP, 1997. 59–79.

Bunch, Lonnie. "Family's Anger Over Their Slave History as Film Shocks Audiences." *The Times* 12 Oct. 2013: 45.

Byatt, A. S. "An American Masterpiece." *The Guardian* 16 Oct 1987. Web. 24 Sept. 2013.

Caruth, Cathy. *Unclaimed Experience: Trauma, Narrative, and History*. Baltimore, MA: Johns Hopkins UP, 1996.

Crouch, Stanley. "Aunt Medea." *New Republic* 19 Oct. 1987: 38–43.

Das, Veena, Arthur Kleinman, Mamphela Ramphele & Pamela Reynolds, eds. *Violence and Subjectivity*. Berkeley & Los Angeles, CA: U of California P, 2000.

Davis, Christina. "An Interview with Toni Morrison." *Toni Morrison: Critical Perspectives Past and Present*. Eds. Henry Louis Gates, Jr. & Anthony K. Appiah. New York: Amistad, 1993. 412–20.

DuCille, Ann. "The Occult of True Black Womanhood: Critical Demeanor and Black Feminist Studies." *Female Subjects in Black and White: Race, Psychoanalysis, Feminism*. Eds. Elizabeth Abel, Barbara Christian, & Helene Moglen. Berkeley, CA: U of California P, 1997. 21–56.

Durrant, Sam. *Postcolonial Narrative and the Work of Mourning: J.M. Coetzee, Wilson Harris, and Toni Morrison*. Albany: State U of New York P, 2004.

Eckard, Paula Gallant. *Maternal Body and Voice in Toni Morrison, Bobbie Ann Mason, and Lee Smith*. Columbia: U of Missouri P, 2002.

Ellison, Ralph. *The Collected Essays of Ralph Ellison*. Ed. John F. Callahan. New York: Modern Library, 1994.

Elkins, Stanley M. *Slavery: A Problem in American Institutional and Intellectual Life.* 2nd ed. Chicago, IL: Chicago UP, 1964.

Felman, Shoshana, & Dori Laub. *Testimony: Crises in Witnessing, Psychoanalysis, and History.* New York: Routledge, 1992.

Fussell, Betty. "All That Jazz." *Conversations with Toni Morrison.* Ed. Danille Taylor-Guthrie. Jackson, Mississippi: UP of Mississippi, 1994. 280–87.

Gossett, Thomas F. *Race: The History of an American Idea.* New Ed. New York: Oxford UP, 1997.

Horsman, Reginald. *Race and Manifest Destiny: The Origins of American Racial Anglo-Saxonism.* Cambridge, MA: Harvard UP, 1981.

Jacobs, Harriet. *Incidents in the Life of a Slave Girl.* Eds. Nellie Y. McKay & Frances Smith Foster. New York: Norton, 2001.

Jones, Bessie W., & Audrey Vinson. "An Interview with Toni Morrison." *Conversations with Toni Morrison.* Ed. Danille Taylor-Guthrie. Jackson, MI: UP of Mississippi, 1994. 171–86.

Jordan, Winthrop D. *White over Black: American Attitudes Toward the Negro, 1550–1812.* New York: Norton, 1977.

Kayser, Wolfgang. *The Grotesque in Art and Literature.* Trans. Ulrich Weisstein. Bloomington: Indiana UP, 1963.

Keenan, Sally. "Four Hundred Years of Silence: Myth, History, and Motherhood in Toni Morrison's *Beloved.*" *Recasting the World: Writing After Colonialism.* London: Johns Hopkins UP, 1993.

Kella, Elizabeth. *Beloved Communities: Solidarity and Difference in Fiction by Michael Ondaatjie, Toni Morrison, and Joy Kogawa.* Sweden: Uppsala, 2000.

Kiernan, V.G. *America: The New Imperialism: From White Settlement to World Hegemony.* Westport, CT: Zed, 1980.

Koenen, Anne. "The One Out of Sequence." *Conversations with Toni Morrison.* Ed. Danille Taylor-Guthrie. Jackson, MI: UP of Mississippi, 1994. 67–82.

Kristeva, Julia. "Stabat Mater." *Feminist Social Thought: A Reader.* Ed. Diana Teitjens Meyers. New York: Routledge, 1997. 302–19.

Mandel, Naomi. *Against the Unspeakable: Complicity, the Holocaust and Slavery in America.* Charlottesville, Virginia: U of Virginia P, 2001.

Michaels, Walter Benn. "'You Who Was Never There': Slavery and the New Historicism, Deconstruction and the Holocaust." *Narrative* 4.1 (1996): 1–16.

Moglen, Helene. "Redeeming History: Toni Morrison's *Beloved.*" *Female Subjects in Black and White: Race, Psychoanalysis, Feminism.* Eds. Elizabeth Abel, Barbara Christian, & Helene Moglen. Berkeley, CA: U of California, 1997. 201–20.

Morrison, Toni. "Unspeakable Things Unspoken: The Afro-American Presence in American Literature." *Michigan Quarterly Review* 28.1 (1989): 1–34.

_____. *Playing in the Dark: Whiteness and the Literary Imagination.* London: Pan, 1992.

_____. *Beloved.* London: Vintage, 2005.

_____. *A Mercy.* London: Chatto, 2008.

_____. "What the Black Woman Thinks about Women's Lib." *What Moves at the Margins: Selected Nonfiction.* Ed. Carolyn Denard. Mississippi: UP of Mississippi, 2008. 18–30.

_____. "The Site of Memory." *What Moves at the Margins: Selected Nonfiction.* Ed. Carolyn Denard. Mississippi: UP of Mississippi, 2008. 65–80.

Moyers, Bill. "A Conversation with Toni Morrison." *Conversations with Toni Morrison.* Ed. Danille Taylor-Guthrie. Jackson, Mississippi: UP of Mississippi, 1994. 262–74.

Nietzsche, Frederick. *On the Genealogy of Morals.* Trans. Walter Kaufmann & R. J. Hollingdale. New York: Vintage, 1989.

Otten, Terry. *The Crime of Innocence in the Fiction of Toni Morrison.* Columbia, MI: U of Missouri P, 1989.

Patterson, Orlando. *Slavery and the Social Death: A Comparative Study.* Cambridge, Massachusetts: Harvard UP, 1982.

Peach, Linden. *Toni Morrison.* Basingstoke: Macmillan, 1995.

Perez-Torres, Rafael. "Between Presence and Absence: *Beloved*, Postmodernism, and Blackness." *Toni Morrison's Beloved: A Casebook.* Eds. William L. Andrews & Nellie Y. McKay. New York: Oxford UP, 1999. 179–201.

Raphael-Hernandez, Heike. *The Utopian Aesthetics of Three African American Women: Toni Morrison, Gloria Naylor, Julie Dash: The Principle of Hope*. Lewiston, NY: Edwin Mellon P, 2008.

Rapport, Nigel. "'Criminals by Instinct': On the 'Tragedy' of Social Structure and the 'Violence' of Individual Creativity." *Meanings of Violence: A Cross Cultural Perspective*. Eds. Aijmer, Goran & John Abbink. Oxford: Berg, 2000. 39–54.

Rich, Adrienne. *Of Woman Born: Motherhood as Experience and Institution*. London: Virago, 1995.

Rigney, Barbara Hill. *The Voices of Toni Morrison*. Columbus, OH: Ohio State UP, 1991.

Rody, Caroline. "Toni Morrison's *Beloved*: History, 'Rememory,' and a 'Clamor for a Kiss'." *American Literary History* 7.1 (1995): 92–119.

Sartre, Jean-Paul. *Existentialism and Humanism*. Trans & Intro. Philip Mairet. Methuen: London, 1973.

Snitow, Ann. "Beloved." *Toni Morrison: Critical Perspectives Past and Present*. Eds. Henry Louis Gates, Jr. & Anthony K. Appiah. New York: Amistad, 1993. 26–32.

Stepto, Robert B. "'Intimate Things in Place': A Conversation with Toni Morrison." *Toni Morrison: Critical Perspectives Past and Present*. Eds. Henry Louis Gates, Jr. & Kwame A. Appiah. New York: Amistad, 1993. 378–95.

Tal, Kalí. *Worlds of Hurt: Reading the Literatures of Trauma*. Cambridge, MA: Cambridge UP, 1996.

Tate, Claudia. "Toni Morrison." *Conversations with Toni Morrison*. Ed. Danille Taylor-Guthrie. Jackson, MI: UP of Mississippi, 1994. 156–70.

Vann Woodward, C. *The Strange Career of Jim Crow*. 3rd ed. New York: Oxford UP, 1974.

Worthington, Kim L. *Self as Narrative: Subjectivity and Community in Contemporary Fiction*. Oxford: Clarendon P, 1996.

Wyatt, Jean. "Failed Messages, Maternal Loss, and Narrative Form in Toni Morrison's *A Mercy*." *Modern Fiction Studies* 58.1 (2012): 128–51.

Excess, (Ir)rationality, and Consumerism: Violence in *No Country for Old Men* and *Fight Club*

James R. Giles

In a 2008 study, Slavoj Žižek discusses three categories of violence, two of which shed light on novels by Cormac McCarthy and Chuck Palahniuk. Žižek's "subjective" violence "includes what people ordinarily mean when they speak of violence—acts of crime and terror, civil unrest, [and] international conflict," while he defines "systemic" violence as the "often catastrophic consequences of the smooth functioning of our economic and political systems" (1–2). Virtually from the beginning, acts of criminal violence dominate McCarthy's *No Country for Old Men* (2005), which evolves, in part, into an exploration of the essential nature and historic presence of violence. Excess and irrationality are usually defining characteristics of violence and are overwhelmingly so in McCarthy's text. In fact, violence is so pervasive and irrational in *No Country for Old Men* that the novel often walks a fine line between reality and unreality. A secret club devoted to violent physical confrontation between consenting males is the central narrative link in Palahniuk's *Fight Club*, which at least on the surface, climaxes in a terroristic attack on American capitalism. In terms of plot, then, both novels are dominated by variations of Žižek's concept of "subjective" violence.

On a more thematic level, both explore variations on Žižek's concept of "systemic" violence. Žižek's argument concerning the "catastrophic" violence resulting from the "smooth functioning" of dominant "economic and political systems" references the regular and ongoing suffering experienced by those at the bottom of, and thus victimized by, such systems. In neither *No Country for Old Men* nor *Fight Club* does the dominant capitalistic system function smoothly. McCarthy's novel takes place in a shadowy realm in which established, "respectable" capitalism has entered into an unacknowledged alliance with savage criminality. In this nightmare world, only the most extreme perpetrators of violence can exercise control. The unnamed protagonist of *Fight Club,* at least in his subconscious, discovers an alternate culture devoted to an initially petty, then increasingly violent, revolt against the corrupt consumerist culture that employs him.

In neither text are the victims of "systemic" violence limited to the lower levels of a dominant economic system. In *No Country for Old Men,* a vicious and unchecked drug war originating in rural west Texas quickly permeates the entire state, destroying virtually anyone who gets caught up in it, intentionally or not. *Fight Club*'s narrator is employed by an automobile company to determine the probable economic consequences of mass recalls of defective cars. He is ordered to work from a formula that makes actually issuing recalls virtually impossible; and, as a result, accidents, sometimes deadly, frequently occur. He is haunted by his complicity in the carnage that results from the car company's cynicism and greed: "Everywhere I go, there's the burned-up wadded-up shell of a car waiting for me. I know where the skeletons are. Consider this my job security" (Palahniuk 31). His reference to "the skeletons" constitutes a grim pun that reflects his awareness of his responsibility in perpetuating a corrupt system. By depicting cynical and illicit perversions of dominant capitalistic systems that, rather than functioning smoothly, destroy individuals at random, *No Country for Old Men* and *Fight Club* extend and enhance Žižek's concept of systemic violence.

While commodification is an important thematic concern of both *Fight Club* and *No Country for Old Men,* it is—because of the contrasting nature of the narrative formats in the two texts—more overtly so in McCarthy's novel. The automobile, the controlling commodity in Palahniuk's novel, could hardly be a more iconic representation of American capitalism. But the corporation's cynical policy toward recalls corrupts it into a deadly weapon, and the narrator's guilt over his participation in the policy contributes to the destruction of his grasp on reality itself. *Fight Club*'s condemnation of corrupt capitalism does, in more than one passage, extend to an indictment of international corporate capitalism, but the novel's real focus is on the deterioration of the narrator's mental stability and his retreat into a fantasy world that shatters his grasp of reality and physically disfigures him. Ultimately, *Fight Club* falls more clearly into the category of the psychological novel than into that of realistic protest.[1] If not precisely a protest, *No Country for Old Men*'s emphasis is upon depicting, in graphic detail, the battleground of the American drug culture. While, at times, violent excess pushes the novel toward a dimension of unreality, its narrative focus, as more than one critic has pointed out, echoes genre fiction, especially the hard-boiled detective novels of Dashiell Hammett and Raymond Chandler. McCarthy explores the subconscious of only one of the novel's three central characters and then primarily in its concluding pages. Illicit, but covertly sanctioned, drugs, the central commodity in *No Country for Old Men*, are pervasive in the landscape of McCarthy's novel, unfailingly bringing violence in their wake.

Despite major differences in focus and narrative mode in Palahniuk's and McCarthy's texts, they employ a parallel narrative device. In each, a pair of personas embody contrasting responses to violence; and their interactions—in one case, indirect and in the other, direct, but ultimately imagined—result in a dialectical exploration of the origins, effects, and essential nature of violence. Georges Bataille's theory of "mankind's double nature" is relevant to these explorations. Bataille writes that:

> One cannot fail to observe mankind's double nature throughout his career. There are two extremes. At one end, existence is basically orderly and decent. Work, concern for the children, kindness and honesty rule men's dealings with their fellows. At the other, violence rages pitilessly. In certain circumstances the same men practice pillage and arson, murder, violence and torture. Excess contrasts with reason. (186)

No Country for Old Men and *Fight Club* depict landscapes, both external and internal, in which Bataille's "extreme" of the "basically orderly and decent" is either in the process of collapsing or has already collapsed. In each, the "excess" of violence overwhelms reason, as the protective barriers of "work, concern for the children, kindness and honesty" are negated. Both texts treat the collapse as a contemporary American phenomenon, though *No Country for Old Men* at least considers it as having roots in the historic violence of American frontier history.

No Country for Old Men

The contrasting personas in *No Country for Old Men* are Anton Chigurh, a psychopathic participant in the drug wars, an "outlaw" employee of a corporation that serves as a front for the drug trade, and Ed Tom Bell, a devoted Texas sheriff struggling in the face of the kind of violence represented by Chigurh to maintain faith in the purpose of his job and his ability and desire to continue in it. A third central character, Llewelyn Moss, sets the novel's plot in motion when he stumbles upon the bloody aftermath of a drug war shootout and discovers, in the process, more than two million dollars. In a fatal choice, Moss appropriates the money for himself. Moss, though, is hardly introspective (in fact, he rarely has the time to be) and is thus not central to the text's dialectic concerning violence.

Of these three protagonists, Chigurh is the most difficult to comprehend. Few characters in fiction are more clearly aligned with violence as sheer excess than Chigurh. While he posits explanations and justifications for his brutal actions in two extended monologues delivered to individuals prior to his murdering them, his argument in both cases is inconsistent and illogical. He kills virtually everyone he encounters, usually with a cattle gun normally used in slaughterhouses. McCarthy's decision to give Chigurh such a unique weapon has inevitably resulted in critical discussion. Jay Ellis provides this insight concerning the cattle gun's symbolic role in the novel: "by killing people with a cattle gun, Chigurh is turning them into livestock, denying their humanity" (229).

Chigurh's own level of humanity is a matter of question. It is difficult to imagine a character more associated with irrational violence than he is. He is an archetypal loner, lacking any family or even close associates. He seems to be have substituted the act of murder for sex, perhaps feeling in part that sexual contact might render him vulnerable. Thus, none of Bataille's barriers against the excess of violence exist for him. Chigurh is inextricably linked to illicit drugs, the novel's pervasive commodity; but there is no indication that he uses them himself. Chirgurh strives to be completely self-sufficient and, to a large degree, succeeds. After being seriously wounded in a gun battle in Eagle Pass, Texas, he performs surgery on himself in a motel room, first buying supplies from a veterinary clinic and stealing medications from a drug store.

It is, then, tempting to view Chigurh from a strictly symbolic perspective, as a personification of violence who merely appears to assume human form. Such an approach would draw support from the difficulty that other characters have in describing him. One teenage boy questioned about Chigurh says first that "he looked like anybody" and then that "he didn't look like anybody" (McCarthy 292). Asked if Chigurh was "Mexican," the boy responds "I don't think so. He was kindly dark complected is all" (McCarthy 291). Moreover, Chigurh, after being seriously injured in an automobile accident, simply walks away from the novel. His primary antagonist, Sheriff Ed Tom Bell, who is strongly representative of Bataille's "orderly and decent" "extreme" of human behavior, begins, in the concluding sections of the novel, to consider Chigurh as existing on some plane other than the human. At one point, Bell describes the killer as being *"pretty much a ghost"* (McCarthy 299).

Still, the realistic mode of McCarthy's narrative calls such an allegorical reading into question. Steven Frye points out that *No Country for Old Men* is strongly reminiscent of not only "the crime novel," but "the western" as well (154), and the introduction of a purely allegorical character into this narrative mode would be jarring indeed. The villains in noir fiction and film and in the western are generally savage, but they are necessarily human so that they can be dispatched at the end. Moreover, Chigurh is finally neither immune from, nor completely in control of, the violence he unleashes. While his self-sufficiency in the aftermath of the Eagle Pass shootout and his subsequent self-surgery verges on the superhuman, he hardly emerges unscathed from the Eagle Pass episode.

On two occasions, Chigurh engages in what Jay Ellis describes as "pre-murder Socratic dialogues" (229). In the first, he prepares to kill Carson Wells, a corporate agent sent to destroy him. Before shooting Wells, an old associate, he forces his victim to listen to an extended dialogue that contains a confession of sorts. In a reference to the Eagle Pass shootout, he tells Wells that "getting hurt changed me. . . . The best way I can put it is that I've sort of caught up with myself" (McCarthy 173). It is difficult to know precisely what Chigurh means by this, but one interpretation would be that his wounds gave him a sense of his own limitations, the realization that he has not transcended mortality.

He then qualifies what he has said, asserting that the change in him occurred before the Eagle Pass gun battle. He tells of killing a man after being provoked in a café and then allowing himself to be arrested by a deputy sheriff near Sonora, Texas: "I'm not sure why I did this but I think I wanted to see if I could extricate myself by an act of will. Because I believe that one can . . . . But it was a foolish thing to do. A vain thing to do" (McCarthy 174–75). In fact, he does "extricate" himself by committing two murders that set in motion the plot of the novel. A psychopath, Chigurh wants to believe that he does exist on a plane beyond the human, that he possesses powers that justify his murderous actions. His comment that allowing himself to be arrested was "foolish" and "vain" is not an expression of regret over killing the deputy and another man, but a self-criticism over exercising his supernatural power in a reckless and arrogant fashion. One can read Chigurh's confession of vanity as an ironic parallel to Christ's temptation in the desert. While Christ resists Satan's temptation, Chigurh succumbs to his sense of omnipotence and, by doing so, allows self-doubt to enter his consciousness. Having failed to maintain control once, he feels it necessary to guard against another such failure. After suffering his Eagle Pass wounds, he may have begun to doubt, on some level, his ability to always extricate himself from dangerous situations. In his confession to Wells, Chigurh describes three murders that are not related to drugs; and, before the novel ends, there will be a fourth that is only tangentially so. The violence that he represents thus goes beyond the drug trade, representing a timeless aspect of the human condition. It is precisely the timelessness of the violence that Chigurh unleashes that Sheriff Ed Tom Bell will struggle to deny.

Chigurh's second "pre-murder Socratic dialogue" occurs with Carla Jean Moss, whom the murderer has relentlessly tracked down to kill in order to carry out a "bargain" that he made with Llewelyn. In fact, Chigurh promised Carla Jean's husband that he would not kill her if Llewelyn would turn over his found money to him. Carla Jean knows nothing about this promise, and it would not matter if she did. Chigurh's explanation of the necessity of his killing Carla Jean is wildly illogical. He first says that he must kill her because "I gave my word" (McCarthy 255); and, after Carla Jean points out that Llewelyn is dead, responds, "but my word is not dead. Nothing can change that" (McCarthy 255). He then asserts that he cannot change his word: "even a nonbeliever might find it useful to model himself after God" (McCarthy 256). Chigurh, even after his Eagle Pass wounding and his Sonora arrest, is still determined to maintain his belief in his own omnipotence. In truly satanic fashion, he offers to spare her if she calls a coin toss correctly, a favorite trick of his. After calling the coin incorrectly, Carla Jean perceptively challenges Chigurh, "you wouldnt of let me off noway" (McCarthy 259).

Chigurh's response is a forced exercise in what Frye describes as "chaos theory" (162), the argument that everything occurs because of random events in the past. In essence, Chigurh argues that because nothing can be changed and since all events are the result of unrelated past occurrences, he has "no say in the matter" (McCarthy 239). If this is so, then Chigurh does not possess the superhuman powers that he claims, since free will is nonexistent. His attempt to "model himself after God" seems to be unraveling at this point—a god with no power to change anything is hardly a god. When Carla Jean begs one last time for her life, Chigurh responds, "You're asking that I make myself vulnerable and that I can never do. I have only one way to live. It doesnt allow for special cases" (McCarthy 259).

Chigurh has, in fact, been feeling vulnerable since the Sonora arrest and the Eagle Pass shootout, concerned that he might yield a second time to vanity and that he might suffer additional physical wounds. He is quickly shown to be justified in so feeling. After he kills Carla Jean, his truck is blindsided, and he is badly injured.

Once again, he patches up his own wounds and limps away from the accident scene. The reader learns more, through Sheriff Bell's investigation of Carla Jean's murder, about the aftermath of the wreck. Chigurh left behind his pistol, which is found by two teenage boys. After one of the boys sells it, it is used to rob a convenience store in Shreveport, Louisiana. Moreover, the passengers in the car that hit Chigurh's truck were three Mexican boys smoking marijuana, passing a joint back and forth and, thereby, distracting the driver. Two of the three were killed.

This time, Chigurh has been indirectly injured by illicit drugs, the commodity he serves and for which he kills. Two young boys are killed while using that commodity and come close to killing Chigurh, and his leaving behind his pistol results in a robbery a state away. More significant than his being injured again is the fact that Chigurh is losing control of the commodity that is a central element to his identity. It is not surprising, then, that he exits the novel at this point. Finally, it makes sense to see him as a very deadly, but still mortal, being, whose capacity for violence is so intense that it appears to take on a supernatural dimension. He embodies the violence as "excess" that results when the collective barriers inherent in Bataille's reason collapse.

Ed Tom Bell, the other persona central to the novel's dialectical exploration of violence, is a firm believer in those collective barriers and struggles to comprehend not only Chigurh, but, more significantly, the plague of violence that threatens to drown the county Bell has sworn to protect as a law enforcement officer. He never completely succeeds, largely because he attempts to understand the sheer irrationality of violence from a rational perspective. In addition, Bell's inherent decency limits his ability to comprehend the fundamentally indecent. Work, concern for others, kindness, and honesty are central values for him. He is completely devoted to his wife, constantly praising her as a better person than he is, and he secretly engages in dialogues with his deceased daughter. His responsibility to the people who elected him is profound, ironically strengthened by his sense of having failed in his obligation to his fellow soldiers in a World War II battle, an action for which he received the Bronze Star.

Chigurh and the violence of the drug trade shatter Bell's faith in his ability to continue as a law enforcement officer, and he retires at the end of the novel. Significantly, he never sees Chigurh, only the destruction that he leaves in his wake; and the nature of the unseen becomes more mysterious and menacing to Bell, who, according to Jay Ellis, indulges in meditations that are reminiscent of "the laments of Jeremiah in the Old Testament." Jeremiah, Ellis points out, was concerned that "he is insufficient to his god's purpose" (243); and Bell, never quite certain about the existence of a god, feels increasingly insufficient to fulfill his obligations to his constituents.

Bell tries to place Chigurh and the outbreak of drug violence in his county and those surrounding it in an historical context as a result of the breakdown of traditional social values, manners, and mores. He wants desperately to believe in some permanence, some kind of continuity of the rational, asserting at one point that "*some things aint changed. Common sense aint changed*" (McCarthy 62). But something *has* changed, he feels, and he struggles to locate the moment when the change began. He believes that people in some earlier period were more "simple" and honorable, telling his Uncle Ellis, after confessing to his act of wartime cowardice, that "I'm not the man of an older time they say I am. I wish I was. I'm a man of this time" (McCarthy 279). That he asserts his relevance only in a negative context reveals his lack of real faith in its continuance.

Bell considers explaining the violence as being a result of the Vietnam War and the 1960s counter-culture, and references to Vietnam and the erosion of faith in authority that resulted from it recur in the novel. Near the end, we learn, for instance, that Llewelyn Moss "was a sniper in Vietnam" (McCarthy 293). But, in a late conversation with Bell, Moss' father refuses to blame either the war or the "hippies" for the present cultural turmoil (McCarthy 294). Bell is not nearly so forgiving of the "hippies," but he also refers to an unspecified earlier time when traditional manners were undermined. He responds to a woman who asks him how he "let crime get so out of hand in your county:" "It starts when you begin to overlook bad manners. Any time you quit hearin Sir and Mam the end is pretty much in sight" (McCarthy 304). This response reflects Bell's social and political conservatism and reveals much about his inability to comprehend the violence threatening him. Anton Chigurh cannot be explained as the result of bad manners.

Bell comes closer to a genuine understanding when he reflects that "this country has got a strange kind of history and a damned bloody one too" (McCarthy 294). He is thinking primarily about the Indian raids that occurred in his region of west Texas, one of which is recounted late in the novel. As Ellis has pointed out, Bell is thinking only of the violence committed against the early white settlers by the Indians, ignoring that committed by whites against the indigenous peoples. (240–41). Still, his insight that the present violence in his county and his state may not be a completely new phenomenon has more validity than his bad manners theory. Chigurh and the drug wars are a truly frightening phenomenon, but the violence they bring forth is not without precedent. Especially ominous is the unacknowledged participation of the dominant economic system in the drug trade. Chigurh visits two corporate offices in the novel, one that of his former employer and the other belonging to a prospective new employer.

The concept of commodities associated with violence is not new to McCarthy's work. David Holloway provides a list of such "things to be bought according to the laws of the marketplace" in McCarthy novels: "scalps, children" and "life itself" (104–5). In their relationship to violence, *Blood Meridian's* scalps are comparable to the illicit drugs in *No Country for Old Men*, and Anton Chigurh has an ancestor in Judge Holden.

Fight Club
The personas in the dialectical examination of violence in Palahniuk's *Fight Club* are not two distinct characters, but rather two aspects of a consciousness in the process of disintegration. The first persona, the unnamed narrator, conjures up, out of a pervasive sense of self-loathing, the second, Tyler Durden, during his rare moments of sleep. For the unnamed narrator, Durden is a figure intended to compensate

for the narrator's perceived inadequacies and "tiny" life in a cynical and deadly consumerist culture. His self-hatred results, in part, from his role in serving his employer—and by extension, international capitalism—by refusing to issue recalls on dangerous vehicles. In one scene, he imagines challenging his boss with his knowledge of the destructive violence that company policy has produced:

> I know about the air-conditioning rheostat that gets so hot it sets fire to the maps in your glove compartment. I know how many people burn alive because of fuel-injector flashback. I've seen people's legs cut off at the knee when turbochargers start exploding and send their vanes through the firewall and into the passenger compartment. (Palahniuk 90)

But he says none of this. His failure to challenge the immorality of his employer and the corporate system in general contributes to his sense of emasculation and impotence, sexually and in virtually every other way.

Initially, his primary release from the self-loathing that this sense of impotence induces in him is in attending support groups for people with serious illnesses, including one for men with testicular cancer significantly named "Remaining Men Together." The narrator does not have cancer, but his manhood is nevertheless threatened. Afraid of death, he paradoxically seeks human contact through association with the dying. He is almost as much an isolate as Anton Chigurh, McCarthy's character, who lacks any of the protective barriers connected with the rational norm of human behavior. His workplace, committed to a policy of dishonesty and unfairness, adds to his alienation; and he has never enjoyed sustaining familial relationships. Marla Singer, an extremely damaged woman whom he meets at "Remaining Men Together," comes closer than anyone else to having a supportive professional relationship with the narrator. He would like to live a rational existence, one from which the chaos of excess is absent, but his disintegrating psychological state will not permit him to do so.

In contrast to Anton Chigurh, the narrator has, until he loses control of his subconscious, avoided violence. But his self-loathing and impotence give birth in his subconscious to Tyler Durden, an alternate ego that equates masculinity with violent excess. The narrator imagines that he first meets Durden at a nude beach, and there is an obvious overtone of homoeroticism in the scene: "Tyler was naked and sweating, gritty with sand, his hair wet and stringy, hanging in his face" (Palahniuk 22). The novel's gay subtext is largely repressed, its relationship to the central themes of the text never made overt. Seeing Tyler nude might well represent the narrator's visualization of the dark and violent side of his character. His physical attraction to his alter-ego also represents the narrator's androgyny, previously repressed as a further threat to his masculinity. At one point, he comes close to acknowledging his sexual attraction to Durden: "we have sort of a triangle going here. I want Tyler. Tyler wants Marla. Marla wants me" (Palahniuk 4). In the narrator's fantasy, it is his alter-ego Durden who has sex with Marla. Even in the realm of his subconscious, he is not in control of his sexuality.

While the narrator sleeps, Tyler Durden takes over his identity and initiates an imagined revolution against the cynical consumerist economy that the narrator is unable to confront during his waking hours. At first, the revolution consists of secret acts of petty sabotage. Durden works as a film projectionist, and he takes perverse pleasure in inserting pornographic images into mainstream family films. In addition, he introduces the narrator to the practice of grossly befouling the food served at dinner parties for business executives. The narrator proudly proclaims that he and Tyler are "the guerrilla terrorists of the service industry" (Palahniuk 72). Such acts are, of course, essentially meaningless in the context of any serious challenge to the consumerist culture.

Tyler begins to move his revolution to a more serious plane through his introduction of fight club. Like Anton Chigurh, Durden attempts to give the chaotic irrationality of his actions a veneer of rational control. Thus, fight club, a fantasized exercise in extreme and pointless male violence, must have rules, its first two rules being that "you don't talk about fight club" (Palahniuk 39). In fact, the central ingredient in, and attraction of, fight club is pain. It equates maleness with the ability to cause pain in others and, even more importantly, to receive and endure pain inflicted by others on oneself. In a preamble to the establishment of fight club, Tyler, in a parking lot outside a bar, suddenly asks the narrator to hit him "as hard as you can" (Palahniuk 43). The two then engage in a fight that the narrator believes confirms his problematic manhood: "if you've never been in a fight, you wonder. About getting hurt, about what you're capable of doing against another man" (Palahniuk 43).

Tyler explains that what they are doing is an initial step in a necessary process of "self-destruction," which the narrator understands to mean that "maybe we have to break everything to make something better out of ourselves" (Palahniuk 43). What is really going on is that the narrator is fantasizing punishment as retribution for the self-loathing induced by his inability to confront the corrupt corporation that employs him, his physical and spiritual isolation, and the androgynous feelings that he consciously wants to deny. Throughout the novel, Tyler is a master at generalizing the personal pain of the narrator, whose alienation is rooted in the absence of any emotional attachment to his father, who abandoned his family. Tyler explains that most of the men who come to fight club, including himself, have had similar experiences with absent fathers and, that when he fights, he imagines that he is fighting his father. The narrator hears all this in the context of his sense of emasculation and then generalizes it as a cultural phenomenon: "what you see at fight club is a generation of men raised by women" (Palahniuk 41).[2]

The central paradox in the narrator's subconscious projection of Tyler Durden as the embodiment of a rebellion against the violence that results from corporate excess and the production of deadly commodities is that Durden is the very personification of senseless violence and destruction. It is inevitable that the narrator will increasingly lose control of his fantasy to the point that he becomes its target. Fight club's practice of a secret and voluntary commitment to violence accelerates into Project Mayhem, an all-out assault on the capitalist culture. Those in Project Mayhem—all men, of course—carry out not only petty warfare against movie theaters

---

and the service industry but violent sabotage against corporate buildings, offices, and executives.

One favorite practice of Project Mayhem is known as "cut-and-run," in which a perceived member of the corporate establishment is kidnapped and threatened with castration by knife. In a climactic scene, the narrator, now identified as Tyler Durden, becomes the target of a "cut-and-run." The fantasy that originates in his sense of impotence and self-loathing has come full circle and threatens to emasculate him. Moreover, he has lost his identity to his imagined alter-ego. Ultimately, in the narrator's sleeping fantasy, everyone he encounters insists that he is Tyler Durden. Finally, the narrator imagines that he is being held hostage by Tyler Durden inside a building that represents the heart of the capitalist system. Durden has thrust a gun in his mouth. The homoerotic associations of this scene are clear. The beginning and end of the novel constitute an abrupt return to realism, in which we learn that the narrator is hospitalized in a mental institution after shooting himself in the face. His fantasy has literally disfigured him.

Conclusion

Both *No Country for Old Men* and *Fight Club* threaten to drown in what Žižek calls acts of "subjective violence," and both are devoted to exploring variations of his concept of "systemic violence." The violence in the two novels results not from the "smooth functioning" of economic systems, but from corruptions of them. In *Fight Club,* the cynical automobile recall policy of the narrator's employer, as well as Tyler Durden's Machiavellian appropriation of his subconscious, are illustrative of how violent excess can be clothed in a guise of rationality. The Socratic dialogues of McCarthy's Anton Chigurh similarly describe subjective acts of violence as examples of an inherently rational inevitability. In addition, McCarthy and Palahniuk utilize conflicting personas to establish a dialectic that echoes Bataille's concept of the "double nature" of human beings, the two extremes of reason and violent excess. Centering their texts in the contrasting modes of genre fiction and fantasy, both create original and challenging novels by probing (ir)rationalily and what often seems to be an epidemic of violence plaguing contemporary America.

Notes

1. For an extended discussion of the narrator's fragmenting consciousness, see my "Violence, Spaces and a Fragmenting Consciousness in *Fight Club*" in *Chuck Palahniuk: Fight Club/Invisible Monsters/Choke,* ed. Francisco Collado-Rodriguez (London: Bloomsbury, 2013): 23–43.

2. Kevin Alexander Boon argues that *Fight Club* "addresses the identity crisis of white, heterosexual, American men in the late twentieth and early twenty-first centuries who grew up in paradoxical cultural environments that make heroes of aggressive men while debasing aggressive impulses" (269).

Works Cited

Bataille, Georges. *Erotism: Death and Sensuality.* Trans. Mary Dalwood. San Francisco: City Lights Books, 1986.

Boon, Kevin Alexander. "Men and Nostalgia for Violence: Culture and Culpability in Chuck Palahniuk's *Fight Club.*" *Journal of Men's Studies,* 11 (2003): 267–76.

Ellis, Jay. *No Place for Home: Spatial Constraint and Character Flight in the Novels of Cormac McCarthy.* New York: Routledge, 2006.

Frye, Steven. *Understanding Cormac McCarthy.* Columbia, SC: University of South Carolina P, 2009.

Holloway, David. *The Late Modernism of Cormac McCarthy.* Westport, CT: Greenwood, 2002.

McCarthy, Cormac. *No Country for Old Men.* New York: Alfred A. Knopf, 2005.

Palahniuk, Chuck. *Fight Club.* New York: Henry Holt, 1997.

Žižek, Slavoj. *Violence.* New York: Picador, 2008.

"Bluffers and Blowhards": Speaking of Violence in Ben Fountain's *Billy Lynn's Long Halftime Walk*

Mark Bresnan

An American combat veteran, traumatized by violence, returns home desperate to share his experience; instead, he is greeted by silence. This basic plot constitutes a substantial strand of twentieth-century war literature, from Ernest Hemingway's Nick Adams and Howard Krebs, veterans of World War I, to Tim O'Brien's Norman Bowker, a Vietnam veteran. An overpowering sense of quiet pervades these stories, whether in the Michigan woods where Nick Adams makes camp or in the silent loops that Norman Bowker drives around an Iowa lake. In O'Brien's "Speaking of Courage," a story in *The Things They Carried*, Bowker drives quietly, remembering past conversations and imagining future ones, but talking to no one. Much of the narrative is in the conditional tense, about stories Bowker would tell if people would listen; as it stands, "The town could not talk, and would not listen" (O'Brien, *Things They Carried* 137). This uncaring silence echoes Hemingway's "Soldier's Home," in which the narrator explains that, after a brief period in which he couldn't verbalize his feelings, Howard Krebs "felt the need to talk but no one wanted to hear about it" (145). Instead, he spends his days in bed, at the library, and reading on his front porch. Even the pool room, where Krebs goes to play billiards, is a "cool dark" place rather than the sort of bustling noisy bar we might expect (Hemingway 146). The silence in these narratives is so powerful that when Nick Adams talks to himself in "Big Two-Hearted River," he immediately regrets it: "His voice sounded strange in the darkening woods. He did not speak again" (Hemingway 215).

Ben Fountain's 2012 novel *Billy Lynn's Long Halftime Walk* is another story about veterans returning home; in this case, the narrative follows Bravo squad, a group of Iraq War soldiers made famous when an embedded reporter recorded and then broadcast their triumph in a violent battle with insurgents at the Al-Ansakar Canal. Like their fictional ancestors, Bravo squad is also traumatized by the violence by the war—especially Billy Lynn, an Army Specialist who witnessed the death of his friend Shroom during the Al-Ansakar firefight. The Bravos, however, are greeted not by silence, but instead by a deafening roar, a ceaseless flow of speeches, conversation, and media broadcasts about war, patriotism, September 11th, and the nobility of battle. Most of the novel takes place at Cowboys Stadium in Dallas, where even the commercials are loud: "The Jumbotron plays the American Heroes graphic again, then grinds through the deafening commercial cycle, the same ads always playing through the same maddening order. FORD TRUCKS BUILT TOUGH! TOYOTA! nissan! TOYOTA! nissan!" (Fountain, *Billy Lynn* 259). This aural assault is driven by much more than technology and mass media, though; its principal source is the everyday speech of patriotic civilians. The novel opens with a description of Bravo squad's experience in their hotel lobby, in which "overcaffeinated tag teams of grateful citizens" repeatedly approach to praise the soldiers (Fountain, *Billy Lynn* 1). "There was one man in particular who attached himself to Billy," explains the narrator, "and the man embarked on a rambling speech about war and God and country as Billy let go, let the words whirl and tumble around his brain" (Fountain, *Billy Lynn* 1).

Despite the inarticulateness of these ramblings, they suggest a cultural willingness to talk to veterans that seems as if it could ameliorate the difficulties long faced by American soldiers. In "The Veterans' Tale: Causes and Consequences," Pat Hoy surveys twentieth-century fiction in which veterans return home from war, both to the United States and to England. He identifies the cultural silencing of war discourse as one of the primary tropes in these narratives:

> [Veterans'] war experiences are nullified when they confront a culture that operates on moral and ethical principles that silence conversation and understanding about the difference between killing on the battlefield and killing elsewhere. At home, bearing the burden of sacrifice and silences becomes increasingly difficult. (Hoy 168)

What are we to make, then, of the outpouring of support, well wishes, and thanks that greets Bravo squad throughout *Billy Lynn*? As the narrator puts it, "being a Bravo means inhabiting a state of semi-celebrity that occasionally flattens you with praise and adulation" (Fountain, *Billy Lynn* 28). The silences that so often greeted twentieth-century veterans have been replaced by the "whirl and tumble" of language as voiced by admiring civilians, sports fans, war protesters, and media personalities. This noise, I argue, is Ben Fountain's primary preoccupation in *Billy Lynn's Long Halftime Walk*.

The bulk of *Billy Lynn* narrates one day in the life of Bravo squad: Thanksgiving 2004, designed to be the high point of Bravo's two-week stateside publicity tour. (Unlike their fictional predecessors Norman Bowker, Howard Krebs, and Nick Adams, Billy and his fellow soldiers are on temporary leave, after which they will return to Iraq.) Although Bravo became famous for charging into a firefight at the Al-Ansakar Canal, they spend most of Fountain's novel in full retreat from this series of verbal assaults, even as they acknowledge the good intentions that motivate them. The culmination of their tour takes place at halftime of the annual Thanksgiving game in Dallas, when they are honored before a live audience of tens of thousands and a television audience of millions more. While they are initially excited by the prospect of being honored (and possibly meeting the pop act Destiny's Child, the halftime performers), Bravo becomes more and more skeptical as the moment draws near. Billy and his fellow Bravos seem to know that talking about the war has the potential to provide catharsis, but they accurately perceive that contemporary discourse about the war has become so impoverished that it is best avoided altogether. Major Mac, Bravo's military chaperone, is hard of hearing, and Billy's distaste for his interlocutors suggests he would not mind a similar condition. One of Billy's biggest concerns is just to find an Advil for his throbbing headache—a physical manifestation of the damage speech can inflict.

Many soldiers, writers, and scholars have acknowledged the difficulty—or perhaps impossibility—of talking about violence

---

and war with honesty and accuracy. In an essay that argues for the importance of war narratives, Thomas Bowie notes how challenging they are to construct. "[I]t is tempting," he suggests, "to simply say that each experience is unique, as is each teller, so in the end we can't ever *tell* a true war story" (Bowie 27). Perhaps in recognition of this difficulty, *Billy Lynn* is a war story in which the violent conflict in Iraq is only portrayed in brief flashbacks. The firefight that made the Bravos famous lasted for only three minutes and forty-eight seconds, a short vignette that was replayed endlessly on cable news, and the football fans who approach Billy throughout the novel frequently explain their reaction to it in the language of spectatorship:

> "I couldn't stop watching!" the woman exclaims to Billy. "It was just like nina leven, I couldn't stop watching those planes crash into the towers, I just couldn't, Bob had to drag me away . . . . Same with yall, when Fox News started showing that video I just sat right down and didn't move for hours. I was just so proud, just so"—she flounders in the swamps of self-expression—"*proud*," she repeats, "it was like, thank *God*, justice is finally being done."
>
> "It was like a movie," chimes her daughter in law, getting into the spirit. (44)

The civilians in *Billy Lynn* consistently employ this rhetorical mode, emphasizing abstractions like justice, patriotism, and glory, while placing themselves in the role of enthusiastic spectators. By setting his war novel in a football stadium, Fountain suggests that the self-proclaimed patriots who shower the Bravos with praise are best understood as fans—passionate and engaged, yes, but also fickle, arbitrary, and rigid in their expectations of what a soldier or football player or pop star should be.

Of course, to act like a fan does not necessarily mean that one is unthinking, solipsistic, and naïve; Henry Jenkins, in his book *Textual Poachers*, shows how contemporary fans craft narratives that rewrite the standard interpretations of all manner of cultural phenomena—television shows, science fiction franchises, and athletic events. In doing so, many of these fans are able to form meaningful communities and, in some cases, talk back in sophisticated ways to the producers of the content they cherish. This level of community and engagement, however, is absent from *Billy Lynn*, in which the most frequent trope is a solitary figure approaching Bravo squad and delivering another hackneyed, vacuous speech that mimics the rhetoric of cable news and other mass media sources. Billy's father, Ray, is a particularly shallow and self-serving example of the slippage between vocal pro-war patriotism and other forms of fanship. After spending the prime of his career as a rock DJ—Rockin' Ray Lynn—only to be laid off in post-September 11th recession, he converted to hosting a hard-right talk radio show:

> Through research Ray concluded that the market could support yet one more aggrieved white male defending faith and flag from America's heartland. He studied the masters, followed the news, logged serious hours on the Internet. He began making demo tapes and sending them out; the family became his test audience for ever more baroque elaborations of conservative creed. "America's Prick," Billy's elder sister, Patty, called him after an especially inspired riff on the welfare state. He'd leaped straight from rock 'n' roll to hard-core right wing with no stops in between. (Fountain, *Billy Lynn* 76)

The certainty with which Ray transforms into right-wing firebrand finds parallels in the certainty of every civilian who approaches Billy, their attachment to the American military as solid as their love for the Dallas Cowboys.

But war, as the Bravo squad knows, is not like football or rock-and-roll. It does not simulate violence or adopt a violent pose (Destiny's Child performs their hit song "Soldier" during halftime)—it enacts violence, often in front of the cameras of embedded newspaper reporters or even the soldiers themselves. In that sense, the violence of war is more clearly visible to Americans than ever. As Fountain pointed out in a September 2013 lecture at the Air Force Academy, "In some ways, the war has never been more accessible to those of us at home. We can find it in the news; we can access the most graphic, horrifying images online" ("Soldiers on the Fault Line" 7). But, as he argues, this does not mean that Americans

---

172

have any truer sense of what war is actually like: "I think that in a profound sense the war remains an abstraction unless and until we have skin in the game, a vital personal stake" (Fountain, "Soldiers on the Fault Line" 7).

"War remains an abstraction"—this is the primary limitation of civilian speech in *Billy Lynn*. In scene after scene, Billy and the Bravos are goaded to talk about sacrifice, duty, and America when they would prefer to be talking about football or women—or perhaps not talking at all. In a VIP reception set up by Dallas Cowboys owner Norm Oglesby (a thinly disguised avatar of real-life Cowboys owner Jerry Jones), Billy and his platoon-mates joke and mingle, willing to accept their hosts' effusive, if sometimes condescending, praise in exchange for food and alcohol. Billy is wary of talking about the war; he "tries to keep it low-key, but people steer the conversation toward drama and passion" (Fountain, *Billy Lynn* 116). But "drama and passion" have little to do with Billy's experience of war. His memories of deployment are mostly disconnected impressions colored by fear, pain, violence, and occasional humor, what Fountain describes in his Air Force Academy lecture as "the real stuff of life, the sweat and worry and blood and guts and sex and pain and pleasure of it" (Fountain, *Billy Lynn* 11). Billy sees his problem in primarily linguistic terms; as the narrator explains, "For two weeks he's been traveling this great nation of ours in the good-faith belief that sooner or later he'll meet someone who can explain his experience, or at least break it down and properly frame the issue" (Fountain, *Billy Lynn* 47). What he finds instead are enthusiastic patriots like "How-Wayne," who promises the Bravos that he is doing his part for the war effort by trying to increase domestic oil production. "And that was cool," thinks Billy, noting that the interaction would have ended there "[i]f he'd just said *enjoy your meal* like everybody else and returned to his lucrative patriotic life, but no, he got greedy" (Fountain, *Billy Lynn* 64). In the world of *Billy Lynn*, to "get greedy" with the Bravos is a purely a matter of communication; not content to wrap up his encounter with the usual bromides, How-Wayne pushes Bravo to give him an assessment of the war's progress. Expecting patriotic platitudes, he is shocked when Sergeant Dime lays bare the violent realities of war: "We *like* violence, we *like going lethal*! I mean, isn't that what you're paying us for? To take the fight to America's enemies and send them straight to hell? If we didn't like killing people then what's the point?" (Fountain, *Billy Lynn* 65).

Dime is intentionally hyperbolic in both language and idea, but the speech locates him clearly on what Billy refers to as "the high ground of experience" (Fountain, *Billy Lynn* 66). He and the rest of Bravos have an unassailable ethos: "They are authentic. They are the Real . . . . Here in the chicken-hawk nation of blowhards and bluffers, Bravo always has the ace of bloods up its sleeve" (Fountain, *Billy Lynn* 66). This "high ground of experience" inspires a rhetoric of war that starkly distinguishes the soldiers in *Billy Lynn* from their civilian counterparts. The Bravos employ a frank and explicit war vocabulary, occasionally resorting to euphemism, but rarely to metaphor and almost never to abstraction. When Billy remembers Shroom, a Bravo who died in the Al-Ansakar incident, he thinks of the way he uses language: "In Shroom World, bricks were 'earth biscuits,' trees were 'sky shrubs,' and all frontline infantry 'meat rabbits'" (Fountain, *Billy Lynn* 61). The euphemism "meat rabbits" suggests that soldiers are both disposable and easily replaceable; the "service" that veterans are always being thanked for is mostly just a matter of showing up and following instructions. When Billy asks him for a description of being in a firefight, Shroom initially resists and then offers a bizarre, but violent analogy: "It's not like anything, except maybe being raped by angels" (Fountain, *Billy Lynn* 61).

The Bravos return to this explicitly violent language throughout their day at Cowboys Stadium, often at especially incongruous moments. Dime ruins a videotaped Thanksgiving greeting to soldiers abroad by adlibbing "PEACE THROUGH SUPERIOR FIREPOWER!" after his scripted speech (Fountain, *Billy Lynn* 167). But despite Dime's bravado in this scene, the Bravos more often express their feelings about war with restrained sincerity. Back in Iraq, the Bravos began saying "I love you" to each other before each combat mission; they followed Shroom's example, who said it "straight, with no joking or smart-ass lilt and no warbly Christian smarm in it either, just that brisk declaration like he was tightening

the seat belts around everyone's soul" (Fountain, *Billy Lynn* 61).
Scholar Samuel Hynes notes this preference for the plainspoken
in his study of first-person nonfiction accounts of war, explaining
that veterans' narratives "work at a level below the big words and
brave sentiments, down on the surface of the earth where men fight.
They don't glorify war, or aestheticize it; they speak in their own
voices, their own plain language" (30). Although the novel's limited
omniscient point of view clearly reveals Billy's thoughts about his
experience in the war, he doesn't often get the opportunity to speak
about it. The most notable exception occurs during his trip back
to his childhood home, an earlier stop on his two-week leave that
the novel flashes back to in the midst of its narration. When his
sister Kathryn asks him for an assessment of the war—an abstract,
political opinion—Billy resists, only opening up when she rephrases
her request: "I just want to know what's going on in your head"
(Fountain, *Billy Lynn* 97). His answer is prosaic, but sincere; he
discusses the work they are trying to do for Iraqis while noting his
frustration at being perceived as the enemy, ultimately concluding
that "You just pull in, you aren't thinking about accomplishing
anything, you just wanna get through the day with all your guys
alive" (Fountain, *Billy Lynn* 97–8).

In an interview with David Lawrence published in *War,
Literature, & the Arts*, Fountain identified the difficulty of creating
a convincing and authentic soldier's voice as one of the central
challenges he faced while writing the novel:

> Given that I've never been in the military, did I even have the right
> to attempt a book like this? . . . Anytime you're dealing with blood,
> with matters of literal life and death, you're obligated to approach it
> with full awareness, and the only way you can possibly justify going
> forward is to ask yourself whether it's possible that you might have
> something new and valid to say, something useful in the deepest
> sense of the word. (Lawrence 96)

Billy Lynn's reception among veterans suggests that Fountain
succeeded. Lawrence, a literary scholar and officer in the Air Force,
read the book shortly after his return from deployment in Afghanistan

and lauds its "astonishing clarity" about the "many things which make our recent martial exploits abroad so complicated" (90). Lawrence also reports that General Martin Dempsey, Chairman of the Joint Chiefs of Staff, read and endorsed the book; Fountain's invitation to lecture at the Air Force Academy suggests that *Billy Lynn* has been embraced by a significant segment of the military. How does Fountain accomplish this depth and verisimilitude—and what does he, as an author, do with his military characters that the fictional civilians in the novel do not?

In the Lawrence interview, Fountain emphasizes the importance of understanding the "minute particulars" of soldiers' experience: "I had to work my way into the soldiers' skins, to the extent such things are possible" (Lawrence 96). Indeed, the preponderance of narrative attention in *Billy Lynn* focuses on these "minute particulars"; the Bravo's day at Cowboys Stadium is captured in extensive detail, from the epic catalogue of football equipment in the locker room, to the commercials Bravo sees on the Jumbotron, to Billy's every thought and sensation during the singing of the national anthem. The narrative is less detailed in its flashbacks to the Al-Ansakar Canal incident, but only because Billy's "memory of the battle is mostly a hot red blur" (Fountain, *Bill Lynn* 43). These flashbacks are most notable for the disjunction between Billy's blurry, confused, and prosaic memories—"Oh fuck or maybe just Fuck, that was the extent of Billy's inner reflections as he scrambled off his belly and made his run"—and the rapturous interpretations of the event crafted by the American public (Fountain, *Bill Lynn* 42). Few, if any, of the civilian characters in *Billy Lynn* are interested in the concrete details of war experience. This preference for the abstract over the particular is not limited to the pro-war patriots who most frequently approach the Bravos, either. In perhaps the novel's most heartbreaking scene, Billy's sister Kathryn responds to his sincere description of his war experience with a clearly pre-rehearsed speech encouraging him to go AWOL. "Kathryn heard him out," explains the narrator, suggesting a clear distinction between "hearing out" and truly listening (Fountain, *Bill Lynn* 98). "She set her jaw" and then launches into a "somewhat frantic speech about a website she'd found that listed how certain people [Dick Cheney, John Ashcroft, George W. Bush] had avoided Vietnam," a talking point familiar to anyone living in the United States during the early Iraq War years (Fountain, *Bill Lynn* 98). Billy's sense of comfort with Kathryn evaporates during this speech, and he spends much of the rest of the novel trying to avoid both her and the pastor she puts in contact with him.

While Kathryn and her father Ray are on opposite poles of the political spectrum, they share the tendency to parrot familiar arguments rather than sincerely engage with Billy. Ray, in fact, has had a stroke and can no longer speak (another indication of the novel's interest in speech, language, and listening), but he makes sure that Bill O'Reilly's conservative, pro-war television news show is on during Billy's welcome-home dinner (Fountain, *Bill Lynn* 79). Billy's interactions with his family suggest another dimension in the relationship between violence and language in Fountain's novel. While the preceding examples have shown how uncomfortable civilian discourse is with the realities of violence, *Billy Lynn* also suggests that language and speech can *themselves* be violent. This violence lies not in the content but in the delivery, the loud aggressiveness with which the Bravos are so often approached.

This is not to equate speech with physical violence; Billy's throbbing headache is a minor nuisance compared to Shroom's death. But while the verbal exchanges between the Bravo squad and their fans do not result in death or physical injury, they exacerbate the traumatic feeling of dislocation that combat veterans so often experience. The violence of language is most vividly captured in Fountain's frequent use of imagistic spacing between words, rendering the speech of the many civilians who approach Billy and the rest of Bravo squad as a form of concrete poetry. The novel's opening scene features the following "cluster" of language, which I quote only in part (all spatial arrangements, capitalization, and spelling are Fountain's own):

terrRist

freedom

---

evil

        nina leven
nina leven

                nina leven

Fountain uses this sort of typographic arrangement nine times in *Billy Lynn*, sometimes in passages that span more than a full page. He exclusively uses it to render the speech (or, in his representation of "The Star-Spangled Banner, song) of civilians—never of the Bravos themselves. These passages are almost completely devoid of verbs, suggesting that no logical relationship existed between the buzzwords that populated the American speech during the early years of the Iraq War. They oscillate with seeming randomness between negative and positive concepts and images, and Fountain's use of phonetic spelling captures the drawl of the many grateful Texans who approach Bravo squad: "terrRr/Eye-rack,/Eaaaar-*rock*,/ Sod'm/freedoms/nina leven, nina leven, nina leven" (38).

    Billy Lynn shows how quickly the American discourse about war exhausted itself in the years after the World Trade Center attacks. September 11th, a date that was mentioned only in somber seriousness for a few weeks after the event, becomes an all-purpose signifier that stands in for bland patriotism. In writing it as "nina leven," Fountain suggested how the phrase so quickly became symbolic discursive shorthand, words with associative but not denotative power. As a candidate for the democratic presidential nomination in 2007, Joe Biden diagnosed a similar linguistic impoverishment in his assessment of former New York City mayor Rudy Giuliani's candidacy, which he famously described as nothing more than "a noun and a verb and 9/11" (Nagourney and Bumiller). "Terrr," "currj," "dem-ock-rah-see," and "ire values" play similar roles in the novel; the logic of their casual patriotism is assumed to be self-evident and is, therefore, never fully articulated. But Fountain's innovative typography and spatial arrangements do more than emphasize the vapidity of civilian reactions to Bravo squad; they also visually recall the many cascades of ordnance deployed over Iraqi cities, especially during the early "shock and awe" phase

---

of the American invasion. In fact, shock and awe are both useful descriptors for Billy's responses to these encounters; while he acknowledges that "people could not be more supportive or kindlier disposed," he "finds these encounters weird and frightening all the same. There's something harsh in his fellow Americans, avid, ecstatic, a burning that comes of the deepest need" (Fountain, *Billy Lynn* 38).

Like most of his fellow Bravos, Billy chooses to detach and dissociate from these encounters, which, as they accumulate, begin to have a numbing effect:

> *We appreciate*, they say, their voices throbbing like a lover's. Sometimes they come right out and say it, *We love you.* We are so grateful. We cherish and bless. We pray, hope, honor-respect-love-and-revere and they *do*, in the act of speaking they experience the mighty words, these verbal arabesques that spark and snap in Billy's ears like bugs impacting an electric bug zapper. (Fountain, *Billy Lynn* 37)

The speeches and cries of support and text messages and halftime ceremonies begin to fade into each other, linguistic fusillades that the Bravos begin to see as the equivalent of friendly fire, no less dangerous for its noble intentions. As the novel continues, Billy becomes more and more detached from his surroundings. Even when he meets Faison, a Dallas Cowboys cheerleader, Billy can think of nothing other than his own lust, and he detaches from her speech about religion in the same way he detached from Norm Oglesby's speeches about patriotism and the frequent cries of "U.S.A.!" on the stadium concourse.

In a 2009 interview with *Ecotone*, Fountain cites a lecture by the historian Shelby Foote as a formative moment in his decision to become a writer: "I looked up there at him lecturing—he was talking brilliantly, yet again with that sense of humility and always with a certain amount of doubt, always questioning himself—and I thought: I want to be that guy" (George 67). Fountain's celebration of doubt in this interview contrasts with the way doubt haunts Billy throughout his visit to Cowboys Stadium. Early in the day, the narrator points out that Billy "knows he doesn't know enough. He doesn't know anything, basically, at least nothing worth knowing, the measure of worth at this point in his life being knowledge that quiets the mind and calms the soul" (Fountain, *Billy Lynn* 52). As any reader familiar with war literature might expect, "knowledge that quiets the mind" proves beyond Billy's reach, but his doubt is redemptive in the way it insulates him from the shallow narratives pressed upon him by both pro- and anti-war civilians. More than once, Billy finds his thoughts separating from his speech, his brain "whispering truer words that [he] couldn't speak" (Fountain, *Billy Lynn* 40). If Billy learns anything during his stateside tour—other than where to find the Advil, which he finally acquires at the end of a very long day—it is that his questions about the meaning of his experience in the war cannot be easily resolved. Instead, he will have to alternate between sincere moments of reflection and deliberate attempts to detach. The novel's final scene finds Billy doing the latter; while en route to the Air Force base where they will re-deploy, Billy "sits back, closes his eyes, and tries to think about nothing as the limo takes them away" (Fountain, *Billy Lynn* 307). To think about nothing has become a bizarre sort of luxury for the Bravos, whose two weeks in the United States have proven even more disorienting, over-stimulating, chaotic, and loud than their time on the front lines of the Iraq War.

"The writer," argues novelist Tom McCarthy in *Transmission and the Individual Remix*, "is not an originating speaker: he or she is a listener. Not a casual listener, but an obsessive one, devoted to their task right up to the point of their own, and the task's, annihilation" (McCarthy n.p.). McCarthy's use of "annihilation" is at least partly metaphorical, referring to the writer's voice within the text. In *Billy Lynn's Long Halftime Walk*, Fountain takes this metaphor a step further, revealing the violent potential of speech. Fountain, the author, can listen to things that his characters can no longer bear, and *Billy Lynn* reveals not only how ill-suited the bombast of contemporary discourse is for a true accounting of veterans' experiences, but also how that bombast stifles the very sort of reflection and dialogue that might eventually lead to catharsis. As readers, we are invited to listen to the shrillness of our own lofty conversations about war, patriotism, and sacrifice, and to hear, if only in their absence, the more prosaic but truer narratives of veterans themselves.

Works Cited

Bowie, Thomas G., Jr. "*Memory and Meaning: The Need for Narrative.* Reflections on the Symposium 'Twentieth Century Warfare and American Memory.' Regis University, Denver, Colorado, November 13-14, 2009." *War, Literature & the Arts* 23 (2011): 22–33.

Fountain, Ben. *Billy Lynn's Long Halftime Walk.* New York: Ecco, 2012.

_____. "Soldiers on the Fault Line: War, Rhetoric, and Reality." *War, Literature & the Arts* 25 (2013): 1–14.

George, Ben. "A Conversation with Ben Fountain." *Ecotone* 9 (2010): 49–67.

Hemingway, Ernest. "Soldier's Home." *The Short Stories.* New York: Scribner, 1995: 145–53.

Hoy II, Pat C. "The Veterans' Tale: Causes and Consequences." *War.* Ipswich, MA: Salem Press 2013: 160–176. Critical Insights Ser.

Hynes, Samuel. *The Soldier's Tale: Bearing Witness to Modern War.* New York: Penguin, 1997.

Jenkins, Henry. *Textual Poachers: Television Fans and Participatory Culture.* New York: Routledge, 1992.

Lawrence, David. "Author Spotlight: Ben Fountain Interviewed by David Lawrence." *War, Literature & the Arts* 24 (2012): 89–97.

McCarthy, Tom. *Transmission and the Individual Remix: How Literature Works.* New York: Vintage, 2012. eBook.

Nagourney, Adam, & Elisabeth Bumiller. "A Pitched Debate: Clinton Hears It From Her Rivals." *New York Times.* 31 Oct. 2007. Web. 7. Jul, 2014.

O'Brien, Tim. *The Things They Carried.* New York: Houghton Mifflin, 1990.

Contemporary War Narratives: Story-Truth, New Journalisms, and Why We Write_____

Lydia Neuman

My friend Tom Druecker tells a joke: "How many Vietnam vets does it take to screw in a light bulb?" Before you can say "I don't know, how many?" he interrupts and growls, "Of course you don't know, you weren't there!" It's a familiar trope, and it works especially well delivered by a big, bearded, sixty-something man who happens to have been a marine in Vietnam. The joke is meaningful because underneath the caricature of the crusty vet, we recognize Tim O'Brien's cluster of axioms about the difficulty of telling the truth about war. "True war stories do not generalize" (O'Brien 84). "In a true war story nothing is ever absolutely true" (O'Brien 88). "A true war story is never about war" (O'Brien 91). "Story-truth," O'Brien famously says in *The Things They Carried*, "is truer sometimes than happening-truth" (203). The firsthand experience of terror is a rapid-fire concatenation of exterior events and interior responses, and memory is a special kind of fiction.

In the chapter "Speaking of Courage," Norman Bowker, recently home from Vietnam, cruises the seven-mile loop around the lake in his hometown. It's the Fourth of July, and he's restive amid the iconic ambience of suburban American summertime—the picture-perfect houses surrounding the lake, the oppressive heat easily displaced by the Chevy's air conditioning, the radio out of Des Moines, the imminent picnics and fireworks, the neon-lit A&W. Bowker is desperate to talk about the night Kiowa died—about his shame at not having saved his friend, and the less permissible shame that his failure of courage cost him a medal. But everyone who might listen is remote. His father, whose car he's driving; the former, now-married girlfriend who lives in one of the neat houses by the lake; the carhop and the intercom operator at the A&W. They're all contentedly ignorant of the horrors of war and the dissonance between inner and outer reality that attends what we now recognize as PTSD.

In the next chapter, "Notes," O'Brien explains that the impetus to write "Speaking of Courage" was a letter in which Norman Bowker asked him to "say something about the field that night. The way Kiowa just disappeared into the crud. You were there—you can tell it" (O'Brien 179). Describing how he wrote and rewrote "Courage," O'Brien affirms the power of language to process trauma, to "objectify your own experience [and] separate it from yourself" (179–180). He adds a disclaimer—"I did not look on my work as therapy" (O'Brien 179)—implying that therapy yields false or feel-good closure. In the 2007 documentary *Operation Homecoming*, O'Brien qualifies: "I think there's a false notion that we all ought to recover from everything—divorce and broken homes and wars— that we all ought to heal. And I don't believe in it. I believe the opposite, that there are some things you shouldn't heal from, that are unhealable. And if they are healable, you oughtn't do it anyway. There's something to be said for remembering, and *not* healing." Confusion and pain are okay, but silence is deadly. Unable to satisfy "the simple need to talk" (O'Brien 180), Bowker ultimately kills himself. In the chapter's final lines, O'Brien reveals that "Norman Bowker was in no way responsible for what happened to Kiowa. Norman did not experience a failure of nerve that night. He did not freeze up or lose the Silver Star for valor. That part of the story is my own" (182). This is the happening-truth that undoes and upholds the story-truth of "Courage," and we would be hard-pressed, from a twenty-first-century liberal standpoint, to deny the therapeutic value of the confession, the narrative, or the meta-narrative.

Writing about violence is thorny. It's prone to sentimentality, false reassurance, self-indulgence. It risks merely inviting Schadenfreude, rendering horror as spectacle, and pandering to prurient interest. In a postscript to *Lolita*, Nabokov frames the danger of the last in artistic rather than moral terms: "[In pornography] obscenity must be mated with banality because every kind of aesthetic enjoyment has to be entirely replaced by simple sexual stimulation" (313). He describes his own standard: "A work of fiction exists only insofar as it affords me what I shall bluntly call aesthetic bliss, that is a sense of being somehow, somewhere, connected with other states of being where art (curiosity, kindness, tenderness, ecstasy) is the norm" (Nabokov 314). The argument is for beauty and sensuousness over morality and message; the suggestion is that compassion may be a requisite feature of art. Perhaps empathy, decency, and humanity are integral to sublime experience. By that logic, a worthy aesthetic of violence would treat "ugliness" not as metaphysical (chance) evil, or simply moral evil, but as a dynamic in which fear is transmuted to anger, and terror to trauma. Conceptualized as a kind of chemical reaction, the products of violence are grief and shame, which themselves breed physical, psychic, social, and institutional damage.

Writing is a potential palliative. Well-chosen words can, in theory, compel a hearing in whatever cosmic court of law adjudicates extralegal injuries. Writing can accuse, and also avenge, affording the opportunity, as George Orwell puts it, "to get your own back on the grown-ups who snubbed you in childhood" (392). In his 1946 essay, "Why I Write," Orwell counts such "sheer egoism" among three other motives: "aesthetic enthusiasm," "historical impulse" and "political purpose" (392). Thirty years later, in 1976, Joan Didion cribs Orwell's title, admiring its "aggressive" first-person imperative and catchy assonance. She describes writing as "a hostile act . . . . an imposition of the writer's sensibility on the reader's most private space" (Didion 5), and denies any political or "intellectual" aspirations. She can't traffic in abstraction, and must focus exclusively on the "periphery," on what she can "see and taste and touch" (Didion 6). Didion's priority is definitely aesthetic; objects dictate form or "grammar." "The picture tells you how to arrange the words" (Didion 7). This dictum recalls the ethos of the modern Imagist poets—and the Structuralist critics who point out that *signifiers* (words) don't reflect *referents* (things) according to natural law. But for Didion, the writer is a gifted medium, an almost passive conduit for language who records phenomena and perception with perfect fidelity, as if such a thing were possible.

Didion and her cohort were the leading practitioners of the New Journalism of the 1960s and 1970s. In narrative or long-

---

form journalism, as the genre came to be known, they pursued a truth-equals-beauty ideal, treating wide-ranging subjects with a sociological bent and novelistic structures. They gathered their stories through rigorous reporting, which endured as the hallmark of the next iteration of the literary journalism tradition. Contemporary New New Journalism, as it's sometimes called, borrows the techniques and attitudes of anthropology: the discipline of field-work, the principles of ethnography, the cultural or sub-cultural immersion now called "embedding." The embedded writer generally keeps a low profile in her finished work; both her person and perspective are practically invisible.

Pam Colloff is a journalist who writes about brutal crimes and the ensuing wrongful convictions that multiply victims and compound ruin. Telling these stories—any stories—she says, requires a great deal of access. She "embeds" with her subjects for brief, intense intervals, and despite her presence in their lives, often at critical moments, she's nowhere to be found in her stories. I ask Colloff what she thinks about Didion's claim that writing is "the tactic of a secret bully, an invasion" (Didion 5). "Didion *would* say that," she laughs. And it's true; Didion is brilliant, but there's a ferocity and an air-tight quality to some of her work that's redolent of narcissism—a constitutional inability to admit other realities. I ask Colloff about her preoccupation with violent subjects, hoping to validate my own fascination with morbidity and tragedy, and to reassure myself that it transcends voyeurism. She describes her inclination toward violence as two-pronged: "There's the inherent dramatic tension of ordinary people in extreme situations," she says. "And then there's the way that violence reverberates through generations" (Colloff). The spiraling ripple effects of trauma are not the voyeur's object. Fully developed portraits of dysfunction ask questions, demand empathy, resist answers. They educate and edify. Is this "advocacy" or "activist" journalism? "I enjoy storytelling," Colloff says, "so the narrative always comes first. But if a story happens to be about social justice—if the story can help someone—that's a bonus" (Colloff).

* * *

"You may well ask why I write," says the narrator in Ford Madox Ford's 1929 novel, *The Good Soldier*. "It is not unusual in human beings who have witnessed the sack of a city or the falling to pieces of a people to desire to set down what they have witnessed for the benefit of unknown heirs or of generations infinitely remote; or, if you please, just to get the sight out of their heads" (Ford 5). Witnessing serves a cautionary, cathartic purpose, and a variety of nonfiction forms testify to traumatic events. Long-form journalism unpacks newsworthy stories with an eye toward detail and deeper meaning. Memoir filters select moments or events through the lens of a particular sensibility. Essays *assay* their contents, weighing them in order to determine significance, sometimes roaming and identifying their "stories" elsewhere. Documentary filmmaking is perhaps the contemporary apotheosis of the witnessing narrative.

The 2010 film *Restrepo* chronicles parts of a fifteen-month deployment of American soldiers in Afghanistan. Sebastian Junger made the film with the late photojournalist Tim Hetherington. The two lived and worked alongside the Second Platoon of the 173rd Airborne's Battle Company in the isolated Korengal Valley, widely considered one the most dangerous positions in the war. The film employs some traditional documentary devices (interviews, captions, an alternating pattern of action and commentary), but there are no talking heads who presume authority beyond their own experience. There are no dramatizations or voiceovers, no reassurance that insight or resolution is forthcoming. Unsteady camera-work derives not from a self-conscious effort toward low-tech authenticity but from the reality of documenting two extremes of unpredictability: combat and boredom. Real-time coverage of the routine produces scenes of rare and wonderful economy, such as one in which a soldier works to adjust the position of a .50 caliber machine gun. He's just climbed onto the ledge of a sandbag bunker's firing hole when a voice sloshes through his walkie-talkie. The otherwise unintelligible words end in a drowsy question—*Howzafaah?*—and the soldier frees up a hand to answer.

"How's the what?"

"The fam," [the voice responds with zero inflection.]

"The family? They're pretty good . . . ." [The soldier has just returned from leave.] "It was a good time, man. I got to hang out at the ranch and everything like that . . ." [He squats, balancing on the ledge.]

"Your family owns a ranch?"

"Of course," [says the soldier, clipping his answer so he can continue to maneuver his body around the gun.]

"Like cows and pigs and chickens and horses ranch?" [his buddy asks].

"No." [The soldier puts the walkie-talkie down and leans out toward what looks like a precipitous drop.]

"Like what kind of ranch then?" [Now the soldier is struggling to adjust the tripod underneath the gun. He mutters "fuck" and grabs the walkie-talkie.]

"It's like a ranch just with like land, you know, with gates and stuff and trucks and whatnot. Some guns, some wildlife, you know, that you shoot at."

"Okay, so just a whole bunch of land that they kill stuff on?" [We appreciate the absurdity and abundance of America.]

"Yeah," [the soldier says.] "Kind of like this."

"Yeaaah," [the friend says, drawing the word out into a kind of little-kid whine.] "But we're not hunting animals, we're hunting people." [The distinction sounds like an effort at accuracy, not irony.]

"Hearts and minds," [the soldier says.]

"Yeah," [the friend says.] "We'll take their hearts and we'll take their minds."

No soundtrack accompanies the film's close-up moments. No music, cutaway edits, or other cues help us to recover as a soldier sobs, having just learned, in the middle of a firefight, that his friend Sergeant Rougle is dead. In another scene, we can't rationalize the catastrophic operation that kills innocent children, and we can't help but sympathize, afterwards, with the stupefaction—likely the hatred—of the villager who watches helplessly as a beast of an American helicopter lands on the roof of the bombed–out house— his own?—to disgorge a colonel who, by way of apology, offers a lecture about holding out for jobs instead of taking money from the Taliban. For all the bravado and genuine courage on display in *Restrepo*, fear is conspicuous, too. We watch American soldiers during a prelude to a firefight, as they register that they are prey. When they respond to enemy fire, their movements are unlike the Hollywood version of battle, in which warriors rush deliberately forward. Here, momentum is sometimes canceled by confusion, and we see split-seconds of terrified hesitation. Later, when members of Second Platoon reflect on their experience in the Korengal, fear and grief manifest in their eyes as something not yet metabolized. The color of their irises is plain and their pores practically visible as they speak, prompted—but just barely—by an unseen interlocutor. Talking about Rougle's death, Sergeant Hijar says, "I still obviously haven't figured out how to deal with it inside. The only hope I have right now is that eventually I'll be able to process it differently. I'm never going to forget it. I'm never going to even let go of it. I don't want to not have that as a memory." On its face, *Restrepo* is utterly apolitical. It doesn't address the war's causes, or its moral or political implications. As with much of the work that exhibits the innovations of the New Journalisms, the film is essentially a series of vignettes without an agenda or a conventional storyline. But our connection to the men of OP Restrepo, while seemingly direct, is mediated by the filmmakers, whose access and approach afford an immediate, intimate level of witnessing.

* * *

Critical Insights

This strain of documentary has a literary counterpart, and war stories—nth-degree examples of "ordinary people in extreme circumstances"—are some of the most successful experiments with a hybrid form that pools the ambition of the novel, the methods of reportage and ethnography, the explicitly personal slant of memoir, the flexibility of the essay, and the graphic power of film to illuminate intersecting narrative arcs and those which approach each other asymptotically. In his own book, *War,* Junger is frank about the impossibility of journalistic distance in certain situations: "You can't write objectively about people who are shooting at you," he says (26). But you can't write objectively about people who are protecting you either, and Junger's life is, to a great extent, in the hands of the soldiers he's covering. He's worked in Afghanistan before, but "this time I'm not interested in the Afghans. I'm interested in the Americans" (Junger 25). The acknowledgement borders on jingoism, but given the isolation and acute danger of the Korengal, Junger can be forgiven for assuming some of the bias of the men he purports to document. He's living, more or less, with the same level of privation and risk. Early in *War*, a soldier admits that "there's nothing like [combat], nothing in the world" (Junger 33). Junger tells us that "for a nineteen-year-old at the working end of a .50 cal during a firefight that everyone comes out of okay, war is life multiplied by some number that no one has ever heard of" (144). His arm's length shrinks as the book proceeds: "The .50 is badass. It doesn't have to hit you and it can still tear you open. It's just a sexy weapon" (Junger 151). Beginning a three-page rumination on the intoxicating effects of firepower, Junger says, "The offers of weapons started on my first trip" (212). He congratulates himself for abstaining, but eventually he and Hetherington half-relent, allowing themselves a tutorial on how to "load and shoot every weapon at the outpost" (Junger 213). "What you *really* wanted to do was use them somehow, but that was so wildly forbidden that it took you a while to even admit you'd had the thought" (Junger 214). In *War,* "you*"* often feels like it means "me" or "I."

Especially since Vietnam, ambivalence toward violence has been a common theme in firsthand war stories. "The truths are contradictory," writes Tim O'Brien in *The Things They Carried.* "It can be argued, for instance, that war is grotesque. But in truth war is also beauty. For all its horror, you can't help but gape at the awful majesty of combat" (O'Brien 87). O'Brien's formulation echoes something that was generally left unsaid until Bill Broyles, Jr.'s' essay, "Why Men Love War," which appeared as a "Documentary" feature in *Esquire* in 1984. Having served as a marine in Vietnam, Broyles considers the "utopian" dimensions of war. He analyzes the guiltiest of pleasures—"the thrill of killing"—and identifies the love of war as a male propensity that "stems from the union, deep in the core of our being, between sex and destruction, beauty and horror, love and death" (Broyles 61). Broyles posits combat as a kind of male analogue to childbirth—a way for men to "touch the mythic domains in our soul" (61). These days, though, the link to gender seems tenuous; women in combat report being similarly impressed with the camaraderie born of singular purpose (stay alive, kill the enemy), the transcendence glimpsed through physical endurance, and the delights of artillery.

Writing about the war in Iraq a quarter-century later, journalist David Finkel encounters the same sentiments in young men from dysfunctional, often violent families who make up a significant demographic of the warrior population. In his 2013 book *Thank You for Your Service*, a soldier named Adam Schumann returns from Iraq with severe PTSD and wistfully recalls his first two deployments— "a front seat to the greatest movie I've ever seen, the sexiest feeling there is" (Finkel, *Thank You* 5). Channeling Adam, Finkel articulates the difficulty of maintaining the kind of intensity that obviates existential angst:

> It is such a lonely life, this life afterward. During the war, it wasn't that way . . . Over time the war came to mean less and less until it meant nothing at all, and meanwhile the other soldiers meant more and more until they came to mean everything. . . . To be a soldier in combat was to fall in love constantly (Finkel, *Thank You* 86).

Adam himself says simply, "I miss it. Holding a gun and being with a group of guys. Camaraderie" (Finkel, *Thank You* 139). Similarly,

O'Brien experiences a gnawing malaise when he's transferred to a "cushy duty" after being shot in Vietnam. He misses the danger of the bush and the potency of friendships forged in terror:

> There were times when I missed the adventure, even the danger, of the real war out in the boonies. It's a hard thing to explain to somebody who hasn't felt it, but the presence of death and danger has a way of bringing you fully awake. It makes you see things vivid. When you're afraid, really afraid, you see things you never saw before, you pay attention to the world. You make close friends. You become part of a tribe and you share the same blood—you give it together, you take it together. (O'Brien 219–220)

O'Brien connects the lure of combat not to sex, but to fear and vulnerability, and to the profound kinds of loyalty and love they inspire. In writing about the seductiveness of violence in war, O'Brien, Finkel, Broyles, and Junger all hint at something missing in the everyday. The vitality of war, it seems, recommends more opportunities for *communion*—with people, with the elements, with tools. The list of reasons that men love war is not a call for violence, but for intimacy, passion, poetry, craftsmanship—concerns that may explain some writers' attraction to danger and violent subject matter, and why traumatic experience often compels people to write.

* * *

Finkel's *Thank You for Your Service* is an account of the psychological fallout of the Iraq War. Several veterans' stories are braided into the central throughline of Adam Schumann's "after-war" (11)—his battle with the demons of three deployments—and the struggles play out against the backdrop of a military culture ill-equipped to handle the vagaries of emotional trauma. The book's prologue splices Schumann's short journal entries, in italics, into Finkel's summary (also italicized) of the soldier's decline. Having effectively merged Schumann's voice with his own (and he's the better writer, after all), Finkel is now authorized to speak for him. Throughout the book, Finkel performs empathy by incorporating his subjects. He preserves their voices (their urgency, their idiomatic quirks, their imperfect grammar) by framing their dialogue with speech and thoughts transposed to a third-person, mostly present tense. As an author, Finkel is both everywhere and absent on every page.

By the penultimate chapter of *Thank You for Your Service*, we're emotionally exhausted by the harrowing stories and relieved when a chef and an aide sit down to work out the menu for an official dinner to be hosted by General Peter Chiarelli. The dinner's theme is "suicide prevention," and the menu-writing scene, which spans five pages (239–243), is a wry look at the business of making meaning. There will be a soup with butternut squash, parsnips and mushrooms.

"You could call it an autumn vegetable bisque trio," the chef says.

"Seasonal?" asks the aide, noting it's not quite autumn yet.

"You could do seasonal," the chef says. "That would be safer."

"Seasonal vegetable," types the aide, and pauses. "What'd you say? Trio?"

"Yeah. Trio," says the chef. "But you might put it at the front."

"Tri? Tri-seasonal?"

"You could use three."

"Tri-Seasonal Vegetable Bisque," types the aide. "Now we're in the main. What's it going to be?"

"Lamb," says the chef.

"What are we going to call it?" asks the aide.

"Lamb," says the chef.

[...]

"S'mores," the chef says, about dessert.

"We gotta make it sound good," the aide says.

"We'll use the new gelato machine and make a chocolate gelato, a meringue for the marshmallow, a graham cracker, and give it a crazy name."

"Newfangled?"

"Uh . . ."

"The Chiarelli s'mores? S'mores . . . s'mores . . . Suicidal s'mores?"

"No . . . How about reconstructed?" the chef says.

"Reconstructed s'mores. That's fun," the aide says. He types it in. He changes Reconstructed to Deconstructed . . . . "That's a pretty good menu." (Finkel, *Thank You* 241–243)

The dinner is ultimately cancelled, the effort to perfect the presentation wasted. But the menu-writing scene underscores the sensitivity of writing itself, where meaning is shaded by the smallest nuances of vocabulary and syntax—Didion's self-evident "grammar." The s'mores are clever because a deconstructed s'more wouldn't be a trio of ingredients but an exercise (ridiculous and altogether less "fun") of separating the idea of the s'more from its constitutive ideology. The invocation of the post-structuralist premise—the inevitable disconnect between representation and reality—reminds us that so much language is fatuous and that journalism itself, with its ideal of transparency, may be folly. We're reminded, too, that Finkel is very good at what he does.

In its own way, the military is compulsive about language and certainly about documenting and witnessing. In *Thank You for Your Service,* Finkel describes a Warrior Screening Matrix that assesses suicide risk and recommends or denies soldiers admission to a Warrior Transition Battalion Complex, or WTB (48). Having made it to the WTB, Tausolo Aieti must collect signatures from thirty-nine of its offices (Finkel, *Thank You* 143), and sign a Contract for Safety promising not to kill himself (Finkel, *Thank You* 145). When Jessie Robinson commits suicide, his wife's counselor presents her with a "Feeling Word List" of three-hundred-forty-seven choices. A suspected suicide generates a "Commander's Suspected Suicide Event Report, also known as a 37-Liner" (Finkel, *Thank You* 155). Autopsy reports and VA medical records record endless clinical details. In *The Good Soldiers*, the Family Contingency Workbook asks deploying soldiers what kind of music they want at their funerals (Finkel, *Good Soldiers* 12). Overseas, "a book called *Counterinsurgency FM 3-24* [contains] 282 pages of lessons" (Finkel, *Good Soldiers* 27–29), and every military operation is illustrated by an "event storyboard . . . that will forever make the event seem different from anything ever before it" (Finkel, *Good Soldiers* 283–284). "Official death narratives," written with varying degrees of literacy—often by soldiers who have watched their friends die—all end with the same excruciating understatement: "Nothing follows" (Finkel, *Good Soldiers* 73). Both of Finkel's books feature moving remembrances composed by non-writers: "a eulogy so overflowing with hurt it was like listening to the exact moment of someone being transformed by heartbreak" (*Good Soldiers*, 122); an obituary for a twenty-one year-old soldier who kills himself: "a Boy Scout, a member of his church's Celebrate Life Science Quiz team [who] loved his dog 'Sarah'" (*Thank You*, 205).

Thank You for Your Service is a kind of mass-portrait of grief and loneliness. "The truth of the after-war is that you're on your own" (Finkel, *Thank You* 148). People write for "therapy," for connection. Banalities, grievances, and memories accumulate in journals. Hurt is telegraphed in the mean shorthand of the text message: "Im not doing this. U don't wanna b mature and pick your phone up then im done" (Finkel, *Thank You* 190). There are references to writing not just as narrative, but as symbol, object, talisman: Adam's "Saskia" tattoo, which spells out his wife's name "in letters constructed of stick figures in various poses of having sex" (Finkel, *Thank You* 12). The words "Always Kiss Me Goodnight" stenciled by Saskia on their bedroom wall (Finkel, *Thank You* 13). Lists, lost and found like artifacts: Adam's soldier-grandfather's "Places I Have Been" list (Finkel, *Thank You* 17), widow Amanda Doster's "Perfect Man" list—"one of those exercises in hope" (Finkel, *Thank You* 121). Number five says that her perfect man is "understanding of my undying love for James and isn't threatened" (Finkel, *Thank You* 121). Amanda's rituals of grief often take the shape of itemized lists, or litanies. The moving foreman estimates her household contents at "fifteen thousand pounds . . . maybe sixteen thousand" (Finkel, *Thank You* 30). Amanda will carry James' ashes herself.

> Into his tool room now. The rider mower will go to the new house, she tells the movers. The four hammers. The three saws. The old boom box up on that shelf. The two chainsaws. The workbenches. The steel wool. The rusty nails. All of it, actually, every bit of it, even an old peanut butter jar filled with sawdust.
>
> On to the bookshelves. Yes to the brochure titled "101 Reasons to Own a Chainsaw," yes to *The Complete Book of Composting*, yes to *Military Widow: A Survival Guide*, yes to *Single Parenting That Works*, yes to the rest . . . .
>
> Yes to the mops. No to the firewood. No to the jacket that James hung on a hook when he came in from splitting the firewood . . . She'll move the jacket, and not that they're asking, but she'll move him. (Finkel, *Thank You* 31–32)

These are the things she carried. It's a peculiar irony that, especially in the fog of grief, *stuff* can weigh heavily, while words often ring hollow. In *Thank You for Your Service,* well-intentioned words often come across as empty, or worse. The title of Finkel's book is itself a phrase that sounds, to many, careless or callous, or both. A flyer blithely advertises a retreat for soldiers suffering from PTSD: "Healing Heroes, Healing Families!" (Finkel, *Thank You* 125). Signs say "We Support the Troops" (Finkel, *Thank You* 127), and bumper stickers exhort drivers to "Pray For Our Troops" (Finkel, *Thank You* 252). Stuck behind one, Saskia's road rage flares.

Finkel's first book, *The Good Soldiers,* tracks the Second Battalion, 16th Infantry Regiment as it moves into Baghdad for the 2007 "surge." Each chapter opens with an anodyne sound bite from

President Bush, and proceeds to a "true" story—e.g., one that "if truly told, makes the stomach believe" (O'Brien 84). Lieutenant Colonel Ralph Kauzlarich, who commands the 2-16, is diligent about bridging linguistic and cultural divides. Kauzlarich learns to say "dear friend" and "what's up" and "thank you for asking" and "I am one sexy bitch" in Arabic, which makes people laugh. He learns to say "It's all bullshit" and "stupid monkey." "*Allah ye sheelack*, he found himself saying. I hope you die" (Finkel, *Good Soldiers* 100). Kauzlarich endears himself to the Iraqi Colonel Qasim, who throws him a birthday party amid the poverty, corruption, and chaos of war-torn Baghdad. "Most astonishing . . . more so than even the pizza, was the cake. It was three chocolate tiers that were covered in icing shaped into swirls and flowers. Each tier had candles, and sparklers, too, and propped on the very top was a big cardboard heart with writing on it. 'HAPPY Birthday KoLoNiL K!' it read" (Finkel, *Good Soldiers* 189). Hearts and minds, and the mysteries of spelling.

Finkel's flood of "documents"—wayward translations, empty slogans, bureaucratic jargon, sanitized accounts of violence and death—argues, against striking examples of heartfelt expression and his own deft prose, for the inadequacies of language in representing violence. To read Finkel's work is to encounter both the failure of words in the face of intense experience and the eloquence of ordinary people as they try to articulate and ease their pain.

* * *

Journalism can function as a conductor of empathy. Dexter Filkins' 2008 book, *The Forever War*, opens with an afternoon's "entertainment" in Kabul—a public Taliban amputation and execution. Like Finkel and Junger, Filkins embeds with military units and covers American soldiers, but he also engages deeply with the people and cultures of Afghanistan and Iraq. He recalls his introduction to Kabul:

> I drove in from the east. I rode in a little taxi on a road mostly erased, moving slowly across the craters as the Big Dipper rose over the

tops of the mountains that encircled the capital on its high plateau .
. . . I passed checkpoints manned by men who searched for music. I
stopped halfway and drank cherry juice from Iran and watched the
river run through the walls of the Kabul gorge. There was very little
electricity then, so I couldn't see much of the city coming in, neither
the people nor the landscape nor the ruined architecture, nothing
much but the twinkling stars. (Filkins, *Forever War* 18–19)

Filkins' voice is lyrical and his sensibility is visual, cinematic. His
mind's eye beholds the imagined as well as the observed, and his
description of entering a war-ravaged city points to the existence of
beauty everywhere—in nature and cities, in the cosmos and society.
The Forever War catalogs the best and worst of human nature;
Filkins observes the capacity for generosity and violence, kindness
and misery, humor and grief—and the frequency with which the first
of each pair arises in the context of the second:

> In my many trips to Afghanistan I grew to adore the place, for its
> beauty and its perversions, for the generosity of its people in the
> face of madness. The brutality one could witness in the course of
> a working day was often astonishing, the casualness of it more so;
> and the way that brutality had seeped into every corner of human life
> was a thing to behold. And yet somewhere, deep down, a place in the
> heart stayed tender.
>
> I sat in a mud-brick hut near Bamiyan . . . and a man and his family
> pressed upon me, their overfed American guest, their final disk of
> bread. (Filkins, *Forever War* 24)

Filkins' appreciation for cultures at war with his own makes him
sound less "heroic" than Finkel or Junger. He's curious about
Americans and "foreigners," about the powerful and the marginal,
about "good guys" and enemies, about the Taliban. "One of them
would be sitting across from you in a restaurant, maybe picking at
a kebab, looking at you from across the centuries" (Filkins, *Forever
War* 25). Filkins is a journalist with an ethnographer's receptivity.
He taps the vein of memoir, too, and is conscious of the tensions
between these approaches. Like his subjects, he's vulnerable to the

effects of violence and war. Back home, the US has become, for him, an alien place where "people were serious about the fillings in their sandwiches, about the winner of last night's ballgame . . . . I got back to the world, and the weddings and the picnics were the same as everything had been in Iraq, silent and slow and heavy and dead . . . . Your days may die but your dreams explode . . . . I couldn't have a conversation with anyone who hadn't been [to Iraq] about anything at all" (Filkins, *Forever War* 339–340).

In 2004, escorted by marines with whom they were embedded, Filkins accompanies his colleague, the photojournalist Ashley Gilbertson, to a recently shelled mosque in Falluja. Gilbertson needs a photo of a dead insurgent for the *Times* and a twenty-two-year-old marine, Billy Miller, is killed when he insists on leading the way as the group ascends the crumbling, narrow stairs of the mosque's minaret to where the body lies.

> Miller was on his back; he'd come out head first. His face was opened in a large V, split like meat, fish maybe, with the two sides jiggling.
>
> "Please tell me he's not dead," Ash said. "Please tell me."
>
> "He's dead," I said.
>
> I felt it then. Darting. Out of reach. You go into these places and they are overrated, they are not nearly as dangerous as people say. Keep your head, keep the gunfire in front of you. You get close and come out unscathed every time, your face as youthful and as untroubled as before. The life of the reporter: always someone else's pain. (Filkins, *Forever War* 210)

Now the pain is Filkins', too. The last line reflects the loss of a marine and an illusion—one that we sense has been under stress for a while. Filkins critiques the ideal of the journalist who is stoic in his detachment—and, implicitly, writers (including himself) who are curiously brave in spite of self-effacing constitutions. Do they aspire to the heroism they document? Does he? Is there a cost to that "courage"?

198

Filkins' "Atonement" appeared in *The New Yorker* in 2012. The piece details Lu Lobello's efforts to locate a woman whose father and two brothers Lobello's unit killed, along with other innocent civilians, in Baghdad in 2003. Nora Kachadoorian was gravely injured when the marines of Fox Company shot at her family's blue Mercedes, but she survived. While still in Iraq, Filkins talked to Nora's mother, Margaret, to members of Fox Company (though not Lobello), and to others. "Atonement" opens in San Diego. It's eight years later, and Lobello is awake on a dark night of the soul. He records a video message for Nora, whom he's finally identified and connected with on Facebook. She lives in Glendale, California, now, not far away, with her mother and husband, whom she met while recovering from the attack. They immigrated to the US after three years as refugees in Damascus. "I need to talk to you, if you let me," Lobello says. "I have so much to say to you. I have so much to say" (Filkins, "Atonement" 94).

Although they've never met, Lobello solicits Filkins' help in facilitating a face-to-face meeting with Nora. Together, they drive to the Kachadoorians' and "Lobello did not quite say it, but . . . I felt that what he was really looking for was absolution" (Filkins, "Atonement" 99). In light of Filkins' own experience in Iraq—and especially Billy Miller's death—confession and forgiveness would seem to weigh heavily and personally. Filkins and Lobello arrive at the Kachadoorians' and sit in the living room, near a "framed photograph of the dead Kachadoorian men" (100). Lobello cries. He apologizes, and the Kachadoorians forgive him. He and Assad, Nora's husband, go outside to smoke a cigarette. The poignancy of the rapprochement is underscored by the presence of Nora's and Assad's little boys, Joseph and Sam, who are playing nearby. Their presence confirms that the cycle of violence has been arrested; the next generation may inherit hurt, but not hatred, and the story they learn will contain friendship.

"Atonement" is a story that "happens to help someone," as Pam Colloff put it. Both Lobello and the Kachadoorians return to the scene of the crime, as it were, and find a measure of healing in the confrontation. Perhaps Filkins, the writer, does, too. While

"Atonement" demonstrates the therapeutic value of dialogue, *The Forever War* contains repeated references to "talking" as the essence of democracy, about which Iraqi citizens are variously hopeful and cynical. Asked for "the best thing about Saddam being gone," a young doctor, now working in a hospital without electricity, replies, "only the free talking" (Filkins, *Forever War* 138–139). A Shiite woman comes out to vote, and is ironically, though not unreasonably, furious about the American occupation: "Democracy . . . . it is just talking," she tells Filkins (*Forever War* 244), who acknowledges, amid an unchecked wave of brutal sectarian murders, that the new Iraqi constitution is "all about words . . . that empowered nobody, restrained no one" (*Forever War* 321). But if "free talking" doesn't provide security or resources, there seems to be consensus, in Filkins' book, that it enables imagination—a way to negotiate the gulf between war and normalcy, despair and hope. Filkins' work—like O'Brien's, Finkel's and Junger's—describes that passage by particularizing the roots and ramifications of violence. Despite the omission of politics per se, this seems like a deeply political project insofar as it agitates and advocates, not for policy, but for more voices and stories—for self-help, for democracy, for literature.

Writing can effect reconciliation—psychic and actual. We write to witness, to remember, to memorialize. To accuse and to avenge. To apologize, to atone, to resolve. To imagine, to create, to progress. Writing is utilitarian. Sometimes, we write to survive. And "sometimes," says Tim O'Brien, "stories can save us" (255). Filkins, Finkel, and Junger impose narrative structure on fundamentally chaotic experience. They mold horror into beauty, as it were, and their texts occasion recognition, empathy, identification. As a reader, the experience is exquisite. Yet this kind of storytelling is ethically fraught. Tom Druecker's joke (*You don't know, you weren't there!*) reminds us that the third-person narrator of stories like these treads on delicate ground. The stereotype of the Vietnam vet, defensively proprietary of his own experience, reminds us additionally that speaking for someone else—the very act of representation—is audacious. Perhaps, though, it's also genuinely courageous.

Works Cited

Broyles, William Jr. "Why Men Love War." *Esquire* Nov. 1984: 55–65.

Colloff, Pamela. Personal interview. 31 Jan. 2014.

Didion, Joan. "Why I Write." *Joan Didion: Essays and Conversations*. Ed. Ellen G. Friedman.

    Princeton, NJ: Ontario Review Press, 1984. 5–10.

Filkins, Dexter. "Atonement." *The New Yorker* 29 Oct. 2012: 92–103.

_____. *The Forever War*. New York: Alfred A. Knopf, 2008.

Finkel, David. *The Good Soldiers*. New York: Picador, 2009.

_____. *Thank You for Your Service*. New York: Sarah Crichton Books, 2013.

Ford, Ford Madox. *The Good Soldier: A Tale of Passion*. 1927. New York: Vintage Books, 1955.

Junger, Sebastian. *War*. New York: Twelve, 2010.

Nabokov, Vladimir. *Lolita*. 1955. New York: Vintage International, 1989.

O'Brien, Tim. *The Things They Carried: A Work of Fiction*. Boston: Houghton Mifflin/Seymour Lawrence, 1990.

Operation Homecoming: Writing the Wartime Experience. Dir. Richard E. Robbins. Perf. Tim

    O'Brien, Tobias Wolff. The Documentary Group, 2007. DVD.

Orwell, George. "Why I Write." *The Orwell Reader: Fiction, Essays, and Reportage by George Orwell*. New York: Harcourt, Brace & World, Inc, 1956. 390–396.

Restrepo. Dir. Tim Hetherington and Sebastian Junger. Perf. Juan 'Doc' Restrepo, Dan Kearney, and Misha Pemble-Belkin. Outpost Films, 2010. DVD.

The War in "Big Two-Hearted River"

Allen Josephs

In memory of Robert W. Lewis

> The story was about coming back from the war but there was no
> mention of the war in it. (Hemingway, *A Moveable Feast* 76)

Heretical as it may sound, I must ask the question: *Was* "Big Two-
Hearted River" about coming back from the war?

Edmund Wilson and then Malcolm Cowley were first to
suggest that there was more going on here than a fishing story. In his
introduction to *The Portable Hemingway* in 1945, Cowley wrote of
"Big Two-Hearted River" as being connected to "Now I Lay Me,"
concluding that "Hemingway himself sometimes seems to regard
writing as an exhausting ceremony of exorcism. And, as a young
man after the First World War, he had painful memories of which he
wanted to rid himself by setting them all down" (Cowley/Weeks 43).
Cowley didn't state flatly that the story was about the unmentioned
war, but he certainly pointed us in a direction that would prove
difficult to reverse.

Other critics followed Cowley's lead. Carlos Baker in 1952
believed it was a "legitimate guess" that Nick was "a returned war-
veteran, going fishing both for fun and for therapeutic purposes"
(127). Philip Young's book appeared the same year, attributing
massive and pervasive importance to Hemingway's wounding.
Specifically, he claimed that within "Big Two-Hearted River" a
"terrible panic is barely under control, and the style—this is the
'Hemingway style' at its most extreme—is the perfect expression
of the content of the story; with its fixation on detail and repetitive,
almost mechanical, movement, it resembles the behavior of a
badly shell-shocked veteran" (Young 46). Young's assertion rather

violently opposed Baker's opinion that "the close reader finds a carefully determined order of virtue and simplicity which goes far towards explaining from below the oddly satisfying effect of the surface story" (Baker 126), yet both critics believed that the story was about the effects of the war.

In 1989, Paul Smith in *A Reader's Guide to the Short Stories of Ernest Hemingway* wrote that Young's theory had a "profound influence" on critics considering "Big Two-Hearted River" and that "few contest his interpretation of the story in the light of the later war stories" (Smith 89). Once Hemingway himself had written in *A Moveable Feast* that the story was about the war, the case was closed, even if only well after the fact, especially since he would reiterate the whole business in his 1959 piece, "The Art of the Short Story," eventually published in the *Paris Review* in 1981: "'Big Two-Hearted River' is about a boy coming home beat to the wide from a war. Beat to the wide was an earlier and possibly more severe form of beat, since those who had it were unable to comment on this condition and could not suffer that it be mentioned in their presence. So the war, all mention of the war, anything about the war, is omitted" (Hemingway, "The Art of . . ." 88). The author's recollection would seem to settle the issue, since, in spite of Hemingway's off-key tone, he cloaked the brilliance of the story, the seven-eighths of the iceberg left out—the war and all its consequent implications—in an invisible cloak of seemingly intentional or even obligatory omission.

Hemingway's fanciful explanation, as though he were fictionalizing the fiction, does not describe what I see happening in 1924, when the young and brilliant and relatively inexperienced Hemingway was actually writing the story, rather than recalling and embellishing the writing of it many years and a few wars later. Maybe in its first iteration, a three-page first-person autobiographical account of a fishing trip to the Fox River in 1919, along with two fishing pals, Al Walker and John Pentecost, it was to have been a story about going fishing after the war. But that first attempt, probably written in late 1923, was "a false start" that went nowhere (Smith 85).

The story then turned into a third-person omniscient account of a solitary expedition made by Nick Adams, with many fictionalized elements, including in its first finished version—one that Hemingway sent out for publication—the notion that "Nick in the stories was never himself. He made him up" (Hemingway, *NAS* 238). As we know, this metafictionalizing—Nick inventing Nick—complicated the story enormously, although that complication of what Hemingway later excised interests me less at this juncture than the problematic chronology of what Philip Young eventually published as "On Writing" in his attempt at a chronological compilation of Nick's life in *The Nick Adams Stories*. This essay will return to the metaphysics later.

In that original version, there is some interesting and pertinent information, chronologically and sentimentally linking Nick Adams and Hemingway. The reader encounters: 1) Ezra, presumably Ezra Pound, a buddy of Nick's who seems to be a poet and thinks fishing is a joke. Hemingway met Pound in mid-February, 1922. 2) Bill Bird, a newsman who, like Pound, is in Paris. Hemingway met Bird in April 1922, when he went to cover the Genoa Conference for the *Toronto Star*. 3) We find Nick is married, not such a surprise, assuming there is some chronological order to *In Our Time*—after all, Nick was already married in the Nick Adams story prior to "Big Two-Hearted River," which is to say "Cross Country Snow," married and with his wife Helen expecting a child. 4) Nick likes to travel to Spain, go to "bullfights," and hang out with historical *figuras*, such as Algabeño and Maera, matadors Hemingway mentions in his correspondence from Pamplona in July of 1924.[1] 5) Nick is in Pamplona with Hemingway's pal, Chink Dorman-Smith, putting us again into July 1924. 6) Nick had been on the road to Karagatch in the fall of 1922, in the Greco-Turkish war, and he's also written a story about it, transferring part of the action, the childbirth, to an Indian camp. Hemingway wrote "Indian Camp" between late 1923 and February 1924. 7) Nick also knows Gertrude Stein and James Joyce. He has read *Ulysses* and even undertakes to criticize it, especially Joyce's autobiographical rendering of Stephen Daedalus (Hemingway, *NAS* 234–240).

Critical Insights

Hemingway included that original version of "Big Two-Hearted River" as the final story of the typescript of *In Our Time*, which he had Donald Ogden Stewart shopping around to publishers in New York during that fall of 1924 (Smith 86). How is that story, which covers some time at least up to mid-1924, about "coming back from the war"? "Soldier's Home," which he wrote the previous spring, was about a boy home from the war, but "Big Two-Hearted River," as he first wrote it, was not. In this first version, Nick is making himself up in the late summer or early fall of 1924, six years after the end of the war, a period that covered a quarter of Hemingway's life and most of his life as a writer. The chronology that Hemingway inculcated into the story assures us, via its many undeniable biographical references, that the story—as originally conceived and submitted for publication as the clincher in a connected collection of stories—could not possibly be construed as being about a boy back from the war. It was about a young man who wanted to write and who was, in fact, doing so, more than six years after his wounding in the summer of 1918.

Three references to the story's passage of time back up the above assertion. The first occurs on the story's first page, when the narrator explains, "It was a *long time* since Nick had looked into a stream and seen trout" (Hemingway, *NAS* 163, my emphasis). At the end of part one, Nick reminisces about his fishing buddy Hopkins: "That was a *long time* ago (Hemingway, *NAS* 169, my emphasis). On the same page, he remarks, "That was a *long time* ago on the Black River" (Hemingway, *NAS* 169, my emphasis). How many times does the reader need to be told that it was indeed a long time ago? It is difficult to know exactly what constitutes a long time, but it is clear that the three iterations of the same phrase are significant. To me, they contradict the notion of "coming back from the war."

Towards the end of October of 1924, Gertrude Stein returned to Paris, read the original version of the story, and told Hemingway bluntly that remarks were not literature (Reynolds 247). She would recall the process nearly a decade later in *The Autobiography of Alice B. Toklas*: "[Hemingway] had added to his stories a little story of meditations and in these he said that The Enormous Room was the greatest book he had ever read. It was then that Gertrude Stein had said, Hemingway, remarks are not literature" (Stein 219).

Whatever she actually said at the time, Hemingway immediately set about excising the so-called remarks, turning the story into the published version we have today. He cut away the offending pages and explained to Robert McAlmon in a letter of November 1, 1924:

> I have decided that all that mental conversation in the long fishing story is the shit and have cut it out. The last nine pages. The story was interrupted you know just when I was going good and I could never get back into it and finish it. I got a hell of a shock when I realized how bad it was and that shocked me back into the river again and I've finished it off the way it ought to have been all along. Just the straight fishing. (Hemingway, *Letters II* 323)

No war, just the fishing. Then he quipped to McAlmon: "Wouldn't it be funny if some publisher had accepted it because of the stuff that I've got to cut?" (Hemingway, *Letters II* 324). The material he cut is not about the war either—it's all about the things Nick loves, the bulls, fishing and above all, writing, which is presumably why Philip Young titled the excised part "On Writing." Another curious chronological point: If "Big Two-Hearted River" is about being back from the war and the wounding, why did Young place the excised "remarks" in his last section, called "Company of Two" (that is, after Nick has married Helen)? For all the reasons I have been adducing—because the original chronology of the story, as Hemingway first wrote it, had nothing to do with coming back from the war. And I can't believe that, interruptions and all, Hemingway started out thinking it was about the war and then forgot about it, going on to write about Paris and Pamplona. The excised parts had nothing to do with the war but did have to do with Gertrude Stein, and there is a wonderful irony in that connection because, as I have pointed out previously, the cut parts (except for a parodic poem or two), are the most Gertrudesque words he ever penned. So the excisions and revisions had the double effect of freeing up the story to its essence and liberating it from her influence (Josephs 9).

Actually there is one minor, skewed mention of the war in the cut portion. Nick is remembering how too much talking ruined everything, as the movies did, and he thinks "That was what had made the war unreal. Too much talking" (Hemingway, *NAS* 237). The use of the past perfect tense—what *had* made the war unreal—distances the war from the young man wading in the river and the adjective *unreal*, both of which are connected not to trauma, but to *too much talking*, as in the movies. Such a connection does not constitute any sort of argument for the unmentioned presence of war. Quite the opposite, especially given the history of talking movies, still in their infancy in 1924.

Two days after the letter to McAlmon, on November 3, 1924, Hemingway wrote to Don Stewart in New York: "I have discovered that the last eleven pages of the last story in the book I sent you are crap. [. . . .] Under this same cover you will find five pages—These five pages are to take the place of the last eleven pages in the story called Big Two Hearted River" (Hemingway, *Letters II* 326–27). He then proceeds to tell Stewart the same thing two more times in the same letter. Still no rumor of war.

In certain letters in the second volume of Hemingway's complete letters (1923–1925), he talks about his swell fishing story, but nowhere does he mention that Nick is back from the war. He tells his father: "I've written a number of stories about the Michigan country—the country is always true—what happens in the stories is fiction. [. . .] The river in it ["Big Two-Hearted River"] is really the Fox above Seney. It's a story I think you will like" (Hemingway, *Letters II* 464). Why will his father like it? Because of how the country is. As he had told Edward J. O'Brien in September 1924, just as he finished the original draft, "It is much better than anything I've done. What I've been doing is trying to do country so you don't remember the words after you read it but actually have the country" (Hemingway, *Letters II* 304). If the story were really about coming back from the war with no mention of the war, wouldn't Hemingway—in his youthful enthusiasm about his experimental fiction—have revealed it? Instead we have the repeated issue of the country, such as in the August 15, 1924 letter to Stein and Toklas, in which he specifies "trying to do the country like Cezanne [. . .] and sometimes getting it a bit. [. . .] and the country is swell [. . .] [and] it is swell about the fish [. . .] (Hemingway, *Letters II* 288). He shares his secret about Cezanne with them, even though "It was a thing you couldn't talk about" (Hemingway, *NAS* 239), but there is no "swell" about the left-out war.

Contrary to Paul Smith's opinion, Michael Reynolds thought all along it was a story about writing. As Hemingway hacked away Nick's "meditations," Reynolds wrote in *The Paris Years* (which appeared the same year as Smith's *Guide*, 1989): "It was still a story about writing, but he did not have to tell the reader directly: fishing was an art form, so was writing" (Reynolds 247). Reynolds ended that section with this comment on the cutting: "Thus his daring experiment disappeared, leaving the collection thematically linked but without the artifice of Nick the writer telling the stories" (248). All the metafictional niceties disappeared—and what replaced them? Nothing. Just the straight fishing. Until the critics came along decades later and decided that the thing left out was the war.

At about the same time, Debra A. Moddelmog, thinking along the same lines, introduced the theory that Nick was the author of all of *In Our Time*. This highly original piece, which I still remember in its prototypical "conference-paper" version, may well have been what initially spurred the present examination, twenty-five years on, of this whole issue of war's precise role in the story, the war as opposed to the subject of writing.

As I have written previously: "In its brilliant and original fusion of style and of substance, of form and content, of *fishing and writing*, 'Big Two-Hearted River' embodies, more than any other story, the early elliptical style that would profoundly influence the way we write today" (Josephs 8, my emphasis here). The unspoken intertwining of fishing and writing carry the story, indeed they are the story. Writing, not the war, is the thing left out. Given the encompassing metaphysical nature of that deleted material, it may well be the definitive instance of omission in all of Hemingway's work, one in which the artificer erases the artifice, but not the art—clearly a reason the finished story is so much finer than the original. What we lose in metafiction—perhaps the most prescient and revealing passage Hemingway ever wrote—we gain in solid composition, as with the painting of Cezanne. By removing Cezanne, he paradoxically achieved the writerly Cezannesque style he was so avidly seeking.

Does that mean that I am categorically denying the presence of the war in the story? Not altogether. There *is* a residual hollowness in the story—something that clearly concerns Nick. But how are readers to know what that is? Is it possible that the story is about fishing and writing on the surface and, in its depths, also about some inchoate expression of the lasting effects of the war? Readers can't know that from the text—nor can they know—what it is that Nick seems to be holding at bay. Not until Hemingway's *later* stories can a reader begin to get possible clues. And from that original uncut version we are textually limited to Nick's concerns, years after the war, about his writing. Early on in both versions of the story, Nick tells us that he had "left everything behind, the need for thinking, the need to write, other needs" (Hemingway, *CSS* 164; *NAS* 179). "The need for thinking," synonymous with worrying, is vague and ubiquitous in Hemingway's work, from at least "The Killers" forward. The ending phrase, "other needs," is downright obscure. Only "the need to write" is specific. As any angler knows, one of the great appeals of fishing is precisely leaving everything behind. It is therefore ironic and poignant that Nick failed to leave thinking and writing behind, especially in the uncut version, in which he thinks about writing more than anything.

Virtually all the criticism that adduces the unmentioned presence of the war does so by quoting late Hemingway or by inferring from later stories—especially "In Another Country" (1926), "Now I Lay Me" (also 1926), and "A Way You'll Never Be" (1932). This inferred interpretation of "Big Two-Hearted River" depends on an extended, eight-year chronology that has nothing to do with the writing of the story in 1924, and it cannot prove the (negative) presence of war in the story. The critics have instead assumed the war and continued to assume it in successive interpretations until we end up with a classic *post hoc ergo propter hoc* argument that bases its conclusions on the order of events, specifically the as-yet-unwritten stories mentioned above—*in the light of the later war stories*, to remember Paul Smith's phrase. The most subtle exercise of this procedure is Joseph M. Flora's conjecture that Nick's state of mind in "Now I Lay Me" forms "the deep memory that Nick in 'Big Two-Hearted River' holds back, the dark swamp" that he is reluctant to enter. I like Flora's idea and have elsewhere quoted it (Josephs 8), but my preference doesn't keep it from being a *post hoc* argument. I think Flora may be right on some subliminal plane, yet the practical problem of the chronology in the original material, which has bothered me for decades, still persists.

Hemingway/Nick did, in fact, make himself up. The stories are by no means strictly autobiographical. By way of example, "Three Shots"—another piece of excision (Hemingway, *NAS* 13–15), in this case the beginning of "Indian Camp"—dealt with Nick's discovery of the fear of death as a child, but it used Hemingway's own concerns about such fears, *after* his wounding and near-death-experience, to introduce the allusion to the silver cord from Ecclesiastes 12:6—"Or ever the silver cord be loosed"—by way of the derivative hymn, "Some Day the Silver Cord Will Break," as well as his own need for a light at night. And as we've already seen, he used the Karagatch birth he witnessed in 1922 to fictionalize the published part of the story "Indian Camp," from Nick's childhood, even going so far as to comment on the exchange in the excised part of "Big Two-Hearted River": "[. . .] he'd never seen an Indian woman having a baby. [. . .] He'd seen a woman have a baby on the road to Karagatch and tried to help her" (Hemingway, *NAS* 238).

Bearing in mind Hemingway's propensity to invent and to re-chronologize when it suited his purposes, let's return to Malcolm Cowley's statement: "Hemingway himself sometimes seems to regard writing as an exhausting ceremony of exorcism." Sounds good, psychologically sound—but what if it's the other way around? What if, instead of exorcism, it's incantation, bewitchment by word? Exorcism is singular, ugly and abortive. "Big Two-Hearted," *au contraire*, lines out a haltingly repetitive, awkwardly original,

---

rhythmic lyricism and we read the story over and over, fascinated, as we would poetry or liturgy.

Cowley continues, "And, as a young man after the First World War, he had painful memories of which he wanted to rid himself by setting them all down" (Weeks 43). What if instead of ridding himself, Hemingway was incorporating, assimilating through the incantation, healing, with the words annealing? No casting out of evil spirits, rather a casting toward the sacred fish that were a salvific fashioning or forging out of his own spirit, something he clearly enunciated in the excised—but never exorcised—part:

> He, Nick, wanted to *write about country* like Cezanne had done it in painting. You had to do it from *inside yourself*. There wasn't any trick. Nobody had ever written about country like that. He felt *almost holy* about it. It was *deadly serious*. You could do it if you would *fight it out. If you'd lived right with your eyes.* (Hemingway, *NAS* 239, my emphasis)

These phrases—giving us an unparalleled sense of Hemingway/ Nick's dedication to his craft—composed a kind of cryptic treasure map to the sacred font. But, as in the case of "Three Shots," they revealed too much about the young author's intentions—doubtless what shocked him *back into the river again*—intentions that had nothing to do with the war and everything to do with learning to write. So, embarrassed by his transparency and scolded by Gertrude Stein, he threw away the map—which Philip Young later exhumed, *mirabile dictu*—and returned to the straight fishing.

As Hemingway delved deeper into his war experiences, always creating, always *making him up*, the more he came to understand, after the fact, the connected nature of those later stories, which, read in reverse order, send us back—even turned Hemingway back—to "Big Two-Hearted River," to the river that was the source, the literal stream of consciousness, the sacred spring that was the fountainhead of the stories to follow. Contrary to what he had written his father, it was not the actual Fox he had put in the story, it was the poetry of the invented, the realer-than-real, Big Two-Hearted River. It was country made immanent. Hemingway was closer to the source of the story when he wrote in *A Moveable Feast*: "What did I know about truly and care for the most? There was no choice at all" (76).

Then, too, what if "Big Two-Hearted River" is not about the memory he would explore two years later in "Now I Lay Me," as Flora would have us believe? What if it's the other way around? In "Now I Lay Me," Nick, avoiding sleep in order to save his soul, invents new rivers to fish: "Some nights too I made up streams and some of them were very exciting and it was like being awake and dreaming" (Hemingway, *CSS* 277). The words *made up* and *very exciting* and *like being awake and dreaming* suggest that in the same way Nick in the stories was never himself, that he *made him up*, so the Big Two-Hearted is not the Fox and that he made it up, exactly as Nick tells us in "Now I Lay Me," and that it is the writing of "Big Two-Hearted River" that had become the source and the inspiration—following the chronology of the writing rather than of Hemingway/Nick's biography—for "Now I Lay Me."

Nick explains that inspiration precisely in "Now I Lay Me": "Some of those streams I still remember and think that I have fished in them, and they are *confused with streams I really know*. I gave them all *names* and went to them *on the train* and sometimes *walked for miles* to get to them" (Hemingway, *CSS* 277, my emphasis). Names like Big Two-Hearted. You can still cross the railroad tracks west of Seney and walk for miles parallel to the Fox, seeing a landscape of river and pines and downed trees and cedar swamps—the swamps are very real—and it can be quite exciting and the river is a classic trout stream. But mere reality does not suffice: for it to be *made up* and *very exciting* and *like being awake and dreaming*—for it to achieve its full Platonic resonance—you have to read the story, itself a river flowing, ever with the same incantational waters.

Reading *The Trip to Echo Spring*, Olivia Laing's fascinating new study of alcohol and writing, I came upon this quote, written about Hemingway's insomniac nights during his separation from Pauline in the autumn of 1926, precisely when he was writing "Now I Lay Me." It seemed written as an illustration of what Nick was explaining: "Lying rigid in his bed listening to the sound of rain. Making up a man who makes up rivers and sits beside them with a rod, fishing for trout and sometimes losing them, until the sun comes up and it is safe to close his eyes" (98). Nick's fear in the story of losing his soul by going to sleep derives from a reversal of Hemingway's actual insomnia of 1926, as he lay awake remembering the creation of the Big Two-Hearted: *I gave them all names and went to them on the train and sometimes walked for miles to get to them.*

Just as many of the critics were seduced by a reverse biographical current, even Hemingway himself seemed to come in time to believe that "Big Two-Hearted River" was about the war (suggested, Heaven forbid, by the critics?). The inexact psychological and physiological experience of the memory of war is never wholly extractable from Nick once he is wounded, just as it is not extractable from Hemingway. It can be argued that some inevitable and unconsciously accretive way, some confabulation, with time and chronology compressing and rearranging in memory—"memory of course is never true" as Hemingway wisely wrote in *Death in the Afternoon* (100)—it became for him a story about the war, *mutatis mutandis*, just as it became one that, in hindsight and seen through the prism of Hemingway's later stories, readers have inevitably associated with the war. But in 1924 when he wrote it, it was not about the war. Nor did he say it was. Not in 1924, not for many years. In 1924, as the text of the original ending makes clear, it was about a young man fishing and learning to write and discovering his commitment to art. As he fought it out—*wading into the picture, living right with his eyes,* then cutting loose the theoretical and aesthetic commitment and conjuring up in its stead the ominous and very real swamp—he was showing us (rather than telling us) how he wrote, working as best he could at the edge of the dark swamp of his creative unconscious, rendering base experience into gold.

Just the straight fishing but ending finally with an unrealized half-lit and tragic fishing to come. Is it there, in the final cutting and rewriting, that the war, in some recurring memory, began to infiltrate and replace the burden of Hemingway's creative consciousness? Or is that deep-water, half-lit, tragic fishing actually a congeries of all those initial feelings about writing, deep within him, tragic with the exposed core of sentience he tells us he was experiencing—*it was deadly serious, he felt almost holy about it*—feelings with which he was not quite ready to cope? Nick thinks, perhaps optimistically, in the story's last line: "There were plenty of days coming when he could fish the swamp" (Hemingway, *CSS* 180). The intentional and opaque ambivalences of the story—half-lit and tragic reflections themselves—will doubtless keep us fishing for another hundred years.

Note

1. See, particularly, the postcard of July 13 to Gertrude Stein and Alice B. Toklas, in *Letters II*, 274.

Works Cited

Baker, Carlos. *Hemingway: The Writer as Artist*. Princeton, NJ: Princeton UP, 1952.

Cowley, Malcolm. Introduction. *The Portable Hemingway*. New York: Viking, 1945; rpt. in *Hemingway: A Collection of Critical Essays*. Ed. Robert P. Weeks. Englewood Cliffs, NJ: Prentice-Hall, 1962.

Flora, Joseph M. *Reading Hemingway's* Men Without Women. Kent, OH: Kent State UP, 2008.

Hemingway, Ernest. "The Art of the Short Story." *Paris Review* 23.79 (Spring 1981): 85–102.

_____. *The Complete Short Stories of Ernest Hemingway*. The Finca Vigía Edition. New York: Scribner's, 1987.

_____. *Death in the Afternoon*. New York: Scribner's, 1932.

_____. *The Letters of Ernest Hemingway, Vol. II, 1923–1925*. New York: Cambridge UP, 2013.

_____. *A Moveable Feast*. New York: Scribner's, 1964.

_____. *The Nick Adams Stories*. Ed. Philip Young. New York: Scribner's, 1972.

Josephs, Allen. "The Meaning of Fishing in Hemingway's Work." *North Dakota Quarterly* 77.4 (Fall 2010): 5–15.

Lang, Olivia. *The Trip to Echo Spring: Why Writers Drink*. Edinburgh, UK: Canongate, 2013.

Moddelmog, Debra A. "The Unifying Consciousness of a Divided Conscience: Nick Adams as Author of *In Our Time*." *American Literature* 60 (December 1988); rpt. in *New Critical Approaches to the Short Stories of Ernest Hemingway*. Ed. Jackson J. Benson. Durham, NC: Duke UP, 1990.

Reynolds, Michael. *Hemingway: The Paris Years*. Oxford & New York: Basil Blackwell, 1989.

Smith, Paul. *A Reader's Guide to the Short Stories of Ernest Hemingway*. Boston: G.K. Hall, 1989.

Stein, Gertrude. *The Autobiography of Alice B. Toklas*. New York: Vintage, 1990.

Wilson, Edmund. *The Wound and the Bow*. London: Oxford UP, 1941.

Young, Philip. *Ernest Hemingway: A Reconsideration*. New York: Harcourt, 1952.

RESOURCES

Works of Literature Exploring Violence_____

Drama

Oresteia by Aeschylus, 458 BCE

Oedipus Rex, *Oedipus at Colonus*, and *Antigone* by Sophocles, 441–406 BCE

The Trojan Women by Euripides, 415 BCE

Titus Andronicus by William Shakespeare, c. 1588–1593

Macbeth by William Shakespeare, c. 1606

Woyzeck by Georg Büchner, 1836–37, posthumously published (with heavy editing by Karl Emil Franzos) 1879

The Conduct of Life by María Irene Fornés, 1985

Death and the Maiden by Ariel Dorfman, 1991

The Lieutenant of Innishmore by Martin McDonagh, 2001

Poetry

Beowulf, 8th–11th century

The Song of Roland, 11th century

The Divine Comedy, Dante Alighieri, 1308–1321, published 1555

John Brown's Body by Stephen Vincent Benét, 1928

Dien Cai Dau by Yusef Komunyakaa, 1988

The War Works Hard by Dunya Mikhail, translated by Elizabeth Winslow, 2005

Here, Bullet by Brian Turner, 2005

The Oxford Book of War Poetry edited by John Stallworthy, 2008

Effacement by Elizabeth Arnold, 2010

Fiction

Satyricon by Petronius, 1st century

Candide by Voltaire, 1759

The Brothers Karamazov by Fyodor Dostoevsky, 1880

The Island of Doctor Moreau by H. G. Wells, 1896

Heart of Darkness by Joseph Conrad, 1899

All Quiet on the Western Front by Erich Maria Remarque, 1929

Johnny Got His Gun by Dalton Trumbo, 1938

Darkness at Noon by Arthur Koestler, 1940

Uncle Tom's Children by Richard Wright, 1940

The Stranger by Albert Camus, 1942

The Diary of a Young Girl by Anne Frank, 1947

The Naked and the Dead by Norman Mailer, 1948

Invisible Man by Ralph Ellison, 1952

Fires on the Plain by Shohei Ooka, 1957

Night by Elie Wiesel, 1960

A Clockwork Orange by Anthony Burgess, 1962

The Painted Bird by Jerzy Kosiński, 1965

Slaughterhouse-Five by Kurt Vonnegut, 1969

The Complete Stories by Flannery O'Connor, 1971

Ceremony by Leslie Marmon Silko, 1977

Schindler's Ark by Thomas Keneally, 1982

The Lover by Marguerite Duras, 1984

The Sorrow of War by Bao Ninh, 1990

American Psycho by Bret Easton Ellis, 1991

Regeneration, *The Eye in the Door*, and *The Ghost Road* by Pat Barker, 1991–1995

Bastard Out of Carolina by Dorothy Allison, 1992

Breath, Eyes, Memory by Edwidge Danticat, 1994

The Autobiography of My Mother by Jamaica Kincaid, 1995

We Need to Talk about Kevin by Lionel Shriver, 2003

Nonfiction

"Of Cannibals" by Michel de Montaigne, 1580

Wisconsin Death Trip by Michael Lesy, 1973

Goodbye to All That by Robert Graves, 1929

Dispatches by Michael Herr, 1977

Bloods: An Oral History of the Vietnam War by Wallace Terry, 1984

Graphic Novels

Watchmen by Alan Moore, Dave Gibbons, and John Higgins, 1987

V for Vendetta by Alan Moore and David Lloyd, 1989

Maus by Art Spiegelman, 1991

Persepolis by Marjane Satrapi, 2000–2003

Safe Area Goražde: The War in Eastern Bosnia 1992–1995 by Joe Sacco, 2002

In the Shadow of No Towers by Art Spiegelman, 2004

Waltz with Bashir: A Lebanon War Story by Ari Folman and David Polonsky, 2009

Bibliography

Ashcroft, Bill, Gareth Griffiths, & Helen Tiffin, eds. *The Empire Writes Back: Theory and Practice in Post-Colonial Literatures.* New York & London: Routledge, 1989.

Bataille, Georges. *Eroticism.* London: Penguin, 2001.

Caruth, Cathy. *Unclaimed Experience: Trauma, Narrative, and History.* Baltimore, MD: Johns Hopkins UP, 1996.

Cawelti, John G. *Mystery, Violence, and Popular Culture.* Madison: U of Wisconsin P, 2004.

Césaire, Aimé. *Discourse on Colonialism.* Trans. J. Pinkham. New York: Monthly Review Press, 2000.

Das, Veena, Arthur Kleinman, Mamphela Ramphele, & Pamela Reynolds, eds. *Violence and Subjectivity.* Berkeley & Los Angeles, CA: U of California P, 2000.

Deleuze, Gilles. *Coldness and Cruelty.* New York: Zone Books, 1989.

Eagleton, Terry. *Sweet Violence: The Idea of the Tragic.* Oxford: Blackwell, 2003.

Foakes, R. A. *Shakespeare and Violence.* Cambridge: Cambridge UP, 2003.

Foucault, Michel. *Discipline and Punish: The Birth of the Prison.* 1975. Trans. Alan Sheridan. New York: Vintage, 1995.

Fraser, John. *Violence in the Arts.* Cambridge: Cambridge UP, 1974.

Frohock, W. M. *The Novel of Violence in America.* Dallas: Southern Methodist UP, 1946.

Fussell, Paul. *The Great War and Modern Memory.* London: Oxford UP, 1975.

Giles, James R. *Violence in the Contemporary American Novel: An End to Innocence.* Columbia, SC: U of South Carolina P, 2000.

Girard, René. *Violence and the Sacred.* 1972. Trans. Patrick Gregory. Baltimore, MD: Johns Hopkins UP, 1977.

Gomel, Elana. *Bloodscripts: Writing the Violent Subject.* Columbus: Ohio State UP, 2003.

Henke, Suzette. *Shattered Subjects: Trauma and Testimony in Women's Life Writing*. New York: Palgrave Macmillan, 2000.

Herlinghaus, Hermann. *Violence Without Guilt: Ethical Narratives from the Global South*. New York: Palgrave Macmillan, 2009.

Herman, Judith. *Trauma and Recovery*. 1992. New York: Basic Books, 1997.

Holmes, Richard. *Acts of War: The Behavior of Men in Battle*. New York: Free, 1985.

Horvitz, Deborah M. *Literary Trauma: Sadism, Memory, and Sexual Violence in American Women's Fiction*. Albany: State U of New York P, 2000.

Hynes, Samuel. *The Soldiers' Tale: Bearing Witness to Modern War*. New York: Allen Lane, 1997.

Kalisa, Chantal. *Violence in Francophone African and Caribbean Women's Literature*. Lincoln, NE: U of Nebraska P, 2009.

Kierkegaard, Søren. *Fear and Trembling*. Trans. Alastair Hannay. New York: Penguin, 1986.

Kowalewski, Michael. *Deadly Musings: Violence and Verbal Form in American Fiction*. Princeton, NJ: Princeton UP, 1993.

Mandel, Naomi. *Against the Unspeakable: Complicity, the Holocaust and Slavery in America*. Charlottesville, Virginia: U of Virginia P, 2001.

Morrison, Toni. "Unspeakable Things Unspoken: The Afro-American Presence in American Literature." *Michigan Quarterly Review* 28.1 (1989): 1–34.

_____. *Playing in the Dark: Whiteness and the Literary Imagination*. London: Pan, 1992.

Ngugi wa Thiong'o. *Decolonizing the Mind: The Politics of Language in African Literature*. London: James Currey, 1986.

Nietzsche, Friedrich. *On the Genealogy of Morality*. Ed. Keith Ansell-Pearson. Trans. Carol Diethe. New York: Cambridge UP, 2007.

Peebles, Stacey. *Welcome to the Suck: Narrating the American Soldier's Experience in Iraq*. New York: Cornell UP, 2011.

Scarry, Elaine. *The Body in Pain*. New York: Oxford UP, 1985.

Shay, Jonathn. *Achilles in Vietnam: Combat Trauma and the Undoing of Character*. New York: Simon & Schuster, 1995.

_____. *Odysseus in America: Combat Trauma and the Trials of Homecoming*. New York: Scribner, 2002.

Slotkin, Richard. *Gunfighter Nation: The Myth of the Frontier in Twentieth-Century America*. New York: Atheneum, 1992.

_____. *The Fatal Environment: The Myth of the Frontier in the Age of Industrialization, 1800–1890*. New York: Atheneum, 1985.

_____. *Regeneration through Violence: The Mythology of the American Frontier, 1600–1860*. Middletown, CT: Wesleyan UP, 1973.

Stewart, Garrett. *Novel Violence: A Narratography of Victorian Fiction*. Chicago: U of Chicago P, 2009.

Tal, Kalí. *Worlds of Hurt: Reading the Literatures of Trauma*. New York: Cambridge UP, 1996.

Tritle, Lawrence. *From Melos to My Lai: War and Survival*. London: Routledge, 2000.

Weil, Simone. *The Iliad, or the Poem of Force*. Wallingford, PA: Pendle Hill Publications, 1956.

Žižek, Slavoj. *Violence*. New York: Picador, 2008.

About the Editor

Stacey Peebles is assistant professor of English and director of film studies at Centre College in Danville, Kentucky. In 2011, she published *Welcome to the Suck: Narrating the American Soldier's Experience in Iraq* (Cornell University Press), which was the first book to cover representations of the Iraq War in literature, film, and new media. Her articles about war and violence have appeared in journals such as *PMLA* and *The Journal of Film and Video*, and she has forthcoming anthology essays that cover the use of digital verité in Iraq War films (*The Philosophy of War Films*, UP of Kentucky) and the legacy of Larry Heinemann's novel *Paco's Story* (*Fictions of the American War in Vietnam*, Bloomsbury Press). With Aaron DeRosa, she will soon guest-edit an issue of *Modern Fiction Studies* devoted to literary responses to the wars in Iraq and Afghanistan. Peebles is also editor of *The Cormac McCarthy Journal* and has published a number of articles on that author's work. Her next book is tentatively titled *Cormac McCarthy and Performance* (University of Texas Press) and covers McCarthy's writing for film and theater as well as the adaptations of his novels by others.

Contributors

Aaron Bady is a post-doctoral fellow in the English Department at the University of Texas at Austin, where he teaches African literature. He runs the blog zunguzungu and has written for *The New Inquiry*, *Al Jazeera America*, and *The Guardian*. His PhD is from the University of California at Berkeley.

Mark Bresnan is assistant professor of academic writing at Marymount Manhattan College in New York City. His research focuses on intersections of contemporary American literature and popular culture, and he has published essays on David Foster Wallace, Jonathan Franzen, and Eric Rolfe Greenberg.

James R. Giles is distinguished professor emeritus at Northern Illinois University, where he taught in the department of English from 1970 to 2007. He is the author of nine books and the coeditor of eight others, including *The Spaces of Violence* (2006), *Violence in the Contemporary American Novel* (2000), and *The Naturalistic Inner-City Novel in America (1995)*. He and Wanda H. Giles have coedited six volumes of the *Dictionary of Literary Biography*. Recently, he published essays in *The Oxford Handbook of American Literary Naturalism* (2011); *A Companion to Twentieth-Century United States Fiction* (2010); *Chuck Palahniuk: Fight Club, Invisible Monsters, Choke* (2013); *The Cambridge Companion to Cormac McCarthy* (2013); and *Critical Insights: The American Dream* (2013).

Lindsay Hallam is a lecturer in film at the University of East London. Her book *Screening the Marquis de Sade: Pleasure, Pain and the Transgressive Body in Film* was published by McFarland, and she recently directed the documentary *Fridey at the Hydey*. She has contributed to the collections *Trauma, Media, Art: New Perspectives* (2010); *Dracula's Daughters: The Female Vampire on Film* (2013); *Fragmented Nightmares: Transnational Horror Across Visual Media* (2014); and the journals *Asian Cinema*, *The Bright Lights Film Journal* and *Senses of Cinema*.

Ty Hawkins is an assistant professor of English at Walsh University of Ohio, where he coordinates the freshman composition program and teaches writing and American literature. Hawkins is the author of *Reading Vietnam Amid the War on Terror* (Palgrave 2012), which examines literatures and rhetorics related to the Vietnam, Persian Gulf, Iraq, and Afghanistan wars. Hawkins' work on authors such as Cormac McCarthy, Jonathan Franzen, and Michael Herr also has appeared or soon will appear in *Critique*; *College Literature*; *Papers on Language and Literature*; and *War, Literature & the Arts*, among other venues.

Allen Josephs is a world-renowned Hemingway scholar and past president of the Ernest Hemingway Foundation and Society. His published works on Spanish culture include the critically acclaimed *White Wall of Spain*, the multiple-prize-winning *Ritual and Sacrifice in the Corrida*, five critical editions and translations of the works of Federico García Lorca, and numerous essays in the *Atlantic*, *New Republic*, and *New York Times Book Review*, among others. He has been university research professor at the University of West Florida since 1986, where he began teaching in 1969. New Street Communications will soon publish his *On Hemingway and Spain: Essays and Reviews, 1979–2013*.

David Mikics is the John and Rebecca Moores Professor of English and Honors College fellow at the University of Houston. He is also a columnist for *Tablet* magazine. He has written a number of books, most recently *Slow Reading in a Hurried Age* (Harvard/Belknap). His website is www.davidmikics.com.

Lydia Neuman is an artist and writer who currently lives in Austin, Texas.

Thomas Palaima, a MacArthur fellow for his research on early Greek scripts, language, and culture (1985–90), is Robert M. Armstrong professor of classics at the University of Texas at Austin. He has long been a regular contributor to the *Austin American-Statesman*, *Times Higher Education*, and *Michigan War Studies Review*. For over twenty years, he has taught a seminar on the human experience of war and violence, ancient and modern, in the Plan II Honors Program at UT Austin. Recent articles include studies of the war poetry of Robert Graves and of the influence of classical warfare on modern western literature.

Aretha Phiri completed her Ph.D. at Edinburgh University in 2014; her thesis involved a comparative, transnational and transatlantic reading of violence and subjectivity in selected fiction of Toni Morrison, Cormac McCarthy, J. M. Coetzee, and Yvonne Vera. Currently a postdoctoral fellow at Rhodes University, South Africa, her research interests include issues of race, gender, and sexuality in comparative, transnational considerations of identity and subjectivity. She has published in various journals including *English Studies in Africa*, *Safundi*, and the *Journal of American Studies*.

Núria Sabaté Llobera is assistant professor of Spanish and Latin American studies at Centre College. She earned a BA in Philology at the Universitat de Lleida (Catalonia) and an MA and PhD in Hispanic Studies at the University of Kentucky. She is the author of a *Critical Anthology of Patagonian Literature* (not yet published) as well as articles exploring the interaction between literature and cultural geography. She teaches Latin American literature with a focus on contemporary Brazil and Argentina. Since 2007, she has been a guest researcher at the Universidad Nacional de la Patagonia, San Juan Bosco in Argentina.

Philip White is an associate professor of English at Centre College, where he teaches courses in Shakespeare, British literature, and humanities. His book of poems, *The Clearing*, won the 2007 Walt Macdonald Award. He has also won a Pushcart Prize for poetry and a Willis Barnstone Prize for poetry translation. He has published scholarly articles in *Hellas* and *Twentieth Century Literature* and poems in *The New Republic*, *Slate*, *Poetry*, *The Yale Review*, *Southern Review*, and elsewhere.

Index

Abbink, John 152
Abel, Elizabeth 149, 151
Abraham viii, 58, 77, 78, 79, 80,
  82
Abrams, David 63
Achebe, Chinua v, ix, 28, 38, 52
Achilles 5, 6, 10, 20, 22, 23, 24,
  26, 36, 224
Adams, Nick 168, 170, 204, 214,
  215
Aeschylus 9, 10, 21, 219
Afghanistan x, 30, 55, 175, 186,
  189, 196, 197, 227, 230
Africa ix, 38, 39, 40, 41, 42, 43,
  47, 52, 53, 231
Agamemnon 5, 9, 10, 26
Aieti, Tausolo 193
Aijmer, Goran 152
Aja, Alexandre 131
akedah 78, 79, 80, 81, 83
Akhmatova, Anna xx
Alexander the Great 60
Algabeño 204
American literature v, 54, 55, 57,
  59, 61, 63, 65, 67, 103, 118,
  140, 151, 215, 224
Andrews, William L. 151
Angelo, Bonnie 140
Ansell-Pearson, Keith 85, 224
Aphrodite 13
Apollo 23
Appiah, Anthony K. 149, 152
Applebaum, Robert 102
Aquinas, Thomas 71
Archer, John 102
Arendt, Hannah 29
Argentina 107, 108, 109, 116, 231
Aristotle 20

Arjuna xiii
Artemis 9
Ashcroft, Bill 28, 34
Ashcroft, John 177
Assad 199
Athena 13
Atwood, Margaret 141

Baker, Carlos 202
Baldwin, James 149
Barkley, Catherine 64
Bataille, Georges 119, 121, 125,
  132, 155
Bathory, Elizabeth 131
Battle of Chancellorsville 56
Battle of Zama 25
Belloc, Hilaire 38, 44
Bell, Sheriff Ed Tom 157, 158
Bellver, Phyllis 117
Benedict, Pinckney 33
Benjamin, Walter 45
Benson, Jackson J. 215
Benvolio 93, 95, 96, 97, 98, 99
Berman, Zev 129
Bernth Lindfors 52
Bhabha, Homi 28
Bhagavad Gita, The xiii
Bird, Bill 204
Black Codes 137
Blanchot, Maurice 121
Bodwin, Mr. 148
Book of Job viii, 79, 80, 83, 84
Boon, Kevin Alexander 167
Borges, Jorge Luis 108
Boudreau, Kristin 145
Bowie, Thomas 171
Bowker, Norman 168, 170, 182,
  183

Braidotti, Rosi 149
Brantlinger, Patrick 52
Braudy, Leo xxi
Braunmuller, A. R. 102
Bravo squad 168, 169, 170, 172, 177, 178
Brazil 115, 116, 231
Breen, Margaret Sönser vii
Breillat, Catherine 131
Brisman, Leslie 82
Brontë, Charlotte xxi
Bronze Age 12, 16
Broyles, Bill, Jr. 190
Brunet, Stephen 21
Bumiller, Elisabeth 181
Bunch, Lonnie 140
Burgos-Debray, Elizabeth 117, 118
Bush, George W. 177
Bustillo, Alexandre 131
Butler, Judith 30
Byatt, A. S. 141

Cain and Abel 72, 73, 76
Callahan, John F. 149
capitalism 153, 154, 163
Capote, Truman 34
Captain White xvi
Carr, Caleb 32
Caruth, Cathy 27
Cary, Joyce 39
Cawelti, John 30
Celdrán, Lynn 105, 117
Cerberus 7
Cervantes 62
Césaire, Aimé 38, 43
Cezanne 208, 209, 211
Chandler, Raymond 155
Chasteen, John Charles 117

Cheney, Dick 177
Chiarelli, Peter 192
Chigurh, Anton 156, 162, 163, 164, 166
Chrisman, Laura 46
Christian, Barbara 149, 151
Chronicles, The 104, 105, 106
Cinema v, 36, 119, 127, 229
Cisneros, Sandra 32
civilians 26, 55, 114, 169, 170, 171, 176, 177, 178, 180, 199
Clairwil 120
Clarissa 32
Clausewitz, Carl von 25
Clover, Carol 127
Clytemnestra 9, 10, 11
Coen 6
Cohen, Derek 102
Cohen, Marshall xxi
Cole, Gary 60
Colette 27
Collado-Rodriguez, Francisco 167
Colloff, Pam 185, 199
colonialism 38, 53, 150, 223
colonization ix, 43
Columbus, Christopher 117
combat x, 5, 10, 25, 27, 56, 57, 60, 62, 65, 168, 174, 177, 186, 189, 190, 191
Conboy, Katie 149
Conrad, Joseph ix, 38, 41, 43, 220
corporeality 144, 146
Cortés, Hernán 104
Cosbi 81
Cosmopoulos, Michael 21
Cowley, Malcolm 202, 210
Crane, Stephen ix, 33, 56, 67
Creon 3, 7
Crouch, Stanley 140

Crow, Jim 137, 152
Curley, Edwin 21
Curtin, Philip D. 52

Daedalus, Stephen 204
Dahlmann, Johannes 108
Dahlmann, Juan 108
Dalwood, Mary 167
Damascus 199
Daniell, David 86
Das, Veena 149, 223
Davis, Christina 149
Deleuze, Gilles 123
DeLillo, Don 33
Dempsey, Martin 176
Denard, Carolyn 151
Denby, David 52
Deodato, Ruggero 131
Destiny's Child 170, 172
Deuteronomy 82, 85
dictatorships 113
Didion, Joan 184, 201
Diethe, Carol 85, 224
documentary 183, 186, 189, 229
Dorfman, Ariel 219
Dorman-Smith, Chink 204
Doster, Amanda 195
Druecker, Tom 182, 200
DuCille, Ann 143
Duras, Marguerite xx, 220
Durden, Tyler 162, 164, 165, 166
Durrant, Sam 149

Eagleton, Terry 31
Easwaran, Eknath xxi
Eckard, Paula Gallant 149
El Dorado 106
Eliot, George 31
Elkins, Stanley M. 150

Ellis, Jay 156, 157, 161
Ellison, Ralph 149, 220
Emancipation Proclamation 137
Eris 12, 13, 19
Eugenie 120
Euphorbus 23
Euripides vii, viii, 3, 6, 7, 8, 20,
    21, 219
Eurystheus 7
evil vii, 9, 13, 14, 16, 17, 48, 74,
    76, 77, 78, 80, 83, 84, 107,
    122, 133, 178, 184, 211
Exodus 72, 81, 82, 85
Eyre, Jane xii, xxi
Ezra 204

Fallon, Stephen 85
fans 129, 170, 171, 177
Felman, Shoshana 145
fictionalization 104, 105, 106,
    108, 112
Fiedler, Leslie 32
Fight Club ix, 153, 154, 155, 162,
    166, 167, 229
Filkins, Dexter x, 196
Finkel, David x, 190
fishing x, 202, 203, 204, 205, 206,
    207, 208, 209, 211, 213, 214
Fleming, Henry 56
Flora, Joseph M. 210
Fonseca, Rubem 114
football x, 171, 172, 173, 176
Foote, Shelby 179
Ford, Ford Madox 186
Ford, Richard 33
Forever War, The 196, 197, 200,
    201
Foster, Frances Smith 150
Foucault, Michel 29

Fountain, Ben v, x, 168, 170, 181
Franco, Jorge 115
Franju, Georges 131
Frappier-Mazur, Lucienne 134
Fraser, John 31
Friedman, David Noel 21
Friedman, Ellen G. 201
friendship 14, 99, 100, 199
Frohock, W. M. 31
Frye, Steven 157
Fugitive Slave Act 137
Fussell, Betty 138
Fussell, Paul 57

Gaea 18
Garner, Margaret viii, 141
Gates, Henry Louis, Jr 149, 152
gender 34, 117, 139, 143, 148,
    190, 231
Genesis viii, 11, 71, 72, 73, 75,
    76, 78, 80, 81, 85
Gens, Xavier 131
George, Ben 181
Gikandi, Simon 40
Gilbertson, Ashley 198
Giles, James 32
Gilman, Charlotte Perkins 27
Girard, René 29
Giuliani, Rudy 178
Glanton, John Joel xviii
glory 56, 66, 171
Golden Age 14, 15
Goldstein, Jeffrey 30
Goldstein, Joshua S. 54
Gomel, Elana 34
Gomorrah 76
Good Soldiers, The 194, 195, 201
Gospels, The 71
Gossett, Thomas F. 137

Graces, The 13
Grant, Ulysses S. 58
Greene, Gayle 102
Greene-McCreight, K. 85
Gregory, Patrick 35, 223
Griffith, Samuel B. 36
Griffiths, Gareth 28, 34, 53, 223
Guatemala 112, 113, 118
Gubar, Susan xiii, xxi

Hammett, Dashiell 155
Hampson, R. G. 53
Hannay, Alastair 85, 224
Hannibal 25
Harper, Graeme 129, 134
Hart, Stephen M 118
Hayes, Christine E. 85
Heart of Darkness ix, 38, 39, 42,
    46, 52, 53, 220
Heller, Joseph ix, 56, 59
Hemingway, Ernest ix, 56, 168,
    203, 214, 215, 230
Henke, Suzette 27
Henry, Frederic 63
Hephaestus 13, 23
Hera 5, 7
Herakles 7, 8, 11, 21
Herlinghaus, Hermann 31
Herman, Judith 27
Hermes 13
Herodotus 14, 19
Hesiod 11, 12, 13, 14, 15, 16, 17,
    18, 19, 21
Hetherington, Tim 186, 201
Hiebert, Theodore 21
Hiroshima Mon Amour xx, xxi
Hitchcock, Alfred 9
Hobbesian war xviii
Hobbes, Thomas 12

Holden, Judge xix, 162
Hollingdale, R. J. 151
Holloway, David 162
Holmes, Richard 25
Holoka, James P. 53
Holst, Kirsten 52
Hopkins 35, 149, 150, 205, 223
Horsman, Reginald 137
Horvitz, Deborah M. 36, 224
Hostel: Part II 129, 130, 131, 133, 135
Hoy II, Pat C. 181
Hoy, Pat 169
hubris 15
Hulme, Keri 28
Hyland, Jenn 134
Hynes, Samuel 175

Iliad ix, 4, 5, 6, 21, 23, 24, 26, 36, 37, 38, 44, 45, 51, 53, 225
Iliad, or the Poem of Force, The 37, 38, 225
indigenous people 106, 109, 112, 113
infanticide viii, 20, 142, 143, 146
Iraqis 175
Iraq War 21, 63, 64, 168, 177, 178, 180, 191, 227
Iron Age 16, 17

Jacobs, Harriet 150
Jameson, Frederic 68
Jane Eyre xii, xxi
Jenkins, Henry 171
Job viii, xii, 79, 80, 83, 84, 85, 138, 154, 156
Jones, Bessie W. 150
Jones, Jerry 173
Jordan, Winthrop D. 136

Joseph ix, 38, 41, 43, 53, 56, 59, 68, 72, 75, 80, 81, 199, 210, 214, 220
Jowett, Benjamin 37
Joyce, James 204
Judge Holden xix, 162
Judge, Mike 60
Junger, Sebastian x, 186, 201

Kachadoorian, Nora 199
Kahn, Coppelia 102
Kalisa, Chantal 31
Kaufmann, Walter 151
Kauzlarich, Ralph 196
Kayser, Wolfgang 136
Kearney, Dan 201
Keenan, Sally 150
Kella, Elizabeth 150
Kendrick, James 30, 36
Kerrigan, Anthony 117
Kerrigan, William 85
Khan, Genghis 25
Kierkegaard, Søren 85, 224
Kiernan, V.G. 137
Killam, G. D. 52
Kleinman, Arthur 149, 223
kleos 10, 11, 20
Knapp, John V. vii
Knossos 12
Koenen, Anne 150
Konstan, David 22
Kowalewski, Michael 33
Krafft-Ebing, Richard von 120
Krebs, Howard 168, 170
Kristeva, Julia 150
Kugel, James 85
Kumel, Harry 131

Laing, Olivia 212

Lang, Olivia 215
Language v, 26, 53, 119, 123, 224, 230
Latin America ix, 103, 113, 114, 116, 117
Laub, Dori 145, 150
Laugier, Pascal 129, 131, 132
Lawrence, David 175, 181
Le Brun, Annie 134
Lee, Robert E. 58
Leigh, Janet 9
Lenz, Carolyn Ruth Swift 102
Levenson, Jill L. 102
Leviathan 21, 83
Lewis, Robert W. 202
libertine 120, 121, 122, 124, 128
Lincoln, Abraham 58
Lindfors, Bernth 52
Llewelyn 156, 159, 161
Llobera, Núria Sabaté v, ix, 103, 231
Lobello, Lu 199
Lombardo, Stanley 21, 36
Lumbergh, Bill 60
Lynn, Billy v, x, 168, 169, 170, 171, 172, 173, 174, 175, 176, 177, 178, 179, 180, 181

MacKendrick, Karmen 124
Mack, Maynard xxi
Madame de Saint-Ange 120
Mairet, Philip 152
Major Danby 62
Major Mac 170
Makward, Edris 52
Mandel, Naomi 145
Marks, Jim 21
Martyrs 129, 131, 132
masculinity 33, 49, 50, 94, 98, 164

Masoch, Leopold von Sacher 123
Mason, Bertha xii
Maury, Julien 131
McAlmon, Robert 206
McCarthy, Cormac ix, xvi, 34, 64, 153, 167, 227, 229, 230, 231
McCarthy, Tom 180
McKay, Nellie Y. 150, 151
Mclean, Greg 129
McQueen, Steve 140
Medea vii, viii, 3, 4, 7, 20, 21, 149
media studies 24
Medina, Nadia 149
Meineck, Peter 21, 22
Menchú, Rigoberta 112, 113, 118
Mendik, Xavier 129, 134
Mercouri, Natasha 21
metafiction 209
Meyers, Diana Teitjens 150
Michaels, Walter Benn 151
military history 24, 25
Milton, John 72, 73, 85
Moddelmog, Debra A. 208
Moglen, Helene 149, 151
Moreau, David 131
Morrison, Toni v, viii, 34, 136, 138, 149, 150, 151, 152, 231
Mosley, Walter 33
Moss, Carla Jean 159
Moss, Llewelyn 156, 161
Moyers, Bill 138
Mphahlele, Ezekiel 52
Mukherjee, Bharati 28
Mulvey, Laura 127
Myth of the Five Ages 14

Nabokov, Vladimir 201
Nagourney, Adam 181
Neely, Carol Thomas 102

neo-Tarzanism 42
Neusner, Jacob 85
New Journalism 184, 185
Newman, Judith H. 85
Nietzsche, Friedrich 85, 224
Nin, Anaïs 27
Nkrumah, Kwame 39
Noah 76
No Country for Old Men ix, 153,
    154, 155, 156, 157, 162,
    166, 167
Noé, Gaspar 131
nonfiction 151, 220
Norris, Frank xiii
Northup, Solomon 140
Norton, David 85
Nunn, Frederick M. 104

Obama, Barak 140
O'Brien, Tim 168, 182, 190, 200
Och, Dana 134
O'Connor, Flannery 33, 220
Odysseus 5, 6, 7, 20, 22, 24, 26,
    36, 225
Oglesby, Norm 173, 179
Okonkwo 45, 46, 47, 48, 49, 50,
    51
O'Kuinghttons, John 118
O'Reilly, Bill 177
Orgel, Stephen 102
Orwell, George 184, 201
Otten, Terry 151
Ousman, Sembene 28

Page, Denys L. vii, 4, 21
Paid, Stamp 141, 142
Palahniuk, Chuck ix, 153, 167,
    229
Palaima, Tom 25
Palud, Xavier 131

Pandora 13, 17
patriotism x, 169, 171, 172, 178,
    179, 181
Patroclus 23, 26
Patterson, Orlando 137
Peach, Linden 151
Peloponnesian War viii, 3, 7, 22,
    25
Pemble-Belkin, Misha 201
Pentecost, John 203
Pinkham, J. 53, 223
Plummer, Luke xiv
Poe, Edgar Allan 33
pornography 123, 130, 132, 133,
    183
postcolonial studies 41
post-traumatic stress disorder 7
Pound, Ezra 204
Powers, Kevin 64
Pratt, Mary Louise 106
Priam 5
Prince, Stephen 30
Project Mayhem 165, 166
Prometheus 13
Puig, Manuel 114
Pynchon, Thomas 33

Qasim 196
Queen Mab 97

Rabbah, Midrash 74, 75
race xvi, 13, 16, 54, 116, 136, 137,
    139, 141, 148, 231
Ramphele, Mamphela 149, 223
Raphael-Hernandez, Heike 152
Rapoport, Anatol 35
Rapport, Nigel 152
realism xiii, 56, 59, 166
Reed, John xii
Requiem xx

Restrepo 186, 188, 201
Reynolds, Michael 208
Reynolds, Pamela 149, 223
Rhys, Jean xiii
Rice, Anne 34
Rich, Adrienne 152
Rigney, Barbara Hill 152
Ringo Kid xiv
river 8, 9, 197, 206, 207, 211, 212
Robbins, Richard E. 201
Robinson, Jessie 194
Rockin' Ray Lynn 172
Rodriguez, Robert 129
Rody, Caroline 152
Rollin, Jean 131
Roth, Eli 129, 131
Rowlandson, Mary 32
Rumrich, John 85
Rutherford, Anna 52

Sacher-Masoch, Leopold von 120
Saddam 200
Sade, Marquis de viii, 119, 134,
    229
Said, Edward 28, 38, 52
Sarmiento, Domingo Faustino 106
Sarmiento, Faustino Domingo 118
Sartre, Jean-Paul 136
Sasdy, Peter 131
satire v, 54
Sawhney, Deepak Narang 135
Schaefer, Jack xv, 32
Scharnhorst, Gary 67
Schumann, Adam 190, 191
Seaver, Richard xxi, 135
separate peace 56, 63, 65, 66, 67
Sergeant Dime 173
Sergeant Hijar 188
Sergeant Rougle 188

Shane xiv, xv, xxi, 32
Shaw, Patrick 33
Shay, Jonathan 20, 24, 25
Sheridan, Alan 35, 223
Shorey, Eric 134
Silko, Leslie Marmon 27, 220
Silver Age 15, 16
Singer, Marla 163
Sleigh, Tom 21
Slotkin, Richard xv, 32, 55
Smith, Paul 203, 208, 210
Smith, R. Scott 21
Smith, Susan viii
Snitow, Ann 140
Snyder, Susan 102
Sodality of the Friends of Crime,
    The 121
Soyinka, Wole 42
speech 34, 80, 142, 145, 146, 169,
    170, 172, 173, 174, 176,
    177, 178, 179, 180, 192
Spivak, Gayatri 28
Stanbury, Sarah 149
Stein, Gertrude 204, 205, 206,
    211, 214
Stepto, Robert B. 152
Stewart, Donald Ogden 205
Stewart, Garrett 31
Stoll, David 112
Stone, Oliver 59
Stowe, Harriet Beecher 143
Strayer, Kirsten 134
subjective violence 166
Subjectivity 141, 149, 152, 223
Suggs, Baby 144, 146, 147
Svarlien, Diane Arnson 21

Tal, Kalí 28, 145
Tanakh, The 71, 84

Tarantino, Quentin 129, 131
Tate, Claudia 152
Taylor-Guthrie, Danille 150, 151, 152
Thank You for Your Service 190, 191, 192, 193, 194, 195, 201
Things They Carried, The 168, 181, 182, 190, 201
Thiong'o, Ngugi wa 28, 39, 53, 224
Third World 54
Thomas, D. M. xx
Toklas, Alice B. 205, 214, 215
torture xiv, 29, 71, 87, 109, 114, 119, 123, 126, 127, 129, 130, 131, 132, 133, 134, 155
tragedy 9, 10, 29, 31, 51, 63, 65, 87, 88, 90, 98, 101, 102, 185
trauma 21, 22, 26, 27, 28, 35, 36, 37, 149, 152, 223, 224, 225, 229
Treaty of Guadalupe Hidalgo xvi
Trend, David 30
Tritle, Lawrence 26
Trojan War 16, 24, 51
Trzaskoma, Stephen 21
Twain, Mark 62
Twitchell, James 29
Tzu, Sun 25, 36

Vadim, Roger 131
Vallejo, Fernando 115
Vann Woodward, C. 152
Vernon, Alex vii
veterans 5, 26, 56, 58, 168, 169, 170, 174, 175, 177, 180, 181, 191
Vietnam War 26, 56, 59, 65, 161, 221
Vinson, Audrey 150

von Clausewitz, Carl 25
von Krafft-Ebing, Richard 120
von Sacher-Masoch, Leopold 120

Wainhouse, Austryn 135
Walker, Al 203
Warrior, Divine 21
Warshow, Robert xiv
Weeks, Robert P. 214
Weil, Simone ix, 6, 21, 24, 38, 43, 44
Weisstein, Ulrich 150
Welchman, Alistair 127
Wells, Carson 157
Wesley, Marilyn 32
Westerns xv
Wilson, Edmund 202
Winters, Yvor 67
witnessing 150, 186
Wolff, Tobias 201
Woodward, Vann 138, 152
Worthington, Kim L. 152
wounding 159, 202, 205, 206, 210
Wright, Ann 118
writing 34, 35, 52, 118, 128, 134, 149, 150, 183, 184, 190, 200, 201, 204, 206, 208, 223, 224
Wyatt, Jean 152
Wylie, Hal 52

Yates, Andrea viii
Young, Philip 202, 204, 206, 211, 214

Zalman, Shneur 73
Zamora, Margarita 118
Žižek, Slavoj 29, 37, 153, 167, 225